AQA Business Studies

AS

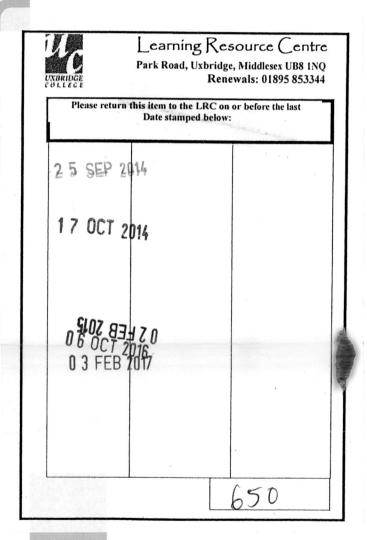
Steven Foden

Diane Mansell

Peter Stimpson

Nelson Thornes

First edition published in 2008 by Nelson Thornes Ltd

This edition published in 2013 by:
Nelson Thornes Ltd
Delta Place
27 Bath Road
CHELTENHAM
GL53 7TH
United Kingdom

13 14 15 16 / 10 9 8 7 6 5 4 3 2 1

A catalogue record for this book is available from the British Library

ISBN 978 1 4085 2319 3

Cover photograph by iStockphoto
Page make-up by OKS Prepress, India

Printed and bound in Spain by GraphyCems

Contents

Introduction

Nelson Thornes has worked hard to ensure this book and the accompanying online resources offer you excellent support for your AS level course.

You can feel assured that they match the specification for this subject and provide you with useful support throughout your course.

These print and online resources together **unlock blended learning**; this means that the links between the activities in the book and the activities online blend together to maximise your understanding of a topic and help you achieve your potential.

These online resources are available on which can be accessed via the internet at **http://www.kerboodle.com/live**
If your school or college subscribes to this service you will be provided with your own personal login details. Once logged in, access your course and locate the required activity.

For more information and help visit
http://www.kerboodle.com

Icons in this book indicate where there is material online related to that topic.

🔅 Learning activity

These resources include a variety of interactive and non-interactive activities to support your learning. These include online presentations of concepts from the student book, worksheets and interactive activities.

✅ Progress tracking

These resources include a variety of tests that you can use to check and expand your knowledge on particular topics (Test yourself) and a range of resources that enable you to analyse and understand examination questions (On your marks . . .).

🔎 Research support

These resources include WebQuests, in which you are assigned a task and provided with a range of web links to use as source material for research.

◰ Case studies

These resources provide detailed coverage of business scenarios, some of which extend material from this textbook and some of which are exclusively online.

How to use this book

The book content is divided into chapters matched to the sections of the AQA Business Studies specification for Units 1 and 2. Sections 1.1 and 1.2 cover Unit 1 (Planning and Financing a Business) and Sections 2.1 – 2.4 cover Unit 2 (Managing a Business). The chapters within each section provide coverage of the AQA specification.

The features in this book include:

In this chapter you will learn to:

At the beginning of each chapter you will find a list of learning objectives that contain targets linked to the requirements of the specification.

Case study

The first case study in each chapter (Setting the scene) provides a real-life context for the theories which are to be discussed in the chapter. The concluding case study in each chapter focuses on testing the theories covered in the chapter. It has five questions attached, each testing knowledge, application, analysis, evaluation and research.

Key terms

Terms that you will need to be able to define and understand.

Links

Highlighting any areas where topics relate to one another.

Activity

Suggestions for practical activities that you can carry out.

Business in action

A real life business example which demonstrates theory being put into practice.

Show the skills

Important hints to help you include the key examination skills in your answers.

Study tip

Tips to help you with your study and to prepare for your exam.

Practice questions

These offer opportunities to practise doing questions in the style that you may encounter in your exam so that you can be fully prepared on the day.

Practice questions are reproduced by permission of the Assessment and Qualifications Alliance.

In this chapter you will have learned to:

A bulleted list of learning outcomes at the end of each chapter summarising core points of knowledge.

Web links in the book

As Nelson Thornes is not responsible for third party content online, there may be some changes to this material that are beyond our control. In order for us to ensure that the links referred to in the book are as up-to-date and stable as possible, the websites are usually homepages with supporting instructions on how to reach the relevant pages if necessary.

Please let us know at **kerboodle@nelsonthornes.com** if you find a link that doesn't work and we will do our best to redirect the link, or to find an alternative site.

Introduction to AS Business Studies

This book is for students following the AQA Business Studies AS level course.

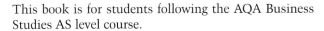 It is written by experienced teachers of Business Studies.

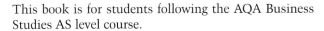 It follows the AQA specification content and sequence of topics.

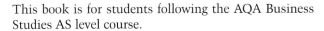 It explains the specification requirements and defines what can and cannot be covered by the final AQA examinations.

Each chapter covers one specification topic and takes the reader logically through each important issue. The key features of this book ensure that:

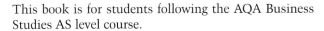 All definitions required by the specification are clearly explained

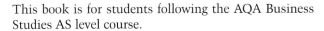 Text is clearly laid out to aid understanding

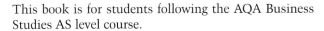 Constant reference is made to actual business situations to allow application of understanding to the real world

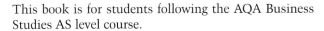 Practice in answering appropriate questions, testing examination skills, is gained at each important stage.

In addition, after every inter-related set of chapters, there are practice questions to test understanding of the material and skills covered in these sections. These offer invaluable preparation for the practice questions that feature on the interactive website.

The final chapter illustrates and reinforces the key skills that students will need to learn. The chapter makes clear that knowledge of appropriate Business Studies material is essential to gain any marks at all – but it is not sufficient to gain full marks. This is because Business Studies students are not just expected to be able to memorise facts, definitions and formulae but also to show real understanding of how to apply them to a business problem. This means that content knowledge needs to be applied to a case study scenario, the problems and possible solutions need to be analysed and the final recommendation must be evaluated.

The authors believe that the

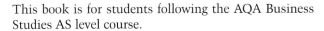 huge variety and number of presentational methods used in the book,

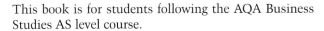 range and diverse style of exercises and practice questions and

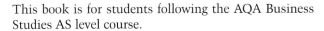 accessibility of the text

will give students who work through it thoroughly, the best possible awareness of what Business Studies is about.

Introduction

Chapters in this section:

Why start a business?

In Unit 1 of *AS Business Studies* you will study many of the issues involved in starting up a business, including the research and planning needed to successfully start a business, and the factors that determine success. So the focus throughout this unit is on small to medium-sized businesses operating in national markets. Case studies of real businesses are used in each chapter to illustrate the main points.

Chapter 1: Enterprise You will study the role, importance and characteristics of entrepreneurs. You will discover why and how entrepreneurs start new businesses. You will also look at the importance of entrepreneurs and small businesses to the UK economy, and how the UK Government supports the creation and survival of small businesses.

Chapter 2: Generating and protecting business ideas Here we look at the way new business ideas are created and protected. You will study how new business ideas arise and the ways that the entrepreneur can carry out small-scale research to investigate the likely success of the product or service and the market in which it will be sold.

Chapter 3: Transforming resources into goods and services This chapter looks at the way businesses transform inputs into finished goods and services. You will look at primary, secondary and tertiary activity, as well as the process of adding value. You will consider the different ways that value can be added in the different sectors of business activity.

Chapter 4: Developing business plans This chapter is concerned with business planning. You will study the benefits of a business plan, its contents and some of the problems a small business would encounter when constructing and using a business plan. You will consider the sources of help and advice available to small businesses in constructing business plans.

Chapter 5: Conducting start-up market research Start-up research is explained and follows logically from the chapter on business planning. This chapter considers the sources of secondary and primary data available to small business start-ups, the sampling methods that can be used and the difference between qualitative and quantitative data.

Chapter 6: Understanding markets Here, we focus on numerical techniques to understand the markets in which small businesses tend to operate. In this chapter you will study the nature of markets and market segmentation. There is a section on numerical techniques and calculations of proportions of totals and percentage changes. These techniques will be applied to calculations of market size, market growth and market share.

Chapter 7: Choosing the right legal structure for the business This chapter is concerned with the key decision of choosing the right legal structure for a new business. You will learn about the benefits and drawbacks of sole traders, partnerships and private and public limited companies, as well as gain an appreciation of the importance of limited and unlimited liability status.

Chapter 8: Raising finance In this chapter you will consider the various sources of finance available to a new business, including internal and external sources. You will assess the advantages and disadvantages of different sources of finance and apply them to a number of different business situations.

Chapter 9: Locating the business This chapter concerns the location decision and considers the factors affecting the decision of where to locate a business. You will consider technology, costs, infrastructure and the market and you will apply your understanding to business case studies to make decisions about the best location in different circumstances.

Chapter 10: Employing people This chapter completes this section of Unit 1 with a look at employing people. You will consider the benefits and drawbacks of full and part time employees, as well as considering the role temporary employees might play alongside permanent staff. You will also analyse data relating to the changing nature of the UK labour market.

1 Enterprise

Fig. 1.1 *Martha Lane Fox is a successful entrepreneur who started Lastminute.com, an online travel and events booking business*

Key terms

Enterprise: the willingness and ability to think of a new business idea and to take risks in starting up a new business.

Setting the scene

Geared Up

Ian and Karen finished A levels with very different ideas about their future. Ian always knew he would go to University, and he chose to study Business and Accounting at a University close to his home town. Karen went to work for a large retailer after Sixth Form College to 'learn the ropes' before setting up her own company. She came from a family of business people; her mother and father ran a successful chain of hotels. The friends kept in touch and regularly talked about running a business together. Karen was unhappy with her current job and suggested they stopped talking about setting up a business and actually did it.

They got on well as friends despite the fact they were very different personalities. Ian was well organised, good with figures and naturally cautious. Karen was outgoing and confident, easily bored and had lots of energy. She liked extreme sports and was a keen cyclist. Karen's interest in cycling convinced her that they could successfully run a business selling top of the range bikes both online and from a shop. She immediately began investigating prices of a number of mountain and racing bikes, accessories and clothing. She asked a friend to build a website for the business so they could sell online. Many of her friends were keen cyclists and agreed with her that the business was certain to succeed. They started their own club, organising rides each weekend and social events.

Ian thought she was rushing things and tried to slow her down. He agreed the idea had potential, and investigated likely locations for the shop and looked around for possible sources of advice and help for small business start-ups. He remembered a unit on his Business course about Government help for small businesses and used his lecture notes to make some enquiries.

Discussion points

1. Describe the key personal characteristics that both Ian and Karen possess that might make them good entrepreneurs.

2. Assess whether Ian or Karen would be the more successful entrepreneur.

3. What do you think Karen's motives were for starting Geared Up?

4. Karen wants to buy stock, get the website going and expand the cycling club. Ian wants to find a good shop location and get some financial help. Draw up a timeline of activities that Karen and Ian should do in the months leading up to starting the business.

What is enterprise?

Enterprise is the willingness and ability to think of a new business idea and to take risks in starting up a new business. Without enterprise, no new business would ever start up because it is hard work and potentially risky.

Fig. 1.2 *Jack Dorsey*

Key terms

Entrepreneur: someone who starts and runs a business and has responsibility for the risks involved. In order to do this, an entrepreneur has to be able to manage the four factors of production effectively. They are:

- land or natural resources
- labour
- capital, which is any kind of equipment used in production
- enterprise.

Study tip

You'll need to understand the numbers involved in setting up, financing and running a business. You're going to come across a few numbers during the course. Make sure you take the time to understand them. You don't need to be a mathematical genius, but if you're not confident with numbers spend *more* time not less trying to understand them.

💡 What is an entrepreneur?

Entrepreneurs have an idea for a new business and risk their time - and usually their savings - to try to make it successful. An entrepreneur needs to make judgements about the likely success of new ideas, and the risks and rewards of putting them into practice.

What makes a good entrepreneur? What makes the difference between a successful new business idea and one that disappears without trace? Here are some quotes about entrepreneurs and their business ideas, including some from Jack Dorsey, co-founder of Twitter and one of the most successful entrepreneurs of recent years.

> Success is never an accident.
>
> *Jack Dorsey*

Entrepreneurs have to work hard!

> Everyone has an idea. But it's really about executing the idea and attracting other people to help you make the idea work.
>
> *Jack Dorsey*

A successful new business often requires an entrepreneur to work closely with others.

> Keep your feet on the ground, understand your trade, live within your means, and grow carefully.
>
> *Sir Paul Smith*

Entrepreneurs clearly need to know about the business and market they are entering , and need to 'live within their means', in other words, keep a careful eye on their cash levels.

> In the modern world of business, it is useless to be a creative, original thinker unless you can also sell what you create.
>
> *David Ogilvy*

Market research is often a starting point for a successful new business, as not being able to sell a brilliant new idea will not lead to success.

> Entrepreneurship is living a few years of your life like most people won't, so that you can spend the rest of your life like most people can't.
>
> *Anonymous*

Making sacrifices – of time, effort and money – is an essential part of becoming a successful entrepreneur.

Finally, entrepreneurs also need to know about 'numbers' and what they are saying about the business.

A restaurant manager said, 'I need to know what makes up our daily sales figures and what they mean for the business. I need to know who spends what and what they spend it on, and I need to know our costs. I have to calculate VAT, staff hours, pay, national insurance and tax. An understanding of maths is crucial in my job.'

So, numerical skills are important to everyone in business - and that includes Business Studies students!

We've established what enterprise is and what an entrepreneur is. How important is enterprise and entrepreneurial activity to the UK economy? Think of the most well-known businesses in the UK today; however large and successful they are, they almost all started as small businesses run by the kind of entrepreneurs featured in *Dragons' Den*.

How important are entrepreneurs to the UK economy?

Entrepreneurs and the new businesses they create are a vital part of the UK economy. These are the economic gains for the UK:

- Entrepreneurs create innovative new businesses that can develop new goods and services for customers.
- New businesses mean additional competition for existing businesses, helping to keep prices low through rivalry.
- Some new businesses will grow to become very large concerns with substantial exports and output levels.
- New businesses help to reduce unemployment.

Activity

TV entrepreneur becomes a millionaire

Peter Moule is an entrepreneur whose invention made him a star of BBC's *Dragons' Den*. He made his first million just three months on, without spending a penny of the £150,000 investment. The exposure the programme gave to his new product led to many retailers and distributors contacting him with potential orders. Peter secured the cash for his innovative plastic electrical wire junction box, called a '*Chocbox*', from two 'dragons'. Since gaining this support, he has:

- obtained export orders from South Africa and USA
- bought two further inventions that may prove to be even more successful than *Chocbox*: one of them is a potential life-saving device
- placed orders for 5 million units per year from the UK manufacturer of his *Chocbox* invention, helping to create many jobs.

Peter was both surprised and pleased by the success and media exposure following his appearance on the show.

Study tip

As with all measurements, think about the context. What's 'small' in one context, could be 'big' in another. Is a business with 15 employees and a £300,000 turnover big or small? It's a pretty big dental surgery, but a tiny manufacturing business.

Questions

1. Why is Peter Moule described as an 'entrepreneur'?
2. Explain ONE reward Peter is gaining from his enterprise.
3. Explain TWO reasons why his business has been so successful in such a short time period.
4. Explain THREE benefits that Peter's business has for the UK economy.

Motives for becoming an entrepreneur

There are a number of reasons why people start their own business:

- to escape an uninteresting job
- to pursue an interest or a hobby
- to exploit a gap in the market
- to market a new or innovative product
- to be innovative in terms of the process of making a product

■ Key terms

Opportunity cost: the cost of an activity expressed in terms of the next best alternative, which has to be given up when making a choice. For example, what could an entrepreneur do with their time, expertise and money if they didn't start a business?

Government grants: sums of money given to a business for a specific purpose or project. They often contribute to the costs of a project rather than fund the whole thing. Grants do not usually have to be paid back.

Study tip

It's worth spending time in the early stages of your course familiarising yourself with the small businesses in your area. The focus of Unit 1 of the AS is on small businesses. The more you can apply your learning to small businesses the better you will perform in the AS exams.

■ Activity

Research a small local business and consider the risks involved in setting up. What do you think are the rewards enjoyed by the owner of that business if it is successful? Consider the risks the owner is taking. How likely, in your view, is it that the business will be a success?

■ Activity

The Prince's Trust

Research The Prince's Trust and investigate the help that the Prince's Trust can give to young people wanting to start their own business. Produce a summary of the help available.

- to be their own boss, be creative and make decisions
- to work from home and reduce travelling time
- to have a second career
- to provide a service or product not for profit
- to have a big business one day!

Risk and reward and opportunity cost

If you ask a successful business person why they started in the first place, they will often quote some of the above reasons, but the most frequently quoted reason is the ability to make your own decisions. Entrepreneurs take risks, often using their own money. In return they expect a reward. That reward is likely to be partly financial, but it is also likely to include the non financial reward of the satisfaction of meeting customer needs and doing a good job. **Opportunity cost** is the cost of the next best alternative. What would an entrepreneur do with their time, expertise and money if they didn't start a business?

💡 Government support for enterprise and entrepreneurs

Small businesses are vulnerable in the early stages, and many fail. However, there are lots of sources of help and guidance for entrepreneurs from the Government and other sources.

Government grants come from a variety of sources, including central and local government, the European Union and organisations that specialise in encouraging business growth in particular areas of the country such as Regional Development Agencies in England, Scottish Enterprise, the Welsh Development Agency and Invest Northern Ireland. There are also some charitable organisations. Grants are often linked to a particular business sector or geographical area. They are usually awarded for one of the following purposes:

- Innovation, Research and Development
- Training
- Economic regeneration
- Encouraging young people to start their own business.

In addition, entrepreneurs can get advice from a wide range of sources. Try typing 'help for small businesses' into your search engine and see how much information you get! Local Business Link websites provide lists of support for small businesses. Put 'Business Link' in your search engine for more information.

■ Case study

Small businesses in the UK

Small businesses play an important role in the UK economy. In 2012 it was estimated that there were over 2.5 million businesses in the UK. Companies House defines small businesses as usually having fewer than 50 employees and an annual sales revenue of less than £6.5 million. Look at the data below and answer the questions that follow.

Table 1.1 *The numbers of businesses of different sizes in various sectors*

Type of industry	Number of businesses				Total number of businesses in industry
	0–4 employees	5–9 employees	10–19 employees	20–49 employees	
Construction	159,925	21,635	10,970	6,595	202,625
Retail	166,430	62,450	28,835	13,180	278,040
Hotels and catering	75,570	32,295	22,790	13,510	151,625
Total all industries	1,391,960	317,745	178,820	120,870	
Total all businesses					2,084,495

www.statistics.gov.uk

Questions

1. What do you understand by the term 'small business'?

2. Calculate the percentage of construction businesses that could be classified as small.

3. From the data above, assess the importance of small businesses in the three sectors.

4. To what extent does the above data show that small businesses are the most important part of the UK economy?

Case study

UK business start-ups rise to new highs

The number of people starting new businesses in the UK rose to record levels in 2012. According to a report from Global Entrepreneurship Monitor in 2011, over 20% of the UK working population either expected to start a business, were actively trying to start one, or were running their own business.

There are many reasons why people set up in business on their own. During difficult economic conditions, some people who lose their jobs are convinced that the only way back into work is through their own enterprise. These are called necessity-based entrepreneurs. The striking thing about the increase in new businesses in 2011 and 2012 was that the main reason given by entrepreneurs was 'to take advantage of an opportunity' rather than out of necessity.

A significant increase in young people starting up their own business was reported in Wales. The Welsh Government has been actively encouraging and supporting new business ventures. In addition, the proportion of young people aged 18–29 in the Welsh population increased from 2.4% to 9.7% in the 10 years since 2002.

Many problems were reported by entrepreneurs such as employing the right workers, excessive regulation and insufficient finance. A growing number of entrepreneurs are turning to crowdfunding and peer-to-peer lending schemes rather than traditional banks.

Around 44,000 new businesses were created in the UK in 2012 reflecting an upsurge in the number of entrepreneurs with passion, new business ideas and enthusiasm who are prepared to risk setting up their own venture. Small start-up businesses are currently one of the driving forces in the UK economy.

Many business analysts are reporting that there is an increase in part-time entrepreneurs. These are people who already have a job, possibly a part-time one, but who want to gain additional independence and security in the future by having a second source of income. This could, of course, become their main source of income if the business really takes off, or if they lose their paid job.

■ Show the skills

An important examination skill you will have to show to examiners is 'analysis'. Question 3 asks you to 'analyse'. There are several ways this skill can be shown. In this case it is best to 'identify and *explain the consequences* of two positive effects' of new business start-ups.

■ Link

For more information on crowdfunding, see Chapter 8 – Raising finance, page 55

Questions

1. Identify TWO characteristics required by successful entrepreneurs.

2. Explain TWO reasons why an increasing number of UK entrepreneurs are setting up their own businesses.

3. Analyse TWO benefits to the UK economy from increasing numbers of start-up businesses.

4. Discuss the likely risks and potential rewards to entrepreneurs in setting up their own businesses in the UK during difficult economic times.

5. Research task:

   a Find out about 'crowdfunding' and why it is becoming an increasingly important source of finance for start-up businesses.

   b Look up the website for Start-up Britain. What are the aims of Start-up Britain, and how does it try to achieve them?

☑ *In this chapter you will have learned to:*

- distinguish between enterprise and entrepreneurs, and be able to provide examples of actual entrepreneurs. You might also be able to recognise examples of enterprising behaviour from your own life

- explain the main motives for becoming an entrepreneur, including notions of risk, reward and opportunity cost. Entrepreneurs are willing to take risks in return for a financial reward

- understand that most entrepreneurs gain much more than just a financial reward from running their own business

- understand the important role that small businesses play in the UK economy, in terms of employment and output. You will also understand that there are different measures of the size of a business

- describe the help that entrepreneurs can get from the Government and other agencies

- evaluate the potential benefits to the UK economy of the small business sector.

For answers to activities and case study questions see kerboodle

2 Generating and protecting business ideas

Setting the scene

The Pure Package

In 2003 Jennifer Irvine had a brilliant idea, but she felt she was the least likely person in the world to make it happen. 'I'm actually a shy, nervous person. I was too scared to approach banks.' But she felt the idea was too good not to have a go. 'I found the idea exciting, and spotted a gap in the market.'

Her brilliant idea was to provide healthy meals, designed specifically for each customer, direct to the home. It's been called a 'healthy meals on wheels' or a 'diet brought to your door'.

The Pure Package establishes the exact diet a customer wants based on information provided in an interview. A profile is built up about the customer based on height, weight, fitness, lifestyle and goals. The Pure Package then makes and delivers all the meals and snacks directly to the customer.

'It's a unique concept, but quite a basic concept, but not something that was ever done in this country before.'

Jennifer had very little money to start with, but she knew she had to find out whether her 'brilliant idea' had a chance of succeeding. She researched existing businesses such as Patak's, who also started small in their own kitchens to find out some of the problems associated with starting that way. She also went on basic Health and Safety courses because she knew she needed to know about Health and Safety when dealing with food.

Jennifer asked friends about the idea, and all of them were very positive about it, but she knew she couldn't just rely on their opinions. She needed other evidence, but she had very little money to spend on market research. It was then she had her next brilliant idea.

She contacted food writers and journalists, asking them to sample some of her food and give her feedback. With the samples she sent out detailed questions. She received lots of useful feedback and amended her recipes. An unexpected outcome of this was that some of the journalists began to write articles about her product in the newspapers, giving her lots of free publicity. As a consequence, orders began to come in, including some from celebrities and supermodels.

Discussion points

1. Explain the main reasons why Jennifer decided to start her business.

2. Discuss the strengths and weaknesses of her early decisions when starting up.

💡 Sources of business ideas

In Chapter 1 we considered the reasons for setting up a business. But how does the entrepreneur go about deciding what product or service to offer? An entrepreneur will often base the decision on his/her own experience, that is on a product or service he/she is familiar with either through a previous job or through a hobby or interest. Alternatively, the decision might be generated by a realisation that there is an unmet need in the market – a gap in the market. This second approach might occur after a **brainstorming** session where possible ideas are considered. Both approaches have advantages and disadvantages.

Table 2.1 *Ways to identify a business opportunity*

Advantage	Benefits	Disadvantages
Knowing the product or service, e.g. based on personal experience	Entrepreneur will have a good knowledge of the features of the product	Is there room for another competitor?
	Entrepreneur may have a passion or interest in the product so will be motivated to do well	The entrepreneur's passion for the product might not be shared by anyone else
	Good contacts in an established market	The entrepreneur's passion may overestimate the size of the potential market
	Entrepreneur may already have a good reputation in the market that he/she can use	Knowledge of the product or service is not the only skill needed – the person may not possess the other skills needed for successful entrepreneurship
Spotting a gap in the market, e.g. based on small-scale market research	Entrepreneur is basing idea on the customer's needs rather than their own, which might improve the chances of success	Entrepreneur will have little or no expertise in the product/service or market – prone to mistakes
	More likely to enjoy 'first mover advantage' – the benefits of being first in the market	Is the gap real? Has someone tried to exploit it before and discovered why it can't be done?
	Little or no competition in the early stages when a business start-up is most vulnerable	Competition may enter quickly and capture market share – how long can 'first mover advantage' last?
	Easier to market a new idea than to persuade people to buy an established idea from one business rather than another?	

A combination of the above approaches is often successful, where an entrepreneur starts a business in a market with which he/she is familiar, but in a unique way that has not been done before. This has the benefit of combining good knowledge with a differentiated approach.

Whichever way an entrepreneur decides upon the initial idea, he/she will need to carry out some initial small budget research. The main ways to do this are:

- Use business directories such as the Yellow Pages, Thomsons Local and the telephone directory.
- Use local maps to locate existing competition and identify gaps in provision.
- Use local and national demographic data to establish potential market features.
- Use small-scale research such as questionnaires or interviews.
- Use market mapping to identify market segments.

Case study

The Pure Package idea

Jennifer Irvine's idea was a combination of her own interest and passion for healthy food and a realisation that no one was providing this service in quite this way. In an interview she gave to the smallbizpod website in August 2007 she admitted that at the start she did not have any money for market research, but tried to make the most of what little information she had about the market.

'I tried to find out about what competition, if any, there was out there, but I didn't know how to do it. Also, I couldn't afford to spend money researching customer tastes, so I used my friends. I cooked lots of recipes and asked them what they thought about the meals. They all gave very positive feedback, so I decided to go for it.'

Jennifer quickly realised that she needed more accurate market information when initial sales were disappointing. A friend suggested she contacted journalists and asked them for feedback. 'I wrote to loads of journalists and offered them free food. In return, they agreed to fill in a detailed questionnaire from which I got really useful feedback, not all positive! As a result I was able to change the product before launching it again. In addition, a few journalists wrote newspaper or magazine articles about the company, which gave us lots of free publicity. As a result, a few celebrities got in touch and wanted to try the product.'

www.purepackage.com

Questions

1 Suggest additional ways Jennifer could have researched the existing competition before deciding whether the idea had potential to be a success. (4 marks)

2 Explain how Jennifer researched whether the idea might be a success in the early stages of the product. (6 marks)

3 Complete a spider diagram to illustrate the strengths and weaknesses of Jennifer's initial idea. (6 marks)

4 Discuss the limitations of small-scale research for Jennifer's business. (10 marks)

💡 Franchises

Some entrepreneurs start a business by buying a **franchise**. This is a business structure in which the owner of a business idea (the **franchisor**) sells the right to use that idea to another person (the **franchisee**), usually in return for a fee and a share in any profit the franchisee makes. See page 12 for the advantages and disadvantages of franchises.

Protecting business ideas

An entrepreneur will want to protect an idea in order to recover the costs of bringing that idea to the market. Businesses often protect their products, processes and images through **copyrights**, **patents** and **trademarks**. If a business has spent time building a brand, or money researching a product, then the entrepreneur will want to make sure there is a return on that investment. In fact, the existence of this kind of protection means that businesses are more willing to invest because they know their efforts will be protected long enough to recover some of the money invested.

Study tip

In Unit 1 the focus is on small businesses with limited resources. If you get asked a question about market research in the early stages of a business start-up remember to be realistic about the kind of research that can be afforded. Small scale research is not perfect, but it is better than none at all, and it is often all that an entrepreneur can afford in the early stages of a start-up.

Key terms

Franchise: a form of business contract in which the franchisor already has a successful product or service, and agrees to sell to the franchisee the right to use the name, logo and trading methods of the business.

Franchisor: the business selling the franchise agreement to the franchisee.

Franchisee: the entrepreneur who buys the franchise agreement from the franchisor business.

Copyright: the protection given to books, plays, films and music.

Patent: an exclusive right to use a process or produce a product, usually for a fixed period of time, up to 20 years.

Trademark: a word, image, sound or smell that enables a business to differentiate itself from its competitors.

Table 2.2 *Advantages and disadvantages of a franchise to the franchisor*

Benefits to franchisor	Disadvantages to franchisor
Franchisor can expand business quickly	Potential loss of control over how the product/service is presented to the customers
Often, franchisor earns revenue from the franchisees' turnover rather than profit – so revenue is reasonably certain	May be difficult to control quality as franchise network expands
Risk is shared – much of the cost is met by the franchisee	Coordination and communication problems may increase as franchise network grows
Franchisee may have very good entrepreneurial skills, which will earn the franchisor revenue	Some franchisees become powerful as they acquire a number of franchises

Table 2.3 *Advantages and disadvantages of a franchise to the franchisee*

Benefits to franchisee	Disadvantages to franchisee
Able to sell an already recognised and successful product/service. Much less risky than setting up a completely new business	Proportion of revenue is paid to franchisor – this can be a substantial burden on a new business
Take advantage of central services such as marketing, purchasing, training, stock control and accounting systems and administration provided by franchisor	Franchisee may not feel that business is his/her own, and may not benefit from the personal rewards of entrepreneurship
Franchisor may have experience in the market that the franchisee can benefit from	Right to operate the franchise could be withdrawn if franchise 'rules' are broken

Activity

Investigate how many well-known high street businesses are in fact franchise networks – you'll be surprised. Also, research the British Franchise Association on the internet for more information on franchises.

Study tip

Make sure you understand the difference between a patent, trademark and copyright. A patent protects a product or process; a trademark is an image or other representation of a commercial idea, whilst copyright protects a piece of creative work such as a song or book.

Case study

Dyson wins Hoover case

In 2000, the domestic appliance giant Hoover suffered a humiliating defeat by rival Dyson in the High Court.

The court ruled that Hoover copied Dyson's designs in the manufacture of its Vortex bagless cleaner range. Sales of the Vortex range could have been suspended as a result of the ruling and Hoover may have had to radically alter the design or cease production altogether. Commenting on the case, victorious company founder James Dyson said, 'I am very pleased to see Hoover, who made a lot of false claims about their product, can't just rip off our designs and copy them.'

Hoover has a history of bitter rivalry with Dyson, which has revolutionised the vacuum cleaner market with its 'dual cyclone' design.

In 1990, a quarter of all vacuum cleaners sold in the UK were made by Hoover, but in 2000 it had less than 10% of the market, according to industry estimates. More than half of the vacuum cleaners sold in the UK are made by Dyson.

Questions

1 Consider the benefits to James Dyson of the protection that a patent gave his business.

2 To what extent does a patent give a business such as Dyson an unfair advantage over competition?

Case study

Domino's Pizza

Have you ever wondered why there are three dots in the Domino's Pizza logo? It's because when the company first started in the US, the original owner set himself the objective of owning three pizza delivery stores. Considering Domino's Pizza now has 8,000 stores in 50 countries, that seems a modest dream. Domino's has achieved rapid growth in the UK recently and predictions are this will continue. One reason for Domino's rapid growth is the fact that most of the branches are franchises.

Fig. 2.1 *Domino's Pizza logo*

The right to set up a Domino's Pizza outlet in the UK is owned exclusively by Domino's Pizza UK and Ireland plc. This company sells franchises to individuals who operate Domino's outlets as separate businesses. There were 772 Domino's Pizza franchises operating in the UK and Ireland at the start of 2013. The company has a target of 1,200 outlets in the UK and Ireland by 2021.

Domino's franchisees benefit from operating a fast food restaurant with one of the best-recognised brand names in the world. They receive support and ongoing training from the Domino's Pizza head office and regional teams. A local fast food franchise consultant is assigned to each franchisee to give advice on issues such as local regulations, health and safety requirements, and stock control. The impact of the national advertising campaigns – paid for by Domino's, because the franchisees themselves could not afford them – lead to increased sales.

However, this level of support and brand recognition does not come cheaply. It is estimated that the total cost of opening a new Domino's fast food restaurant is at least £280,000, with a major proportion of that being the franchise fee. A share of revenue is paid annually to Domino's. All supplies must be purchased from the franchisor too. Domino's franchisees are not allowed to have other business interests. They must keep at least a 51% share in the franchise business, and they should be personally responsible for operating their restaurant. All these measures are designed by Domino's to try to maintain the highest quality standards.

Domino's is confident of its future growth potential in the UK. The total pizza market is growing by 10% a year and Domino's share is currently around 20%. The company must choose new franchisees carefully. It does sell some new franchises to existing franchisees as long as they can prove that they will still be able to control a larger business. These existing operators know the market well, and they are already successful in selling the brand. However, does Domino's want to deal with large franchisee businesses? Selling to new franchisees might be more risky, but they might be even more entrepreneurial and keener to succeed than existing operators.

Questions

1. Explain what the term 'franchise' means. (2 marks)

2. Calculate the percentage increase in Domino's Pizza outlets from 2013 if the company is to meet its 2021 target. (3 marks)

3. Analyse TWO benefits to Domino's of selling franchises rather than opening its own managed outlets. (6 marks)

4 Analyse TWO benefits to Domino's of selling additional franchises to existing franchisees. (6 marks)

5 Discuss whether an entrepreneur, with some experience in catering, should open a Domino's franchise or set up a new fast food business. (10 marks)

6 Research task: Look into the main features of another major UK franchised business such as Subway or KFC. If you wanted to open a franchised fast food business, which company's franchise would you choose? Justify your answer.

Show the skills

Carefully apply your answers to the case study by using information you have gained from reading it. For example, the cost of setting up a Domino's franchise should be discussed in answer to question 5.

☑ *In this chapter you will have learned to:*

- understand how entrepreneurs generate new business ideas, often relying on their own experience or brain storming in order to identify gaps in the market. Most entrepreneurs do not have much money at the start, so their options are limited

- understand how entrepreneurs identify and exploit a market niche through small-scale research

- appreciate how limited the resources of a small business are initially, and how difficult it is to spend large amounts of money on research

- analyse the role of patents, copyrights and trademarks in protecting new business ideas and understand the crucial role that these methods of protecting ideas are because they enable an entrepreneur to recover the money invested in the new product, service or process

- evaluate the benefits and disadvantages of franchises and be able to judge whether a franchise is the right structure for a given business situation.

For answers to activities and case study questions see

3 Transforming resources into goods and services

In this chapter you will learn to:

- understand and explain the basic input-process-output model of business activity
- understand and apply the classification of business activity by sector
- understand and explain the benefits of added value to a product or service
- analyse the ways in which different businesses add value to their product or service.

Setting the scene

The Royal Oak

Pierre Cordin bought the Royal Oak pub to add to the three he already owned. He was the Managing Director of The Suffolk Pub Company, a business he started three years ago with the intention of providing a real alternative to the pubs owned by the larger breweries. He wanted to provide a restaurant quality menu in a pub environment. He researched each location carefully, choosing only those with a relatively high income earning local population.

Premium beers and lagers, good quality wine (including English wine which was growing in reputation) were on offer as well as food cooked by renowned chefs lured from London with the promise of high wages and a share in the profits. The first two had been very successful. He had learned that the more you add to the experience, beyond just the food, the more people wanted to visit, and the more they were willing to pay. When he trained as a chef, he had done a business course as well, and he had remembered the bit about adding value to his product.

Discussion points

1 Is a meal in a pub or restaurant a product or a service?

2 In what ways could a restaurant add value to a meal?

🔆 Business inputs and outputs

In the chapters so far, you have looked at the ways in which entrepreneurs turn ideas into businesses. In this chapter you will learn how the various factors that go to make a product or service are combined successfully to add value and meet customer needs.

At its simplest, a business is a process whereby **inputs** are processed to produce **outputs**.

Business activity tends to be classified in terms of whether it is primary, secondary, tertiary or quaternary.

Primary production is the extraction of resources at the first stage of production, involving resources such as land and raw materials. Farming is the obvious example.

Secondary production is the transformation of resources to produce finished goods and components. Car manufacture is an example.

Tertiary production is the transformation of resources to provide a service, which is why it is sometimes referred to as the service sector. It includes retailing, which is the selling of products from the primary and secondary sectors.

Other examples of tertiary activity include the public services such as health care and education, transport, tourism and finance. It also includes those activities which recently have proven to be in short supply such as plumbers, electricians and builders. The biggest growth

Key terms

Input: something that contributes to the production of a product or service.

Output: something that occurs as a result of the transformation of business inputs.

Study tip

The idea of transforming inputs to produce an output is as relevant to services as it is to products. In the exam you may face a service sector business, but remember there is still a process of transforming inputs such as people's time, expertise, skills and experience to providing that service. Added value is as much a feature of a haircut as it is of a car.

Fig. 3.1 *An example of primary production*

Fig. 3.2 *Car manufacture is an example of secondary production*

Fig. 3.4 *An example of tertiary production*

area in tertiary production is in business and financial services, where it is estimated that one in five people now work.

Quaternary production is the name given to industries whose main purpose is the transformation of information.

IT-based businesses are included in this definition, as are consultancy and Research and Development businesses. This sector continues to grow as the 'knowledge economy' becomes more important. The tertiary and quaternary sectors are sometimes referred to together, as they are both service based. They are by far the most important parts of the UK economy, accounting for about 75 per cent of total employment.

The changing importance of different sectors of business activity

It is tempting to assume that this process of transformation only takes place in the secondary sector of the economy, but as the primary and secondary sectors of advanced economies such as the UK decline, and tertiary and quaternary sectors expand, it is important to understand that the process of transformation of inputs to produce outputs is just as relevant for a service or an information based business as it is for a farm or a factory.

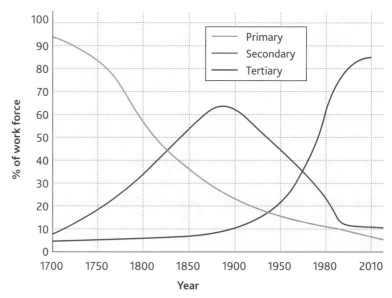

Fig. 3.3 *Primary, secondary and tertiary output adapted from www.bbc.co.uk*

Consider the data above, which shows clearly the change in significance of the various sectors.

It is becoming more difficult to provide precise definitions of each sector for two main reasons. Firstly, the significance of the sectors changes over time as economies evolve. Secondly, and more importantly, it is becoming increasingly difficult to classify individual businesses as they expand and innovate their product range to become successful. For example, it used to be easy to classify a farm as primary. But more and more farms have holiday accommodation or farm shops or activity centres attached. Some make local products such as wine or cider. Does that make them primary, secondary or tertiary, or a bit of all three! The innovation of entrepreneurs is making classifications such as this increasingly inaccurate.

Inputs include the raw materials, which are the basic 'ingredients' that go to make up a product or service. These will include component parts, semi assembled parts, energy and labour. But for service based businesses it will also include expertise, skills and information.

The production processes are those activities that transform the raw materials. Some examples are included in the activity below.

The outputs are the finished product, service or other benefit to the customer. Other outputs that are becoming increasingly recognised are waste and pollution.

💡 🗂 Adding value

Added value is the value of the process of transformation of inputs into outputs. It is measured by the difference in value between the price of the finished product or service and the cost of the raw materials. When a business adds value, the value of the finished product is greater than the sum of the values of all the inputs.

It can be represented with a diagram:

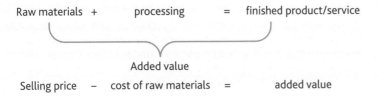

Fig. 3.5 *Adding value to a product*

Businesses add value in a number of ways: For example:

- Advertising – creates interest in a product or service and may convince a customer to pay a higher price, thereby increasing the added value.
- Branding – achieves a similar outcome because customers are often willing to pay more for a branded item than a non-branded one, even if the actual physical process of transformation is the same.
- Product features – value can be added by innovative design and adding new features to existing products. Mobile phone makers will charge higher prices for phones with the latest and most advanced features.
- Location – may enable a business to add value, for instance if the location is seen as particularly desirable.
- Personal service – allows a business to differentiate its product or service.
- Reduce input costs – this could be done by using cheaper materials, or using materials more efficiently, for example, less waste. Consumers may perceive cheaper materials as lowering quality. The price might then have to be *reduced*.

There are a number of benefits to businesses of adding value:

- Differentiation from the competition – customers might be more willing to choose a particular brand over its rivals.
- Charging a higher price.
- Reducing the sensitivity of demand to changes in price.
- Higher profit margins.
- Targeting product or service at a different market segment.

■ Case study

Penelope's

Penny and James hit on their idea for Penelope's after their daughter's prom night. They'd heard about limo services that take people to events and then bring them back again, but had been disappointed to find none existed in their area. Also, they had experienced a bad example of one themselves where they were made to feel lucky to be in the car and that they should be grateful to ride in the back of a (not very well looked after) Rolls Royce.

■ Key terms

Added value: the difference in value between the price of the finished product and the cost of materials used.

■ Activity

Some examples of adding value

Consider the following businesses and try to identify the process of transformation of inputs that adds value to the finished product or service. Make a list of each raw material, then briefly describe the transformational process that takes place.

1. A themed hotel
2. A wedding cake manufacturer
3. A hand-built sports car manufacturer
4. A real ale brewery
5. A tax consultant
6. An author of children's books

Study tip

Consider the relationship between the changes in business sectors and added value. As the UK economy moves away from agriculture and low cost manufacturing and towards services and niche manufacturing, the ability to add value increases. In farming, it is often much easier to add value (and therefore make more profit) from selling holiday accommodation on the farm than farming the land.

Penny was convinced that a market existed for a genuinely top quality service involving a chauffeur-driven limousine. 'What we need to focus on is not the transport bit of the product, but everything else. A limo is just a posh taxi unless you do other things to make it special.' James was not convinced at first, worried that it wasn't possible to offer anything but a posh taxi ride.

'Think of all the things you could do to make that journey even more special!' said Penny. 'You mean like champagne on the way there?' said James. 'Obviously not if you're taking students to their Year 11 prom!' warned Penny, 'but if your customers are a couple celebrating a wedding anniversary then that would be a great idea'.

They sat down and tried to think of ways they could add to the value of the experience of a limo ride. At the same time, it became clear to James that their potential market could be broken down into different segments, so they first of all identified the potential segment, then tried to think of ways to add value for that type of customer.

1 Wedding anniversary/romantic occasion.
2 Young person's event such as a prom.
3 Business event.

Questions

1 Explain which sector of business activity Penelope's is in. (4 marks)

2 Describe the small-scale research that Penny and James might have done to establish existing competition in the market. (4 marks)

3 Analyse THREE ways Penelope's could add value to each of the market segments. (9 marks)

4 To what extent is it always easier to add value to a product than a service? Use other real business examples to support your answer. (10 marks)

5 Research task: Investigate ONE other industry, e.g. soft drinks or sports shoes. Find out the measures that manufacturers and retailers of these products use to 'add value' to try to convince consumers to pay higher prices.

■ Show the skills

'To what extent' requires you to evaluate your answer and come to a final, supported conclusion.

☑ *In this chapter you will have learned to:*

■ understand how a business transforms inputs into outputs when making products or providing services, and appreciate that a service is as much a transformation of resources as a product

■ explain the primary/secondary/tertiary/quaternary classification of business activity and apply it to different businesses

■ understand also that these classifications evolve over time as the economy changes; with primary and secondary production declining and tertiary and quaternary production expanding

■ understand added value and how it arises in products and services and you'll begin to understand the relationship between added value and service sector activity

■ analyse the benefits of adding value in terms of a business's ability to differentiate itself from competition and its ability to generate profit.

For answers to activities and case study questions see

Practice questions

Chapters 1–3

1   What do you understand by the term enterprise? *(2 marks)*

2   List THREE likely characteristics of a successful entrepreneur. *(3 marks)*

3   Analyse THREE possible benefits to the UK economy of a thriving small business sector. *(9 marks)*

4   Describe THREE possible ways to measure the size of a business in the supermarket industry. *(3 marks)*

5   Describe TWO possible sources of advice and help available to a young person starting a mobile catering business. *(4 marks)*

6   What do you understand by the term opportunity cost? *(3 marks)*

7   Distinguish between patents, trademarks and copyrights. *(6 marks)*

8   Louise Murray imports jewellery from India and China and sells it in her West London shop and via her website. She has been in business for three years and has struggled to grow after an initial period of success. She decided to start this type of business because she was aware that a number of similar businesses in London had been successful and she was convinced there was room for more competition.

    a)   Evaluate the advantages and disadvantages of Louise starting a business in an existing market rather than attempting to meet the needs of a new market. *(8 marks)*

    b)   Analyse THREE possible benefits to Louise, who wishes to expand the business throughout the north of England, of franchising the business. *(3 marks)*

9   Define the term 'value added'. *(3 marks)*

10   Analyse THREE possible benefits of adding value to a restaurant specialising in sea food. *(6 marks)*

11   Describe TWO ways that a restaurant specialising in sea food could increase its added value. *(4 marks)*

12   Is a restaurant that specialises in sea food a primary, secondary or tertiary business? Explain your answer. *(4 marks)*

13   Based near Chichester in West Sussex, East Head Ltd is a designer and manufacturer of a variety of safety helmets for surfers and windsurfers. The owner Paul Bradley said 'I designed and made the first helmet for myself and when I asked around my friends who are also surfers, they all said they thought it was a great idea. I began selling initially just to friends, then word spread. Soon I couldn't

make them quick enough to meet demand. I didn't do any research to discover if there was a demand out there, I just got started and it grew.

I also was worried my design might be copied by other businesses, but I wasn't sure how to go about protecting my invention. I also needed to take on staff, which meant the company needed investment. An adviser from Business Link suggested I look for support from government or other agencies to help me in the first few months of trading.

My objective is to open up outlets in many of the main surfing and watersport areas in the UK within the next five years. I'm only 25 years old, and I expect to have a nationwide network of outlets before I'm thirty."

a) Describe the main reasons why Paul decided to start his own business. *(3 marks)*

b) Is East Head Ltd in the primary, secondary or tertiary sector of business? Explain your answer. *(3 marks)*

c) Describe THREE possible sources of help and advice Paul could have sought in the early stages of the business. *(6 marks)*

d) Analyse the possible benefits to East Head Ltd of patenting its designs. *(3 marks)*

e) To what extent would Paul's future objectives be guaranteed by the franchising of East Head? *(10 marks)*

4 Developing business plans

In this chapter you will learn to:

- understand the purpose and content of business plans and some of the problems small businesses encounter when planning

- understand the sources of information and guidance available to help businesses plan for competitive advantage

- explain the resources needed to construct a successful business plan

- evaluate the benefits of business planning for small business start-ups.

Study tip

Many people assume a business plan is something done for the bank manager or other lender. Whilst this is true sometimes, that is not the only purpose. If you are asked an exam question on business planning, remember the other benefits of planning, both at the start of the business, but also as the business is trading.

Setting the scene

AKC Home Support Services

Darren Jones launched his care business, AKC Home Support Services, in 1991 with his wife Sharron. Although writing their business plan was one of the first things the couple did, Darren admits he originally saw it as a bit of a chore. Now, he takes a different view, believing it has helped the business stay on track and true to its goals.

'When we started the firm I knew we needed a business plan but saw it more as a document for everyone else than something to help us. If I started another business tomorrow I would write one much more willingly as it brings a number of benefits – from helping you secure finance to keeping you focused on your goals. We got help from our local enterprise centre, looked at examples from other businesses and a template from the bank. We mixed and matched bits from these sources because not everything applied to us. For example, because we were going into a new market we couldn't write about our competitors but needed a lot of information about the market for care services.'

'We used our business plan to set out the financial and strategic goals we wanted to achieve in the short and long-term. We review it annually now unless there's a significant shift in our market and then we use it to immediately re-evaluate our goals. Our business plan has also helped us to avoid expanding too quickly. Early on, we were offered work in another county. This seemed great but when we looked at our business plan – and particularly our cashflow forecasts – we realised it was important to establish a firm base in one county before taking on work in another otherwise we would overstretch ourselves.'

'We purchased a residential unit four years ago and our business plan definitely helped us demonstrate why the bank should lend us the money. Without it being put down on paper I don't think it would have sounded like a very viable suggestion.'

'Our plan also helped us to get support from Shell LiveWire – the organisation that assists 16–30 year olds to start and develop businesses – as you must have a business plan to enter its competitions. We were awarded prizes twice – not only bringing in extra money but publicity too.'

www.businesslink.gov.uk

Discussion points

1. What appeared to be the main benefits to AKC of having a business plan at the start of the business?

2. What appear to be the main benefits of the business plan during the later stages of the business, as it grows?

21

■ Link

For more information on venture capitalists and business angels, see Chapter 8 – Raising finance, page 55.

■ Activity

Consider how much more successful most activities are when they are planned. The initial idea will probably be mapped out, and the plan might continue to be useful as you carry out your activity.

Often, the best way to decide whether you've been successful in something is to look back on what it was you initially set out to do. A business plan fulfils all these functions.

■ Key terms

Business plan: a written document describing the nature of the business, its objectives, marketing strategy, and projected cash flow forecast and income statement.

💡 What is a business plan?

A **business plan** is a document designed to allow a business to plan for the future, allocate resources, identify key decisions and prepare for problems and opportunities. It is particularly useful for business start-ups, but is also useful for applying for finance and for planning for growth.

A business plan has a number of purposes. It helps to plan for the future because it requires the entrepreneur to think carefully about the business, and commit all the main information and ideas to paper. The entrepreneur will therefore understand the business better and the market in which it operates. It will enable the entrepreneur to identify the main courses of action needed to start and run the business, and to set objectives against which the performance of the business can be measured.

A business plan allows an entrepreneur to present a request for extra funding. In the early stages of a business it is likely that money will be in short supply, so often entrepreneurs will need additional funding. A business plan will provide all the information a potential lender or investor will need to decide whether they wish to invest. Banks, venture capitalists and business angels all require detailed information before they make a decision.

Even after the business is up and running, a business plan continues to be an essential planning tool. It will provide a regular check on progress regarding things such as cash flow, objectives and financial forecasts.

The contents of a business plan

There is no single format for business plans, because they differ according to the type and size of business, the expertise of the entrepreneur and the precise purpose of the business plan, but a number of key elements are present in most business plans.

Executive summary: This is a summary of the main features of the business. It will be one or two pages in length and is often the most important part of your business plan. It is the first part that people see, and often it is the only part they will read! It should include highlights from each section of the rest of the plan and it is intended to explain the basics of the business in an interesting and informative way.

Business description: This is a description of the history of the business, its start-up plans, the type of business structure it has. It will tend to include:

■ start date (for new businesses) or how long the business has been trading, its history and any previous owners (for established businesses)

■ the type of business and sector of the market

■ the legal structure – is it a sole trader, partnership or limited company?

■ the entrepreneur's vision for the business.

Product or service: This is a description of the product or service being sold, its key features and how the customer will benefit. This will include:

■ what makes it different from the competition

■ what benefits the customers will gain

- plans for the further development of the product/service
- information on any copyrights, designs or trademarks.

Market analysis: This is an analysis of the market and competition. It also will include an analysis of the customers' needs, where they are, how to reach them and how the product or service meets the needs. This section will include:

- the market – data about the size and growth of the market as a whole
- the customer – the key features including who they are and where they are
- the competition – who they are, their strengths and weaknesses
- the future – how might the market change in the future and how can the business respond.

Strategy and implementation: This is an analysis of the key decisions and strategies that need to be carried out, together with who is responsible for carrying them out, when they have to do it by, and the money they have to do it with. The most important element here will be the marketing and sales strategies, which will include information on:

- pricing
- promotion
- sales strategies.

Production strategies might include:

- location – is it owned or rented, what are its advantages and disadvantages?
- production – are they owned or leased, how old are they, what is the capacity in relation to forecast demand?
- systems – stock control, quality control and financial management, IT.

Management team: This is a description of the key members of the business, together with their skills and experience. This section is also likely to include data on the number of employees, how the business is structured and salaries.

Financial plan: This will include a number of key financial documents such as the profit and loss account, cash flow forecast, balance sheet and break-even analysis. It might include some key financial ratios, as well any assumptions the business has made in putting its financial forecasts together.

Sources of help and guidance for business planning

Entrepreneurs can get a lot of help in the early stages of their business start-ups, particularly in writing a business plan. Some provide guidance on what to include, others provide templates that entrepreneurs can fill in with their own details.

Small business advisers

There is a wide range of help for small businesses. One example is Business Link, which provides detailed advice on the contents of a plan, templates, examples of completed business plans, as well as case studies of how small businesses have constructed and used business plans.

Study tip

Rather than try to memorise the precise contents of a business plan, have a look at a number of different ones and get an overall picture of the kinds of things that seem to appear. It's much better to understand **why** lenders and other interested parties would be interested in the information than it is to remember a precise format. If you understand the purpose and audience of business plans, you'll much more likely be able to recall the main contents.

Fig. 4.1 *Bytestart is one example of a source of help for business planning*

Accountants and bank managers

Most of the main high street banks offer a small business service, which includes advice about how to write and present a business plan. For example, Barclays Bank offer a small business advice service, a range of guides, in hard copy or on CD-ROM, a Local Business Manager, as well as a range of small business seminars.

Government agencies

The Government sees small business success as a key feature of a healthy economy. For example, the Department for Business, Enterprise and Regulatory Reform website describes its mission as being

> *to create the conditions for business success through competitive and flexible markets that create value for businesses, consumers and employees.*

www.businesslink.gov.uk

The Department offers a range of help and guidance, including a Business Plan competition, which provides the winners with £25,000 to help start up a business.

There are Government grants available also to small businesses to help them set up and write their business plans.

■ Resources needed to create a business plan

It seems clear, therefore, that a business plan is an essential planning tool for new business. So what does it take to draw up a good business plan?

Time – this is not an unlimited or free resource. Many entrepreneurs begin thinking about their new business venture while they are still in employment in their old jobs, or are still at home looking after their children. It is a time consuming activity, and the more time taken, the better the plan is likely to be.

Determination – an entrepreneur needs to remain determined to complete the plan accurately and fully, even if it proves difficult.

Vision – the entrepreneur needs a clear idea of the business and its USP.

Numbers – an entrepreneur cannot avoid financial information, and can't afford to be afraid of numbers.

Planning – this is a skill in itself, the ability to be organised and to plan a number of activities at once.

■ Problems for small business planning

Despite the benefits for a small business of a business plan, there are potential problems.

- Time – an entrepreneur may not feel he/she has the time to devote to putting together a business plan. This might be true if the entrepreneur wants to start trading as quickly as possible, perhaps because he/she is excited about the product, or just wants to get going.

- Money – although not expensive, a business plan costs some money, even if it is just in terms of the entrepreneur's own time. Any advice about planning might cost money.

■ Link

For more information on Government support for enterprise and entrepreneurs, see Chapter 1 – Enterprise, page 6.

- Expertise – an entrepreneur may not know enough about the product/service or market initially to be able to construct a business plan accurately. For instance, the financial elements of the plan require some forecasts about sales, which the entrepreneur may not know.

- Opportunity cost – some people may feel that the time spent on a business plan is 'wasted' when it could be spent actually trading.

- On balance, most people would agree that a business plan is worth the time and resources it takes to put it together. It might depend on the circumstances the entrepreneur is in. For instance, someone with a clear idea of the market and good existing knowledge of the product and no need of extra finance may decide a plan is less important than someone moving into a new area or needing financial support from a bank, venture capitalist or business angel.

Show the skills

If you are answering a question about the importance of business plans, you must evaluate their significance. For example, although they can reduce risks for new businesses and increase chances of funding, they do not guarantee success if, for instance, economic conditions worsen quickly.

Case study

The Old Railway Station Hotel

Six months ago Barry Morgan and his brother James bought the Old Railway Station Hotel near York from the previous owner who had spent large sums of money converting it from a dilapidated railway station on an abandoned line into a small, luxury hotel. The previous owner had converted the station building itself into the reception, restaurant and bar, whilst a number of carriages had been converted into hotel rooms. The conversion had taken six months, and expectations had been high that it would be a success. Indeed, the first three months trading had been healthy, but soon the bookings declined and the business struggled to meet its high costs.

Before Barry and James bought the hotel, they realised that the main problem was the substantial loan repayments that the original owner had to pay due to the high costs of conversion. The Morgans produced a business plan for the hotel to show to potential investors in their business. They wanted to raise £175,000 which, when added to their own capital, would be enough to buy the hotel and pay off some of the outstanding debts.

They were successful in raising the finance. The Morgans took over the hotel, and they were convinced it would be a profitable business if they could operate it efficiently. The potential market was large, especially with so many foreign tourists visiting the nearby city of York. The new owners changed the marketing strategy of the hotel. They based prices on the results of market research that they had undertaken when drawing up the business plan. The former owner had set prices based on his previous experience of running a London hotel.

Six months after buying the hotel, the Morgans were pleased with its success. They had not realised though, when they wrote the business plan, that a major hotel company had plans to build a large golf and hotel complex five miles away. James was also worried about the recent decline in foreign tourists to the UK, and increases in income taxes proposed by the government.

Questions

1. Identify TWO ways in which James and Barry might have researched the hotel market. (4 marks)

2. Analyse the likely information that James and Barry included in their business plan. (8 marks)

3. To what extent would a business plan guarantee the success of the Old Railway Station Hotel? (12 marks)

4. Research task: Use the link below to investigate in more detail the importance of business planning, and the key contents of a good plan. There are video clips to watch too, for example, why plans are important to investors. http://www.entrepreneur.com/businessplan/index.html

✔ *In this chapter you will have learned to:*

■ understand the purposes of a business plan and its value to small businesses, both before trading, but also as a useful analytical tool as the business is trading

■ appreciate that a plan allows an entrepreneur to decide where he or she wants to go with the business, and assess whether he/she is getting there

■ explain the sources of information that are needed to construct a business plan, and the various sources of help and guidance that a small business can call upon. You'll understand that a range of government, bank and other agencies are willing to help business start-ups

■ explain the time and skills needed to construct a business plan and appreciate why on occasion, entrepreneurs choose not to do a business plan. You'll understand that in the vast majority of cases, this is not a good idea

■ evaluate the benefits of a business plan for small business start-ups in particular situations.

For answers to activities and case study questions see kerboodle

Conducting start-up market research

In this chapter you will learn to:

- explain the methods of primary and secondary market research

- understand the benefits of different methods of market research

- explain the difference between quantitative and qualitative research data

- analyse the importance of sampling, and the factors influencing the choice of sample

- evaluate the usefulness of various research methods for small business start-ups.

Link

For more information on how many entrepreneurs start up a business based on a hobby or interest, see Chapter 2 – Generating and protecting business ideas, page 9.

Key terms

Market research: the process of gathering, analysing and interpreting data about a market.

Primary market research data: data collected by the entrepreneur, or paid to be collected, which does not already exist.

Secondary market research data: data already in existence that has not been collected specifically for the purposes of the entrepreneur.

Setting the scene

Star Financial Services

Jeremy and Jenny Bellinger had quit their well paid jobs in banking to start their own financial consultancy business. They were both convinced that their home town of Bedford could provide sufficient customers who needed advice on pensions, investments, savings and insurance. They had asked a number of friends and family and all had been very positive.

Jeremy had spent a useful morning looking through the phonebook for existing businesses in the same market and had only found a few. All of them were large, well-known high street names. Jeremy and Jenny believed there was a gap in the market for a small business giving personal financial advice.

Jenny agreed, but was nervous about going to the bank for a start-up loan without more evidence that their hunch was right. She had sat in too many meetings as a Small Business Adviser when she worked in a bank listening to poorly researched ideas. She knew the bank wanted evidence of a market, not a hunch there might be one.

Discussion points

1. What evidence could Jenny and Jeremy collect to support their request to the bank?

2. What limiting factors exist for Jenny and Jeremy preventing them from obtaining accurate information about the potential market?

Start-up market research

The benefits of setting up a business based on a hobby or interest include a passion for the product and knowledge of it. However, this can also be a disadvantage if the entrepreneur just assumes that his/her interest will automatically be shared by others. Entrepreneurs, and those looking carefully at the business plan to decide whether to invest in the new business start-up, will need evidence that there is likely to be a demand for the product or service. The problem that entrepreneurs face is that gathering this evidence can be costly, and money is often in very short supply at the start of the business. So the entrepreneur is often trying to balance the need to gather data about the market with the need to keep costs as low as possible. This chapter looks at the methods of market research that a small business start-up might reasonably hope to afford.

The first decision an entrepreneur faces is whether to use data that already exists – **secondary market research data** – or to collect data specifically for the purposes of the business start-up – **primary market research data**. Each has its own benefits and drawbacks. Often, the most successful strategy is to combine some secondary research, with a small amount of carefully collected primary research.

There is no perfect source of information or method of collecting data, but overall some data is better than none at all.

Fig. 5.1 *Yell.com is a useful source of secondary market research data*

Activity

Secondary research

There exists a lot of possible sources of market research data, and the internet has made this much more accessible. Included in this chapter is a range of possible sources. Use these, and any others you feel are appropriate to analyse a market of your choice in order to assess whether a new product or service could be successful. This could be done as part of a Young Enterprise company.

■ Secondary market research data

An existing business may have lots of useful data internally that it could use, such as sales figures, stock records, geographical analysis of sales, financial records, reports from sales staff about customer opinions and even customer complaints! These can be very useful in analysing the performance of the business. However, the entrepreneur attempting a business start-up has no such data. There are many examples of sources of secondary market research that an entrepreneur might use for a small business start-up. Some will assist the entrepreneur to understand the market itself. These include:

■ Many entrepreneurs forget to use the most obvious source of information about their local market: the listings of businesses in the BT phone book, Thomson Local or Yellow Pages.

■ Trade Associations – most industries have an organisation which exists to advise and assist the businesses in it.

■ The Chartered Institute of Marketing has a marketing library.

■ Chambers of Commerce.

■ Enterprise Agencies.

■ Business Link (government organisation providing advice and support to start, maintain and grow a business).

■ The trade press – most industries have their own magazines and newspapers. These will include articles on the latest trends in the market, useful contacts and information about suppliers.

■ Source reference materials such as surveys and directories. The Institute of Directors website at www.iod.com has a useful directory, as does www.is4profit.com/business-directory.html.

■ Competition – competitors will issue brochures, price lists, special offers, product details. All of this is valuable information.

Other sources of secondary research to help understand the economy, and the demographics of the country or region include:

■ Government publications such as the National Statistics online at www.statistics.gov.uk and the Department for Business Enterprise and Regulatory Reform at www.statistics.gov.uk. Also, there is information provided by the EU through Eurostat at www.epp.eurostat.cec.eu.int.

■ If the entrepreneur is willing and able to spend some money purchasing secondary research, there are companies that specialise in collecting and analysing market information. Some well-known ones include Mintel (www.mintel.com), Dun and Bradstreet (www.dbuk.dnb.com) and Verdict (www.verdict.co.uk). These tend to be quite expensive, although they are detailed, so will tend only to be used by established businesses or entrepreneurs with money to spend (perhaps those that have a business angel or Dragon to invest in their business!)

■ Primary market research data

If an entrepreneur wants detailed, precise information about the market, it is often necessary to collect it specifically for that purpose. This is primary market research data.

Business start-up entrepreneurs may not be able to afford to pay someone to collect primary research, so may have to do it themselves. A number of decisions need to be made by the entrepreneur when deciding on collecting primary research.

Sampling methods

Who shall I collect information from?

Ideally, the answer to this question is **everyone**. However, it is likely the entrepreneur does not have the resources or time or skills to research everyone so a choice has to be made to select a proportion of those that could be researched. This means sampling. The sample size is important, because the smaller the size of the sample the less confident, generally, an entrepreneur can be about its accuracy.

A **random sample** does not mean haphazard. It takes a lot of thought and care to get a truly random sample. Asking people in the street on a Thursday afternoon in a town centre is not going to get a random sample, because many people will not be able to be in town at that time. Computers are increasingly used to generate randomly chosen lists of people.

A **quota sample** is one in which the characteristics of the market as a whole are mirrored in the sample. For instance, a researcher might be given targets to ask 50 males between 20 and 29 years of age, 30 females between 30 and 39 years of age. Once the researcher has reached that number no more are asked. It can be cheaper to do however, and accurate if the entrepreneur knows about the key characteristics of the potential market. A quota sample can be collected on a street corner because the researcher just stays there until he/she has the required number of people with the key characteristics.

A **stratified sample** is one where a selection of people is randomly chosen from within a sub-group. For instance, a business might want to know the views of females aged between 17 and 24. People would be selected randomly from within that group.

Factors affecting choice of sampling methods

■ Available finance – a small business start-up is unlikely to have large amounts of capital available, and the entrepreneur may be unwilling to spend money researching the market. So any market research in the initial stages is likely to be low cost, or free.

■ The nature of the product – an existing product or service will already have created secondary data in the form of information about competitors, their location, sales, etc. New, innovative ideas are less likely to have data already in existence. Local products or services are easier to research than those with larger geographical markets. Many entrepreneurs find it easier to research customers' attitudes to a physical product than a service because there is something physical to see and try out.

■ The level of risk – the newer the product the greater the risk (and the greater the potential rewards!). It is probably true that the greater the risk the more important the need for research.

■ The target market – a clearly defined target market, whether in terms of age, income or some other factor, is easier to target in terms of sample.

Primary research methods

■ Observation – sometimes, the most useful information is gathered by an entrepreneur just watching people walking through a shop, or past a particular location.

■ **Key terms**

Random sample: one in which each potential member of a group has an equal chance of being in the sample.

Quota sample: the sample of a certain number of people is taken from one specific group of the population, for example 100 females or 50 people aged between 18 and 30.

Stratified sample: the population is divided into groups with common characteristics, for example, people earning over £100,000, and a sample is randomly selected from this group.

■ Link

For more information on market segmentation, see Chapter 6 – Understanding markets, page 36.

Fig. 5.2 *Call centres can conduct primary market research with speed and efficiency*

■ IT allows for far more detailed and accurate 'observation' through sales records on EPOS systems, loyalty card schemes, CCTV and interactive websites.

■ Written questionnaire – the most obvious (and most over-used) method of primary research. The benefits are that a large number can be distributed quickly. However, badly designed questionnaires are worse than none at all. It is essential to avoid asking leading questions that encourage one answer more than others, and to be sure to use open and closed questions correctly. Written questionnaires are limited to collecting only the information from the questions; it isn't easy to respond on the spot to an answer with a follow up question.

■ Face-to-face questionnaire – difficult and time consuming, but has the benefit of being able to respond to answers with follow up questions.

■ Telephone and online surveys – have many of the same benefits of face-to-face contact, but are cheaper and quicker to do.

■ Focus groups – people discussing a product can reveal information and opinions that might not be revealed by interviewing people individually. This method can reveal issues the business had not thought of. Focus groups can be useful in discovering the psychology of purchasing decisions, such as the importance of peer influences and image. The danger of this method is in drawing conclusions about the whole market based on a relatively small sample size.

■ Test marketing – selling a product in a small segment of the market can generate useful data that can improve the product before a full launch. The small scale of many business start-ups means this may not be feasible.

Primary research has a number of disadvantages:

■ It can be expensive, so it is often difficult for a small business to afford it.

■ It is difficult to carry out accurately.

■ It can be inaccurate, therefore the business might make inappropriate decisions.

■ Entrepreneurs often lack the skills and time to carry out primary research.

Study tip

Market research is another area where numbers play a key part. Be sure you are confident in assessing simple numerical information such as the percentage of people who respond to a question in a certain way. Keep practising those numbers!

Case study

Market research at Bladonmore

Bladonmore is a financial training business, based in London. A customised service and a gritty, real-world approach to training have enabled the company to grow rapidly during its first two years. Director Richard Rivlin explains how effective use of market research has contributed to Bladonmore's development.

'Like most companies starting out, we needed to research our target market but didn't have limitless cash to pay someone to do it for us. Doing it yourself is cheap in money terms – but you have to invest your time if you expect to get anything useful out of it.'

'Over a period of three months, I went on a virtual fact-finding mission using the internet. If you persevere, you can find an incredible amount of quality information for free, including market reports and expert analysis. Business consultants' websites, industry bodies and sector-leading companies are a good place to start.'

'I wanted to know the size of the market, to learn from competitors' successes and mistakes and to understand what potential clients want.'

'Research isn't just about reading the occasional market report. It should be an on-going process that keeps you up to date with your market, your rivals and your clients. I find newspapers one of the best research sources. There's something relevant to our business in the press almost every day.'

'I didn't wake up to the wonders of free expert research soon enough. If I had my time again, I'd head straight for the websites of top consultants like Ernst & Young and McKinsey. You may not be able to afford their research fees, but they publish enough in the public domain to meet the needs of many smaller businesses.'

'I now make it part of my daily routine to clip useful research out of newspapers. I even carry around a small pair of scissors for the purpose. It's yielded several business development ideas and I wish I'd got into the habit sooner.'

www.businesslink.gov.uk

Questions

1. Assess the benefits of secondary market research to Bladonmore. (10 marks)

2. Suggest THREE ways that Bladonmore could use primary market research data to add to the information provided by secondary techniques. (6 marks)

3. Discuss the most appropriate primary research method for Bladonmore. Justify your answer. (10 marks)

💡 Quantitative and qualitative data

Some of the information will be in numerical form. For example, a business might discover that 70 per cent of its potential customers dislike the image of a product. This is **quantitative data** because it refers to numerical information. Quantitative data is good for establishing key information about a business and its market.

Techniques to collect quantitative data include:

- questionnaire
- telephone surveys
- online surveys.

Other types of research generate **qualitative data**, which is information about attitudes, feelings and opinions. This kind of data is often more revealing and useful, but it is more difficult and expensive to collect. This is probably especially true for the business start-up.

Techniques to collect qualitative data include:

- in-depth interviews
- group discussions, such as focus groups.

It is often said that quantitative data reveals what is happening, whilst qualitative data explains why it is happening. To illustrate, it is often quoted that 'eight out of ten owners who expressed a preference said

■ Key terms

Quantitative data: data in numerical form. An example of this is '8 out of 10 owners who expressed a preference said their cats preferred Whiskers'. Quantitative data is usually collected from larger scale research in order to generate statistically reliable results.

Qualitative data: data about opinions, attitudes and feelings. It is usually expressed in terms of why people feel or behave the way they do.

their cats preferred Whiskers'. That piece of quantitative data is a good advertising slogan, but a more revealing piece of market research would be the qualitative data behind why two out of ten didn't.

Case study

Market research plan: making the right decisions

For each of the scenarios below, discuss in groups and answer the questions in order to create a market research plan for each one.

- A dry cleaning business is planning to open in a high street location in a small town. This is a franchise of a well-known national chain. The franchisee wants to know the size of the potential market, the price customers are willing to pay and the best location for the outlet.

- An employee of a large car manufacturer has been made redundant and is hoping to start up a business as a manufacturer of specialist parts for car engines. His customers are likely to be other car manufacturers in the UK and, eventually, other parts of the EU. He needs to know about existing competitors in the UK, possible trends in car purchasing and likely changes in the economy.

- An entrepreneur is convinced there's a gap in the market for her theme hotel, which has a number of rooms decorated in themes such as 'Hollywood glamour', '1950s romance', 'space age', etc. She wants to know people's attitudes to themed hotels and whether they would be prepared to pay extra to stay in this type of room. She also wants to know how best to promote this product.

For each of the above scenarios, answer the following questions. **In each case, be prepared to justify your answer.**

Questions

1. Identify and explain TWO sources of secondary data that the entrepreneur planning to open the themed hotel could use.   (4 marks)

2. Identify and explain TWO sampling methods that this entrepreneur could use if she conducted primary research.   (4 marks)

3. Analyse TWO primary research methods that the dry cleaning business could use.   (6 marks)

4. Discuss the importance of market research to the success of the car-part manufacturing business being planned by the employee who was made redundant.   (10 marks)

5. Research task: Assume that you are planning to open a new café in your home town. Undertake preliminary market research into this market by using a combination of secondary research and primary research methods.

✔ *In this chapter you will have learned to:*

- explain the different methods of secondary and primary research available to a small business start-up and realise that the limited resources of a small business is likely to determine what data is collected and how it is collected

- understand the benefits of various methods of collecting market research information for small businesses, whilst also understanding that limited resources may mean a less than perfect picture of how the market is generated

- explain the difference between qualitative and quantitative data and understand how each type of data is likely to be collected

- analyse how sampling can be used effectively by an entrepreneur, and understand the factors behind sampling decisions

- evaluate the usefulness of various research methods for small business start-ups and be able to make justified recommendations on the most appropriate market research strategy in a given situation.

For answers to activities and case study questions see **kerboodle**

6 Understanding markets

In this chapter you will learn to:

- understand the key features of physical and virtual markets and the main factors affecting demand

- explain the features, benefits and limitations of different methods of market segmentation

- understand and use numerical techniques to analyse data such as calculating proportions and percentages, changes in values and rates of change

- use these numerical techniques to calculate market size, market growth and market share and to analyse market conditions.

Setting the scene

New Horizons Travel

Kate and Anna have operated their small travel business in Colchester for just six months. Business has been steady but not as good as the business plan forecasts. 'We need to promote certain kinds of destinations, the places that UK and foreign tourists really want to visit,' said Kate. 'But how do we find that out?' asked Anna. 'I looked at the government's statistics website and found this section. I thought this would be a good start,' said Kate.

> *Visits abroad by UK residents increased by 6% from January 2012 to January 2013, with over half of those visits to Europe. Over this period visits to the USA fell by 5%.*
>
> *Over the same period visits by overseas residents into the UK fell by 1% to 2,220,000 although the amount spent increased by 11%.*
>
> *Over the three months to the end of January 2013, there were 9,880,000 visits abroad by UK residents and they spent over £5.56bn.*
>
> *Between Nov 2012 and Jan 2103 there were 7,990,000 visits to the UK and these visitors spent over £4bn. Nearly 10% were from the USA and 75% from Europe. London proved to be the most popular destination followed by Edinburgh and Manchester.*

'These figures are very interesting, but could we not get data that is more relevant to our business in Colchester?' said Anna.

www.statistics.gov.uk

Discussion points

1. How useful is this information to a small travel firm, and what other sources of information could Anna and Kate use?

2. Why is it important for entrepreneurs to know and understand trends in the markets their businesses operate in?

Link

For more information on how small business collect data about their product, market and competition, see Chapter 5 – Conducting start-up market research, page 27.

Understanding the nature and type of markets

Market research data can help a business to understand its market, for example whether it is operating in a local or national market.

Table 6.1 *Features of local and national markets*

Type of market	Features
Is the market a **local market**?	Business may have a very good relationship with, and understanding of, the customers
	Communication with customers is likely to be easy, and relatively cheap
	Reputation will spread quickly and easily to customers and potential customers
	It is relatively easy to collect primary data from customers
	Changes in customer tastes are likely to be apparent quickly
	Market size may be small, or at least there is limited possibility for continuous growth
Is the market a **national market**?	More costly distribution of products/services to customers
	Slower communication with customers
	Competitors nearer to customers
	Slow spread of reputation – good or bad! – to customers
	Larger potential market

In the above examples, the assumption is that there is a physical location for the business around which the customers are distributed. However, increasingly businesses do not have a physical presence in the market, but the market is an **electronic market**.

There is also open source software available that can build web pages, linked to a database, which a small business could use to create an online presence. Companies such as Pay Pal and World Pay can handle the financial transactions.

Factors affecting demand

The importance of demand

All businesses want their products to sell. Estimating customers' **demand** for products and the factors affecting demand is an essential part of market research. Demand rarely stays constant and, for some products, can vary substantially over even a short time period. Understanding the forces that influence demand is very important for all entrepreneurs.

The factors most likely to affect demand for a good or service include:

Price – normally, if the price is reduced, demand will rise. This might not be the case if other factors are changing too, such as competitors' prices. The demand for some products is very responsive to a price change, e.g. if there are many rival products. However, for some products, such as essential goods or branded products with customer loyalty, a change in prices may not impact greatly on the quantity sold.

Competition – prices charged by competitors can affect the demand for a business's product. If rivals' prices are reduced and if the business does not follow suit, a fall in demand can be expected. Relative price is not the only consideration though, as new features, celebrity endorsements and successful branding by competitors can also impact on demand.

Key terms

Local market: customers are only a short distance away.

National market: a geographically dispersed market where customers are spread over a large area.

Electronic market: does not have a physical presence, but exists in terms of a virtual presence via the internet. Many businesses have gone from 'brick to click'.

Demand: the quantity of a product that customers are willing and able to buy at a given price over a certain time period.

Study tip

Too often in exams, candidates give the impression that only one factor affects price, when in fact it is likely to be a combination of factors that determine the price of a product. Consider the list of factors affecting demand and, choosing a number of different products and services, rank the factors in terms of the most influential for each product/service. See if you can draw conclusions about what types of products/services feature which factor most prominently.

Table 6.2 *Advantages and disadvantages of online marketing*

The advantages of online marketing	The disadvantages of online marketing
The world is the market	Price transparency means that any business that can't or won't keep its prices down will lose customers
Less expensive than a physical presence, both in terms of reaching customers with marketing information and distributing products	A website might get a lot of 'hits', but it doesn't mean people will buy. There are no sales staff to encourage and advise customers
24/7 opening. No need to close	
No requirement for an expensive, highly visible high street location. An effective link to search engines will work just as well	A website crash is the equivalent of all the branches of a business having to close at the same time
Start-up and running costs are lower than a physical presence	Security issues can be a problem, e.g. credit card fraud
Business can react much more quickly to customer requests. Often products are distributed immediately upon payment which itself is often instant	Some people like to go to a shop and browse – there are some purchases where the customer needs to see/hear/taste/smell the product
Real time information is gathered by the database as it interacts with customers, so the entrepreneur is constantly in touch with the performance of business	Some people complain of a lack of help and support from online retailers if things go wrong
Customers expect businesses to have an online presence, so to not have one would be damaging to its reputation	

Incomes – if consumer incomes rise, demand for many products will increase as more can be afforded. The reverse is the case if incomes fall. However, the demand for luxury goods is likely to be more income sensitive than the demand for necessities.

Marketing – there is often a positive relationship between the amount spent on advertising and other forms of marketing and demand.

Seasonal demand – this is particularly important for some products such as clothing and energy, but less significant for many food products and consumer services.

Market segmentation

Market segmentation involves identifying groups of consumers with similar characteristics and then focusing marketing on one or more of these groups.

The most frequently-used method of segmenting markets is demographic segmentation. This breaks the market down into customers' characteristics such as age, income levels, gender, ethnicity and socio-economic groups. Other types of segmentation are based on differences in lifestyle or personality, or regional/national differences between customers.

There are both advantages and disadvantages in developing different products for some of these different groups:

Advantages of market segmentation:

- Leads to a better understanding of customers' needs in that **market segment** and a greater chance that these needs will be met
- Less wasteful of resources than when trying to sell the same product to 'everyone'
- More effective targeting of promotion to specific groups
- Segmentation can help a business differentiate its products from those of competitors and this might allow higher prices to be charged.

Key terms

Market segmentation: the technique where the market is broken down into smaller sections with similar characteristics.

Market segment: a group of consumers within a larger market who have similar characteristics such as age or income level.

Fig. 6.1 *Tui segment the holiday market by targeting certain destinations to families, but other resorts to adventurous, sports oriented customers*

Disadvantages of segmentation:

- Requires effective – and perhaps expensive – market research to establish customer segments and needs within these groups
- May be inaccurate to assume that all customers in a segment, for example, the 18–25 year olds, all want the same type of product
- May not be appropriate for new businesses operating in a market that is already small.

Case study

Segmentation in UK cinema industry

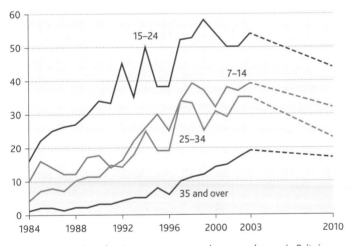

Fig. 6.2 *Attending the cinema once a month or more by age in Britain*

There were 31 million visits to UK cinemas in the first two months of 2013: an increase of 7% compared with 2012. This increase reflected the great popularity of the recent releases such as *Les Misérables* and *Lincoln*. There are hopes in the UK film industry that total admissions in 2013 will exceed the figure for 2012 of 172 million. Young people aged 15–24 are still the most likely age group to visit the cinema frequently, that is, more than once a month. 44% of the group recorded this level of cinema attendance. Only 17% of the over 35 age group visited cinemas more than once a month.

Almost all children (98%) aged 4 to 9 are accompanied to the cinema by an adult. Children start to go to the cinema with friends from around 10 years old. Over 70% of the 10–14 age group visit the cinema with friends. In January 2013, the most popular films aimed at this age group were *Wreck it Ralph* and *Oz the Great and Powerful*.

The majority of cinema admissions are to modern multiplex cinemas which show up to 30 different films per day in many different screening rooms. However, independent cinemas are continuing to survive and even thrive in some areas of the country. These usually target specific segments of the market, such as people interested in older films, foreign films or non-commercial films that would not be shown in the big national chains.

Questions

1. Explain THREE ways in which a cinema owner could segment the market for films. (6 marks)

2. Assess the value of the information above to an entrepreneur planning to open an independent cinema in the north of England. (10 marks)

3. Discuss whether the entrepreneur should focus the cinema on just one segment of the market. (10 marks)

Using data to understand the market – numerical techniques

Proportions of a total – market share

One of the ways in which data can be analysed is in terms of how much a value is in relation to a total. Proportions can be expressed in many different ways, which is why they are often confusing. Many people find they understand proportions if they think of pieces of a cake or pizza.

If you were faced with a piece of data such as '47 out of 94 people interviewed said yes they liked the product' it might not be easy to see what proportion that is. If you saw the pizza in Figure 6.3, you'd instantly see the proportions saying yes and no.

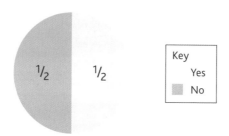

Fig. 6.3

So a good way to begin to understand proportions is to 'see' them as pieces of a pizza. Proportions are often expressed as fractions. So in the above example, the proportion saying 'yes' is half, or ½. How do we arrive at ½? Well, we have *1 pizza, and we've split it in 2*. The number of pizzas we've got goes at the top, and the number of times it's divided up goes at the bottom.

Let's do another one. Suppose you went with two friends to a pizza restaurant and ordered the biggest pizza they had and wanted it divided so you each got a piece. The number of pizzas (1) goes at the top, and the number of pieces (3) goes at the bottom. So you'd each get ⅓ of the pizza. Again it might be worth 'seeing' what that proportion looks like. See Figure 6.4.

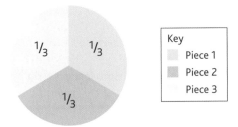

Fig. 6.4

So, proportions might be expressed as pieces of a pizza or as fractions, but they also come in percentages. How does a fraction get turned into a percentage? Let's go back to our first example. In it we said a half is 1 over 2, or ½. Replace the number 1 at the top with 100. Then it becomes $^{100}\!/_2$, which is 50. So a half, or ½ is 50%. Try it with the pizza example. Each friend got ⅓ of the pizza. Replace the 1 at the top of the fraction with 100, and it becomes $^{100}\!/_3$, which is 33.3%.

So to turn a fraction into a percentage, replace the 1 at the top with 100.

Suppose two more friends arrived just as the pizza was brought to the table. What proportion of the pizza would each of you get? There's still only one pizza, so the number on the top is still 1, but there are now five of you, so the number on the bottom becomes 5. You'll get ⅕ of the pizza. What does that proportion look like? See Figure 6.5.

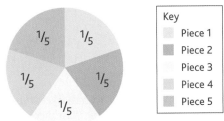

Fig. 6.5

Let's finally turn that piece of pizza into a percentage. Remember, to do this you replace the 1 at the top with 100. So now it's $^{100}\!/_5$, which is 20%.

A pie chart looks just like a pizza, so that's why it's such a good way to display information such as proportions. One particularly useful way that pie charts are used is to calculate **market share**.

■ Key terms

Market share: the proportion of a total market accounted for by one product or company.

■ Case study

Calculating market share

Brian Henderson had been staring at the figures for what seemed like the whole of the day. 'I can't make sense of this' he said. 'Hendersons' sales last year were £125,000. I know that the total sales in the market were £625,000. So how do I work out our market share?'

'Let me show you . . . again' his wife Penny said patiently. 'How many times do our sales divide into the total sales of the market?' 'Er . . . 5' said Brian after he'd used the calculator. 'OK, so we have ⅕ of the market' said Penny. 'Can you remember how to turn ⅕ into a percentage?' she asked. 'Yes I do! You replace the 1 at the top with 100 then divide by 5' said Brian, rather pleased with himself. 'So, our market share is 100/5, which is 20%'.

Brian was getting confident now, so Penny said, 'look at the rest of the data and calculate the other companies' market shares'.

Table 6.3

Company	Sales
Hendersons	125,000
Williamson	250,000
Bryant	200,000
Topping	50,000
Total	**625,000**

Study tip

When completing calculations, it's often useful to do a check to see if your answer makes sense. In the above example, sales changed by £125,000 and they were originally £300,000.

Half of £300,000 is £150,000, which is quite close to £125,000, so you know that the correct answer is not going to be far from half – which you also know is 50%. 41% is close to 50%, so you can be quite sure you've probably got your calculation right.

■ Key terms

Market growth: the measurement of the change in market size, usually expressed as a percentage of its original size.

Market size: the measurement of the size of total sales for a whole market, either expressed in terms of the value of sales (in currency) or the volume of sales (in units).

Study tip

Market share questions can be asked in different ways. For example:

Company A recorded sales revenue of £4.8m in 2012. Its market share was 25.6%. What was the total size of the market?

Total market size = $\dfrac{£4.8m}{0.256}$

= £18.75m

Questions

1. Calculate the market share for each competitor and display this information in a pie chart.

2. Using this information, assess the position of Hendersons in the market.

Changes in values – market size and growth

As well as looking at the way proportions of totals are calculated, market research data will often analyse how values are changing.

Suppose a business had sales last year of £300,000, and this year sales were £425,000. How do you calculate the size of the increase compared to what it was?

First you have to calculate by how much sales in a market have changed. £425,000 – £300,000 is £125,000. Now we divide £125,000 by the original figure of £300,000 and finally multiply the answer by 100. The answer is 41.67%.

Let's go through that again.

$$\frac{\text{How much has the value changed?}}{\text{What was the original value?}} \times 100$$

In numbers this is:

$$\frac{£125,000}{£300,000} \times 100 = 41.67\%$$

This is a calculation of **market growth**, which is different from market share. In terms we used before, market share is a measure of how big your piece of pizza is. Market size is how big the pizza itself is. Market growth is how much the pizza has grown! Both **market size** and market growth are likely to be affected most by external factors such as economic growth. Market share is the most precise measure of the success of an individual business.

■ Case study

Hendersons' market calculations

Having correctly calculated Hendersons' current market share, Brian was feeling smug, so his wife decided to give him some more calculations to do. She put the following information in front of him:

Table 6.4

	Sales in 2011	Market share in 2011	Sales in 2012	Market share in 2012	% change in sales between 2011 and 2012
Hendersons	90,000		125,000		
Williamson	210,000		250,000		
Bryant	190,000		200,000		
Topping	60,000		50,000		
Total	550,000	100%	625,000	100%	

Penny asked Brian to answer the following questions:

Questions

1 Complete Table 6.4 showing the market share for each business for 2011 and 2012 and calculate the % change in sales for each business and for the market as a whole. (10 marks)

2 Copy and complete Table 6.5 identifying which six of the following statements are true. (12 marks)

Table 6.5

Statement	Tick or cross to indicate true or false
Hendersons' sales have fallen.	
Hendersons' sales have risen.	
Hendersons' market share has fallen.	
Hendersons' market share has risen.	
The market as a whole has grown at a greater rate than Hendersons' sales.	
The market as a whole has grown at a slower rate than Hendersons' sales.	
Hendersons' market share has grown by 4 percentage points.	
Hendersons' market share has grown by 39%.	
Hendersons' and Williamson's sales have grown at a faster rate than the market as a whole.	
Hendersons' has the biggest market share in 2012.	
Bryant's sales have grown by 5%.	
Bryant's market share had risen by 3%.	

3 Analyse the relationship between the rate of growth of an individual business and the rate of growth of the market as a whole. (10 marks)

4 To what extent is it easier for a business to increase its market share in a growing market compared to a static or shrinking market? (14 marks)

Show the skills

The skill of analysis can be demonstrated by using and interpreting quantitative data. In your answer to question 3, try to illustrate your analysis with numerical examples.

✓ *In this chapter you will have learned to:*

- understand the key features of physical and online markets and be able to distinguish between local and national markets. You'll be able to explain the main benefits and drawbacks of each type of market

- explain the key factors affecting demand and be able to appreciate that it is likely that a combination of such factors will determine the price of a product or service. You'll understand that different products and services will have different priorities

- explain the features, benefits and limitations of market segmentation

- use accurately some of the numerical techniques to calculate proportions, percentages and changes and be able to use these techniques to analyse market size, growth and share and be able to distinguish between them.

For answers to activities and case study questions see kerboodle

Practice questions

Chapters 4–6

1. Define the term 'business plan'. *(3 marks)*

2. Describe THREE possible pieces of information that a venture capitalist might need before deciding whether to invest in a business that builds loft conversions. *(6 marks)*

3. Describe THREE possible problems that an entrepreneur might have when constructing a business plan for a window cleaning business. *(5 marks)*

4. Explain to an entrepreneur who is setting up a tanning salon the benefits of small business banking services. *(5 marks)*

5. Describe TWO sources of government help that an entrepreneur starting a business making organic sausages could use. *(4 marks)*

6. Explain TWO possible reasons why an entrepreneur might choose not to construct a business plan. *(4 marks)*

7. Clive Malcolm has had a window cleaning business for nearly 6 months, since he bought it from his brother, who decided to sell it because he couldn't make it a success. Clive has 150 customers who have their windows cleaned every 2 weeks. So far, Clive has not tried to get any new business, and in fact, he has lost 20 customers since he took the business over. He knows he needs to do something if he is to make the business a success.

    a) Explain TWO benefits to Clive of conducting primary market research. *(4 marks)*

    b) Distinguish between quantitative and qualitative market research data in the context of Clive's business. *(6 marks)*

    c) Explain THREE problems Clive might have in selecting a random sample. *(6 marks)*

    d) Evaluate the likely impact on Clive's business of a detailed market research strategy. *(10 marks)*

8. List THREE possible methods of primary research that an entrepreneur starting a hairdressers might use to find out about the likely demand for her service. *(3 marks)*

9. Analyse THREE possible difficulties to a clothes shop of seeking to expand from a local to a national market. *(6 marks)*

10. Analyse THREE likely factors affecting the demand for takeaway pizza. *(6 marks)*

11. Explain what you understand by the term 'market segmentation'. *(3 marks)*

12. Describe TWO benefits that a restaurant might gain from market segmentation. *(6 marks)*

13. Distinguish between market size, market growth and market share. Use the mobile phone market to illustrate your points. *(8 marks)*

14   Bill and Anne operated a smoothie bar – a business that sold healthy fruit and vegetable drinks and snacks. In the first 10 weeks of trading the business had attracted an average of only 350 customers per week and had yet to break even. Secondary market research had shown that the value of UK smoothie sales had risen from £34 million in 2006 to £56 million in 2011.

At the start they drew up a detailed business plan and carried out detailed primary market research in several towns. They borrowed £50,000 from the bank and funded the remaining £60,000 from the sale of their London house.

From the start, things went wrong. They opened late because of late delivery of supplies so missed the busy summer trading period. A competitor set up nearby and opened a month before them. Finally, they found it difficult to recruit good quality part time staff.

a)   What is meant by the term, 'entrepreneurs'?   *(2 marks)*

b)   Explain TWO non-financial items that the Bank Manager would have expected to see in the Business Plan for Just Juice Ltd before agreeing to the loan.   *(4 marks)*

c)   Explain ONE reason why Bill and Anne might have decided to use primary market research as part of their business planning.   *(3 marks)*

d)   Calculate the percentage growth in the UK market for smoothies between 2006 and 2011.   *(3 marks)*

e)   To what extent might the drawing up of a detailed business plan guarantee the success of Just Juice Ltd?   *(10 marks)*

7   Choosing the right legal structure for the business

Setting the scene

Compass Point counselling

Jane Howlett had been a manager at a counselling centre for 10 years before she set up her own sole trader business, specialising in counselling children and young adults in a range of areas such as depression, eating disorders and family problems. She was used to difficult situations, having to help people in distressing circumstances, but she wasn't ready for the enormous difference she found between being the manager and being the owner of a business.

Jane was happiest in her counselling room with her clients. She employed her husband John to deal with all the finance and administration, but inevitably wanted to get involved in all the decisions.

The business started small, with a bank loan and just the two of them, but quickly began to grow. Jane was very keen to make sure that all business decisions taken were for the benefit of the clients rather than with profit making in mind.

Discussion points

1. What do you think are the main differences between being the owner and manager of a business?

2. Which would you prefer and why?

3. Make a list of the main objectives that you think Jane might have had at the start of Compass Point.

Which is the right legal structure?

The decision about which legal structure a new business is to adopt is probably one of the earliest decisions to make, usually taken shortly after deciding on the product or service to be offered. This decision is important as it affects a number of things:

- How much tax and National Insurance the business pays.
- The records and accounts that have to be kept.
- The liability faced by the owner if the business fails.
- The sources of finance available to the business.
- The way decisions are made.

Sole traders

Features

This is the most common and simplest form of business organisation. At its very simplest, it is one person operating a business alone. There is very little procedure needed to start a sole trader business. It is usually just a matter of starting to trade. Once up and running, a sole trader is obliged to keep basic records for tax, National Insurance and VAT purposes.

Although sole traders are the most numerous of all types of business structure, they contribute less to total UK output than other types such as limited companies.

Table 7.1 *Benefits and drawbacks of sole trader status*

Benefits of a sole trader	Drawbacks of a sole trader
Simple and quick to set up – just the thing for the entrepreneur with the brilliant idea who can't wait to start trading	The most significant is that sole traders have **unlimited liability**, which means they are personally liable for all debts incurred by the business
Inexpensive to set up – the entrepreneur with only a little money may choose this structure	Difficult to raise additional finance, because sole traders often have limited funds of their own and very little security against which to raise more. Banks may be willing to help if there is a good business plan
Any profit made by the business is the owners to keep, or reinvest	
The owner has complete control of the business; all the decisions are hers/his	All the decisions rest with the owner, who may not possess all the necessary expertise. This is often the reason small businesses fail, because the owner knows everything about the product, but little about finance or insurance or other areas
Often a close relationship between business and customer can be built up because of the size and simplicity of the business structure	
Hours of work etc. can be tailored to suit the entrepreneur	The drive comes from the owner, so the business is vulnerable if the owner becomes ill, or interested or other things happen in her/his life

Key terms

Unlimited liability: a feature of unincorporated businesses where the owners are personally liable for all debts incurred by a business. All sole traders and most partnerships have unlimited liability.

Partnerships

Features

This is the simplest way that two or more people can be in business together. In a partnership, partners share the risks, costs, and responsibilities of the business. The partners take a share of the profits and share in the decision making. The partners are jointly and personally responsible for any debts that the business runs up.

A partnership does not have a legal existence of its own so if one of the partners resigns or dies, the partnership is dissolved. A new partnership must be formed with the remaining partners, or with new partners for the business to continue.

Although it is not a requirement, often partners draw up a Deed of Partnership. This specifies many of the key features of the partnership such as:

■ How much of the finance each has contributed.
■ How much control over decisions each partner has.
■ How the profits will be shared.
■ How the partnership can be ended.

Study tip

With business structures, the drawbacks are often the 'flipside' of the benefits. For example, although it's inexpensive to set up a sole trader, it's also difficult to raise extra money. Similarly, although there is very little bureaucracy associated with setting up, there's also very little protection if things go wrong.

So, in an exam, if you have trouble remembering any drawbacks, but can remember benefits, try to turn them around.

Table 7.2 *Benefits and drawbacks of partnership status*

Benefits of a partnership	Drawbacks of a partnership
As with sole traders, there are very few procedures to follow in order to set up a partnership	As with sole traders, the partners have unlimited liability. This is complicated by the fact that each partner is jointly liable for the debts incurred by the business. So a wrong decision by one of the partners can have consequences for all the partners
Unlike sole traders, the expertise of more than one person can be brought into the business for decision making and for sharing the work load	Profits are shared amongst the partners (according to the distribution agreed in the Deed of Partnership)
Often different partners specialise in different aspects of the business	The partners are legally bound to honour the decisions of the others
There are more sources of finance as each partner can contribute a share of the start-up funds	The partnership ends on the death or resignation of a partner
	A maximum of 20 people can join a partnership, thus limiting the size of the business and the sources of funds

Show the skills

In the exam, you may have to justify a decision about which is the best form of legal structure for a particular business. Don't just restate all the various benefits and drawbacks itemised here. Apply your points by considering why the particular business in the question would benefit most from one form of legal structure rather than another. If you do not *apply* the points you make, you will be unlikely to gain many marks for evaluation.

Incorporated and unincorporated businesses

Before going on to talk about limited companies, it's worth pausing to consider the process of incorporation. Sole traders and partnerships are examples of unincorporated businesses, whilst private limited companies and public limited companies are incorporated. There is no requirement for you to understand the exact procedure, but it's worth knowing the basics. Incorporation basically creates a legal entity, something that exists as far as the law is concerned. This has a significant impact on the owners of a business. For example, if J. Smith is a sole trader and the business accumulates debts, or is sued by a customer, then it is J. Smith the person that is liable for the debts, or J. Smith the person who will appear in court. If the business is J. Smith Ltd, then the debts are the businesses, not the owners, and it is the business that is represented in court. So with incorporated businesses, it is true to say that the business itself exists, whereas with an unincorporated business, the owner (or owners in the case of partnerships) is in fact the business.

Business in action

Jennings Cycles Ltd

Adam Jennings spent ages thinking about whether to remain a sole trader or become a limited company. His bank manager (and cycling-mad friend) advised him. 'When considering the difference between unincorporated and incorporated businesses it's worth thinking abut risk. For a sole trader and partners, there's a lot of risk, but it's all yours. You put the money into the business, and you take the risks. But you're risking your own money, so there is very little you have to do in terms of a start-up process or documentation. For limited companies, both private and public, there may be less risk, but you're risking other peoples' money. The shareholders need to know that their investment is reasonably secure, and that if the business is unsuccessful, they won't lose all of their assets. Hence there is limited liability. They also need to be sure that the business is using their money appropriately, hence the need to produce detailed financial information. The limited liability and the need to provide detailed records are both because, essentially, limited companies use other people's money.'

'So if I want long-term growth and security, and I don't mind a more formal process to set up and a bit more paperwork, I should go for limited company status,' Adam summarised.

Private limited companies

Features

The key feature of a private limited company is that the owners are the shareholders, and their ownership of the business is determined by the proportion of the total shares each person holds. So, for instance, if there are 100 shares in a business, and a particular shareholder owns 20, then he/she owns 20% of the shares. This is sometimes referred to as 20% of the equity in the business. The business must have Ltd in its name. A shareholder in a limited company has **limited liability**, which means that they are not liable for the debts the business might incur, beyond what they might have invested into the business. As a consequence of limited liability, limited companies are required by law to go through a much more complicated process when they are created, and are required to keep much more detailed records once they begin trading. The main reason for this is so that potential investors and lenders can make sure the company is being run properly. This form of business is the popular form for family businesses and for small, well established businesses. Shares can only be sold privately and with the consent of the other shareholders.

■ **Key terms**

Limited liability: a feature of incorporated businesses such as private and public limited companies, which means that the owners' liability is limited to the amount they have invested in the business.

Benefits and drawbacks

Table 7.3 *Benefits and drawbacks of a private limited company*

Benefits of a limited company	Drawbacks of a limited company
Access to funds through the issue of shares	More complicated set up process than unincorporated business structures
Higher status of business structure than a sole-trader	Limited liability might be a benefit for shareholders, but lenders may see it as a risk
Limited liability is a benefit for the shareholders, who may see the risk as more acceptable than if the business were unincorporated	Some disclosure of accounts is necessary as these must be sent to Companies House.
Incorporation means the business exists, and will continue to exist even if a shareholders resigns or dies	

Public limited companies

Features

The key feature that distinguishes a public limited company from a private limited company is that the shares are bought and sold publicly. Both types of structure are owned by shareholders, but whereas in a limited company the shares are only bought and sold privately between individuals, with a public limited company, shares are traded publicly, and anyone can buy them. This means they have a market value. On any given day, the shares in a plc can be bought and sold, and this affects the share price. The share price of a plc is important because it indicates how popular the business is, and it can influence how successful future issues of shares might be. The share price of a plc is also a crucial factor in determining how easy it would be to take it over by buying a proportion of the shares. The initial sale of shares to the public is known as flotation.

Many of the benefits and drawbacks of a plc are the same as for a private limited company. There are additional things to bear in mind.

Study tip

There's a lot of confusion in students' minds about shares and share prices. Often students claim that a rising share price means the plc gets more money. But the Stock Exchange, which is where these shares are bought and sold, is just a second hand market. So share price movements are important to a plc, but a rising share price doesn't directly generate more funds, any more than a falling share price would mean the plc had to give money back.

Table 7.4 Benefits and drawbacks of a public limited company

Benefits of a public limited company	Drawbacks of a public limited company
The main benefit is the scale of the funds that can be raised from a flotation. A successful business that wants to grow may find many investors wanting to buy shares in the initial share offer, which means large sums of money can be raised. Future funds can be raised because banks and lenders see a plc as a very stable, secure type of business and they are willing to lend large sums of money.	The process of flotation is expensive. Documents have to be produced to advertise the company and explain its financial situation, there are legal fees, and shares have to be underwritten. What that means is that someone has to guarantee to buy any unwanted shares. The underwriters are paid a fee for this. In addition, the company must have a minimum of £50,000 in share capital, of which 25% must have been sold before the plc can trade. So, you can see, it's a very different process from starting a sole trader! It is not possible to control who owns the shares in a plc as the shares are traded publicly. This has a number of implications. Firstly, there's nothing stopping competitors, customers or suppliers buying shares. Secondly, a takeover cannot be prevented if someone is willing and able to buy enough shares. The plc must provide regular, detailed financial information. This is so that any investor, or potential investor can see how well, or badly, the company is doing. A drawback often quoted is the **separation of ownership and control**. A plc is owned by shareholders, but often run by managers. The two groups of stakeholders are different people, with different objectives. This can cause conflict and can make decision making difficult.

Fig. 7.1 The Eden Project in Cornwall is an example of a not-for-profit business

Not-for-profit businesses – social enterprises

Features

So far, we've assumed that entrepreneurs are motivated to make a profit. Some, however, have other objectives. These not-for-profit businesses are growing in importance. The Government estimates that there are now 55,000 social enterprises in the UK, employing more than 775,000 people and contributing £8.4bn each year to the economy. Examples include The Eden Project, Café Direct and Jamie Oliver's restaurant Fifteen.

One type of business that does not have profit as its main objective is a social enterprise organisation. This type of business mainly aims to provide a social benefit. It may make a profit, but often those profits are reinvested back into the business so that the social aims can be met, rather than paid out to the owners.

Table 7.5 Benefits and drawbacks of a not-for-profit business

Benefits of a not-for-profit structure	Drawbacks of a not-for-profit structure
Entrepreneurs can earn a living doing something valuable, which can be motivating The more successful the social enterprise the more society benefits Customers may be more willing to buy from a social enterprise It might be easier to recruit, motivate and retain employees in a social enterprise Grants or other forms of finance might be available from sources sharing the same social aim	Profits and social aims may conflict, leading to difficult choices The entrepreneur will always have to accept a lower return than with a profit-making business because a proportion of the profits will go towards the social aim

Compass Point Counselling – the way forward

When Jane Howlett looked back, it didn't feel like five years had passed since she started her own business, a not-for-profit counselling service for young people called Compass Point Counselling. In those five years Jane had seen her business grow from just her and her husband to a total staff of 10 people, including eight full- or part-time counsellors, as well as Jane and her husband.

The business was a victim of its own success. Jane had started as a sole trader and employed John, to look after the finance while she counselled. This worked well initially, because they were able to begin operating quickly and the business was cheap to run. John's background in accountancy meant he could run the office side of things, but as the business grew, and took on more employees, it became clear that neither of them had experience in managing people. They'd taken out a second mortgage to turn their garage into an office and counselling room, and used the income from the business to pay it off. All employees including Jane and John were paid a salary, and any spare money they had was reinvested.

The business didn't struggle to pay its bills on a day-to-day basis, but the potential to expand remained limited. The couple had a derelict barn in the grounds of their house, and Jane had always felt this would make a perfect counselling centre. However, it would cost a lot to convert it, and there were probably legal issues to consider. Also, the possibility existed for other people to join the business. John's friend Sahir was keen to invest an inheritance in a business which made a contribution to the local community. He currently worked as a Human Resources Manager in the local council, but was looking for a different challenge.

Although Jane had put it off so far, she knew she had to sit down and make some decisions about the future of the business, but she didn't know when she was going to find the time or what she should do. One thing was certain, she couldn't carry on much longer as a sole trader.

Questions

1 Explain the main benefits to Jane of initially setting up as a sole trader. (6 marks)

2 Explain the benefits and drawbacks of Jane forming a partnership with John and Sahir. (6 marks)

3 Analyse the impact of Compass Point's not-for-profit objective on the likely type of business structure chosen. (8 marks)

4 To what extent would the future success of Compass Point be guaranteed by the formation of a limited company? (14 marks)

5 Research task: Find out about the housebuilder, Crest Nicholson. It has converted to a public limited company twice! Discover why and when it did this.

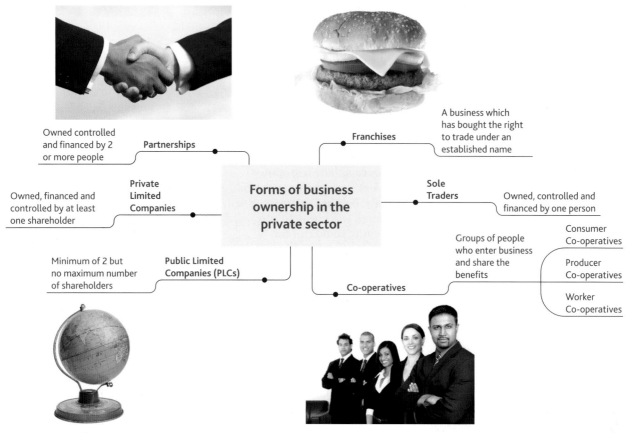

Fig. 7.2 *Types of business organisation adapted from www.businesslink.co.uk*

☑ *In this chapter you will have learned to:*

■ understand the main features of the different types of business structure, and their benefits and drawbacks

■ understand the difference between unincorporated and incorporated business structures and in particular understand the significance of incorporation in terms of the liability of the owners of the business

■ explain the process of starting different types of business structure

■ evaluate the benefits and drawbacks of each type of business structure for specific situations and be able to make reasoned conclusions about the most appropriate.

For answers to activities and case study questions see

Raising finance

In this chapter you will learn to:

- explain the difference between internal and external sources of finance

- understand the various sources of internal and external finance

- analyse the appropriateness of various sources of internal and external finance for different needs.

Study tip

Think back to Chapter 4 on business planning – if you were the friend or relative of someone about to start a business and who wanted to borrow money from you, what would you need to know before you said yes. Most of the answers to your questions should be in the business plan.

Key terms

Internal sources of finance: finances raised from within the business

Setting the scene

Geared Up gets bigger

So far, Karen had been right. Her initial enthusiasm for the bike shop, and her absolute confidence that it could be a success had proved right. Ian's cautious words had not been necessary, as the business grew from one shop and a website, to three shops and an online business with an annual turnover of over £1,000,000.

'We're ready for the next big step,' said Karen one day and, although he felt scared and convinced it was too soon, Ian knew he'd go along with Karen's latest plan.

'We need to get bigger if we're going to be more successful,' she said. 'You and I are the biggest shareholders, and we've now got my dad and your mum as minority shareholders,' she added. 'Their investment was crucial at the time,' Ian reminded her, as they both remembered the time two years ago when the business nearly went under.

'But we need to think much bigger,' argued Karen, 'I want to supply a supermarket chain with a range of bikes endorsed by a professional cyclist and branded with the Geared Up brand, and that's only going to happen with a massive injection of capital.'

At the start of every new business, decisions have to be made about where to get money from. Usually, the entrepreneur has to put some of his/her own money into the business. Sometimes, friends and family contribute, but often the entrepreneur has to approach a lender for loan capital. If the new business is a limited company, then share capital is a possible source. It is usually the case that the new business start-up has a number of things it needs to spend money on before any revenue is earned from the sale of the product or service. Premises have to be rented or bought, machinery and equipment, stocks of raw materials and components and various professional service fees all need to be paid for. This is usually before a single item has been made or sold.

Discussion points

1. What factors should Karen and Ian take into account when deciding whether to expand further?

2. Draw up a list of factors to consider when choosing the source of finance should they decide to expand.

Internal sources of finance

Internal sources of finance come from within the business. These include the owner's savings (for unincorporated businesses), retained earnings, or retained profit and income from a sale of the assets of the business. New businesses will have no retained earnings yet and they will have no assets that can be sold. Therefore, owner's savings are the only common form of internal finance for a new business start-up.

Personal sources of finance

It's very rare that a small business start-up doesn't require some investment from the owner. So the most important source of finance is the owner's own money. Sometimes entrepreneurs will borrow from friends or family.

Table 8.1 *Advantages and disadvantages of personal sources of finance*

Advantages of personal sources of finance	Disadvantages of personal sources of finance
There's no cost to using this money, in terms of interest costs on a loan	It's not strictly true there's no cost to an owner using his/her own money. There's the opportunity cost in terms of the alternative uses to which the money could have been put
An entrepreneur putting his/her own money into a business start-up is a sign of confidence. If they're willing to put their own money at risk, maybe others will as well	
The entrepreneur doesn't have to worry about the money being withdrawn, which could happen if the money was borrowed	Most entrepreneurs have limited finance at the start, which limits what the business can purchase
There's no risk of interference in decision making by a lender	New business start-ups are risky, so the entrepreneur could lose everything if the business is not a limited company
The entrepreneur does not have to pay out anything from profits if he/she does not want to, it's all available for reinvesting	
Borrowing from friends or family means it is rare for interest to be paid	Borrowing from friends or family can cause a strain on relationships if the business does not do well
Friends and family may be more willing to lend than other lenders	

Case study

Reliance Garage

Reliance Garage was set up two years ago by two brothers, Al and Mark. They used some of their own savings (£5,000 each) to take out a lease on a small workshop and to buy essential tools. The purchase of stocks of oils and spare parts was made possible with an overdraft.

The business made a slow start, and it was only in the second year that a small profit was made. The brothers agreed to use this to buy a computer to help diagnose problems with car engines.

During the third year, the number of customers increased and Al and Mark decided to spend £10,000, obtained from a bank loan, to convert part of the workshop into an MOT testing station. This loan has to be repaid within five years and has a fixed interest rate.

Further equipment was bought with the help of a loan from their parents who said that 'it could be repaid when their sons could afford it or when the parents really needed it'.

At the end of the fourth year, the brothers sold some tyre fitting equipment, which had been used much less than expected. They used the money from this to pay off part of the bank loan.

External sources of finance

External sources of finance are ones which come from outside the business. These include the issue of new shares in a limited company, bank loans, overdrafts and venture capital.

Loan capital – overdraft

An **overdraft** is a very flexible source of finance, particularly useful for managing cash flow during periods when the money going out of a business is temporarily greater than the money coming in. The banks usually charge a fee for arranging an overdraft, and usually charge interest. Sometimes, there's an interest-free amount before interest is charged.

It is not a good source of finance for longer term uses, such as buying equipment or machinery because the interest rates tend to be high and the bank could remove the overdraft at any time.

Table 8.2 *Advantages and disadvantages of an overdraft*

Advantages of an overdraft	Disadvantages of an overdraft
It is a flexible source of finance, because it is only used when it is needed	It is expensive if used for a long period of time or for large amounts
	Arrangement fees and fees for going over the overdraft limit can be high
It is quick and easy to arrange	The overdraft can be removed at short notice
	The business has to have a bank account with that bank in order to get an overdraft

Loan capital – bank loan

A **loan** is a sum of money lent for a fixed period of time, repaid over an agreed schedule. The price of the loan is a rate of interest, which is a percentage of the loan amount and added to the repayments. The actual rate of interest will depend upon a range of factors including the size of the loan, the length of the repayment period and the level of risk.

Key terms

External sources of finance: those that are outside the business, such as banks and shareholders.

Overdraft: a temporary arrangement which allows the business to draw out more money than is in its account, up to an agreed limit.

Loan: a good source of finance for assets such as machinery and equipment and other start-up costs.

Study tip

Always try to match the period of need to the life of the loan. In other words, if the business needs money for a short period of time, only borrow the money for a short period of time. If the business is going to use the money for an asset it intends to keep and use for a long time, use a longer term source of finance.

Table 8.3 *Advantages and disadvantages of a loan*

Advantages of a loan	Disadvantages of a loan
The length of the loan can be matched to the length of the need for the loan. The business can then plan for the repayments	Interest is paid regardless of whether the business is making a profit or not
The interest is fixed for the period of the loan, so it is easier to budget for the loan	The loan may have to be secured against a personal asset or an asset of the business, placing it at risk if the business cannot keep up the payments
The loan is guaranteed for the period, so the business knows it has got the money	The length of the loan may turn out to be longer than the life of the asset purchased with it. This means a business is paying for something it no longer needs
There is no need to give the lender a proportion of the profits earned by the business	
The lender does not have any say in how the business is run	

Business in action

Advice about loan capital

There is a large range of sources of advice about loan capital for small business start-ups. Here are just a few:

Table 8.4

Source of advice		Features
The Prince's Trust www.princes-trust.org.uk	 **Prince's Trust** **Fig. 8.1** *Prince's Trust*	Provides advice and support for young people starting up in business
Prince's Initiative for Mature Enterprise www.prime.org.uk	**prime** **The Prince's Initiative for Mature Enterprise** **www.prime.org.uk** **Fig. 8.2** *PRIME*	Provides advice and support to unemployed over 50s, helping them to explore self-employment
Small Business Loan Guarantee Scheme www.berr.gov.uk	**BERR** Department for Business Enterprise & Regulatory Reform **Fig. 8.4** *BERR*	Help for businesses that find it difficult to get a loan. This is operated by the Department for Business Enterprise and Regulatory Reform

Share capital

Another source of finance is to ask an investor to put money into a company in return for a share of the business. This is known as share capital or equity capital. It is called share capital because the people who provide it are entitled to a share of the profits earned by the business, and usually own a share of the business itself. It is sometimes known as equity because each share is an equal part of the business.

People who invest share capital in a business aren't entitled to regular interest payments. They may, however, receive a proportion of any profit the business makes at the end of the year in the form of dividends. The other big difference between share capital and loan capital is that share capital is never paid back. So it is best used for very long term purposes.

The selling of shares in a business represents the selling of parts of the ownership of the business. So an entrepreneur loses some control over a business as soon as he/she sells shares in it.

In many cases, small businesses grow by becoming **incorporated** so that friends, family or other private investors can buy shares in the business in return for a lump sum investment.

If a business has a lot of growth potential, or it is seeking to grow rapidly, it could look for investment from other, more formal, investors such as **venture capitalists** or **business angels**.

Business angels differ from venture capitalists in two main ways, they are often individuals rather than companies, and they tend to look for smaller investments of between £10,000 and £250,000. In return for a capital investment, a business angel would expect a share in the business. Sometimes angels group together to provide a larger investment. Business angels often work closely with the owners of the business.

Crowdfunding

The difficult economic conditions in the UK and USA after 2008 have led to a significant increase in this method of financing new businesses. By posting details of proposed new business start-ups online, for example by using social media, entrepreneurs have been able to raise finance from large numbers of people who have been convinced by the prospects of their new businesses. These investors provide small sums either in the form of a loan – which has to be repaid at a specified time plus interest – or share/equity finance. In the latter case, the small sum made available to the business is invested in exchange for a small part-ownership of the new business.

Case study

Show me the money

Gavin Thomas had been at his work placement for just three weeks and already he felt he'd learnt more about business than in all the two years of his Business Studies degree. He'd managed to get a place at a large well-known investment bank in Manchester for the third year of his degree. Already he was looking forward to his final year when he could add his business theory and practice together. His manager had been showing him how the bank advised clients, particularly small businesses, on the various sources of finance available to them. Now his manager wanted to test him on what he'd picked up. 'I'm going to give you a project; I want you to

Study tip

The vast majority of limited companies are private, so their shares are bought and sold privately, often between family members, employees or other individuals, and not on the Stock Exchange.

Key terms

Incorporated: the process of forming a limited liability company. The process involves creating a separate legal identity for the business, and the creation of shares, or equity.

Venture capitalist: usually a professional investor, often another company, interested in high growth, high risk businesses, who will invest an amount into a business in return for shares, and an expectation for a high return. Venture capitalists are usually interested in larger investments of around £250,000 or more.

Business angel: a wealthy, entrepreneurial individual willing to invest in a small, high risk business who expects a high return. The business is likely to have a high growth potential.

Crowdfunding: the practice of funding a new business by raising small amounts of money from a large number of people, typically via the internet.

advise a number of my clients on the most appropriate sources of finance for their various needs. I want to know why you choose each source'. Below is a summary of the clients and their needs.

Table 8.5 *Client's finance needs*

Client and need	Suggested source of finance	Reasons for choice of source of finance
a A newsagent needs to cover expenditure over a short period of time. She is expecting high sales at the end of the month.		
b A new business in a high tech market needs £100,000 to fund expenditure on equipment. The business is looking for an innovative solution to house design which will reduce fuel consumption. The owner is willing to consider giving up some of the control of the company.		
c A dry cleaners needs to update its equipment following a series of breakdowns which have damaged its reputation. It expects the new equipment to cost approximately £30,000, and have a useful life of about 5 years.		
d A self-employed builder needs a new van.		
e An unemployed woman, aged 23, is hoping to set up a business designing and making greetings cards from her home. She has no finance of her own, and has been turned down by a number of high street banks.		
f A very successful, profitable business selling sports cars wants to expand and purchase a second showroom. The owner is unwilling to consider giving up any control of his business.		
g Two brothers operate a partnership which does loft conversions. They are looking to expand the business in order to do a wider range of construction work.		

Show the skills

When evaluating appropriate sources of finance, consider the amount required, whether the business is a new start-up, interest rates, and the willingness of owners to give up a share of the business.

Questions

1 Copy out and complete the table above. Explain your choice of sources of finance in each case. (14 marks)

2 Explain the potential benefits of converting the partnership to a private limited company in example **g**. (6 marks)

3 Assume that you are a business angel with £100,000 to invest. Analyse these businesses and draw up a list of six questions you would ask their owners before deciding in which to invest. Justify each question briefly. (12 marks)

4 Evaluate each business and its need for finance. Recommend the most appropriate one for the business angel to invest in. Justify your choice. (14 marks)

5 Research task: Undertake further research on the sources of external finance referred to in this chapter. Which source would be most appropriate for a local business you know to use to fund expansion?

✒ ✓ *In this chapter you will have learned to:*

- distinguish between internal and external sources of finance for small business start-ups and be able to explain the various sources

- understand the importance of matching the period of the need for the finance to the length of the source

- understand the benefits and drawbacks of each source of finance and be able to analyse the appropriateness of various sources of finance in particular situations.

For answers to activities and case study questions see **kerboodle**

In this chapter you will learn to:

- describe the main quantitative and qualitative factors affecting location decisions

- explain the benefits and drawbacks of starting a business from home

- understand how different businesses will place different emphasis on location factors

- use location factors to justify location decisions.

Setting the scene

Teleworking is not always the best choice

Flexible working from home – or teleworking – has become very popular in recent years. Many entrepreneurs start their businesses from their own homes. There are some clear advantages for both the worker and the business.

The worker has greater flexibility over how and when work is undertaken, as long as business deadlines are met. There is no lengthy or expensive commute to work, and some parents are more able to combine childcare with teleworking than they would be if they worked from the office or factory of the employer.

The business gains from lower costs, a crucial consideration for newly set up enterprises. If the entrepreneur works from home, there will be no additional rent, rates, heating and lighting costs. If an established business encourages workers to operate from home, then it can usually manage with smaller premises and achieve cost savings through this.

Working at home does have its drawbacks too. There is no clear separation between working life and home life. Recent research by Nottingham Business School suggests that many workers often work longer hours than they would normally in order to convince work colleagues that they are not taking advantage of the more flexible working.

There are also social issues. There is no interaction with work colleagues, although this might be less of an issue for a single entrepreneur who would probably be working alone anyway. Some people also appreciate the structure and formality offered by a typical working day at the office or factory, and find it difficult to organise their time effectively at home.

Entrepreneurs will always ask themselves whether the potential cost savings of working from home are more important than the prestige, and perhaps better location, of having their own business premises.

Discussion points

1. Under what circumstances would you advise a new entrepreneur to work from home, at least initially?

2. What limitations are there for entrepreneurs if they decide to operate their business from home?

Factors affecting location decisions

There are various factors affecting the choice of location for a business start-up. With a small business start-up, there may be different priorities

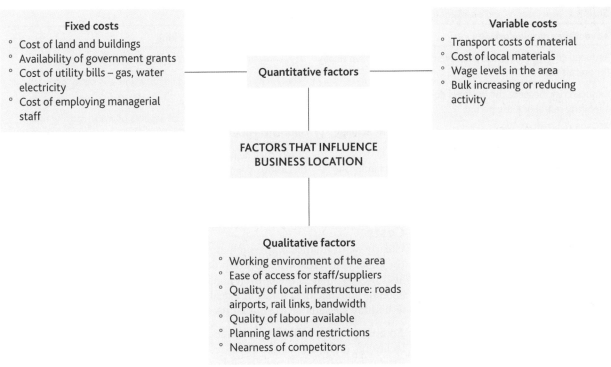

Fixed costs
° Cost of land and buildings
° Availability of government grants
° Cost of utility bills – gas, water electricity
° Cost of employing managerial staff

Quantitative factors

Variable costs
° Transport costs of material
° Cost of local materials
° Wage levels in the area
° Bulk increasing or reducing activity

FACTORS THAT INFLUENCE BUSINESS LOCATION

Qualitative factors
° Working environment of the area
° Ease of access for staff/suppliers
° Quality of local infrastructure: roads airports, rail links, bandwidth
° Quality of labour available
° Planning laws and restrictions
° Nearness of competitors

Fig. 9.1 *Location factors*

for different **stakeholders.** The most important factor for some businesses is to be close to customers. For retail outlets, being close to the customer, or at least in a location that the customer expects the business to be, is essential. Passing trade influences footfall, the number of people entering a premises in a given time period, and this can be crucial to the success of a new business because it is trying to establish itself. To an employee, transport to and from work is perhaps the most important factor, so proximity to transport links becomes important. Transport might be the most important factor in relation to suppliers, particularly if the products or parts are expensive to transport. The location of competitors might be a relevant factor, either in terms of avoiding being near them, or perhaps the opposite; in some cases, it pays to be located near to competition so that customers can easily visit all alternatives.

As IT influences business more, the physical location of companies becomes less important. Businesses are becoming more 'footloose' and less dependant on the traditional locational factors.

For some entrepreneurs, the chance to work from home is a key decision to go into business in the first place, so the location is determined by non-business factors.

Technology – teleworking

Undoubtedly technology is affecting location decisions for many small businesses. The most significant is the impact of the internet on the ability of entrepreneurs to work from home. This is sometimes referred to as teleworking. Improvements in communications mean that for many people, the home is either an extension of the office, or it is the office. There are a number of benefits and drawbacks in running a business from home.

■ **Key terms**

Stakeholder: an individual or group with an interest in a business. Stakeholders include employees, management, shareholders, customers, suppliers and competitors.

Study tip

In the exam, be prepared to justify why particular location factors are relevant to businesses in specific circumstances. The significance of a factor will vary according to the precise circumstances in which the business finds itself.

Table 9.1 *Advantages and disadvantages of teleworking*

Advantages of teleworking	Disadvantages of teleworking
Reduced costs, because the entrepreneur does not have to pay for premises	It is sometimes difficult to separate work from home life
Reduced risk, because the business does not have to commit to a lengthy rental or lease period	There may be initial set up costs, a house is rarely perfectly suitable as a workplace
Reduced travelling so that more time can be spent actually working as opposed to travelling to work	There may be a loss of social aspects of work, causing the entrepreneur to feel lonely
Allows some entrepreneurs to plan work around family and other commitments	There may be hidden costs such as the effect on house insurance, council tax or a tenancy agreement
Family are on hand to help if needed	It might not be possible to avoid distractions such as children, pets and TV

■ Link

For more information on costs (such as fixed and variable) see Chapter 11 – Calculating costs, revenues and profits, page 75.

Costs

Clearly, with finance being such an issue at the start of a business, the costs associated with location decisions are likely to be crucial. Techniques such as break-even analysis and investment appraisal can be used to help decide a location based on financial information, and you will study these later in your course.

An entrepreneur is likely to consider the costs associated with particular locations, and compare the revenues gained. There will be a number of fixed costs, which will not depend on the level of output, but will differ in different locations. These include the cost of purchasing or renting the building. A location that is cheap to buy may save money in the short term, but will the location maximise revenue? Also, its value as an asset for resale will be lower if it is an unattractive place. In addition, there might be costs associated with transforming the location into suitable premises. If the business needs staff who will be paid a fixed salary, then that fixed cost will need to be taken into account. In areas which are high cost, salaries tend to be high also to compensate, pushing up the fixed costs of the business start-up. If skilled staff are needed, this might push costs up even more if they are in short supply. Costs of utilities will also need to be considered.

Some of these fixed costs might be reduced if there are incentives to locate in particular areas. For example, the Department for Business, Enterprise and Regulatory Reform is responsible for the nine Regional Development Agencies, whose role it is to improve efficiency, employment and skill levels in particular areas of England. Scotland, Wales and Ireland have similar arrangements.

Variable costs may differ at different locations. Transport costs may differ because of the distances travelled, and the quality of the transport links. The impact of this will depend upon whether the product becomes more costly to transport as a finished product or as component parts. If labour is needed as a variable cost, this may also differ between locations. Some skilled labour costs can vary significantly in different parts of the country.

■ Case study

Boodles Beers

Karen Hodges opened Boodles in 2007 in a recently converted building in Chichester. She and her husband Tom had both worked for a large brewery running pubs throughout the South of England. When the possibility came up to buy their own pub and make the beer on the premises, they didn't have a moment's hesitation.

A key to locating in Chichester was proximity to the key ingredients of malt, yeast and Kent and Sussex hops. They use a brewing technique largely unchanged for decades and have begun to attract customers from throughout Sussex, Kent and Hampshire.

Questions

1. List the main factors other than raw materials likely to affect the location of a brewery such as Boodles. (4 marks)

2. Analyse whether a brewery such as Boodles is likely to locate near its raw materials or near its market. (8 marks)

3. To what extent is location likely to be the most significant factor affecting the price of Boodles' finished product? (10 marks)

Infrastructure

In the majority of cases, transport links will be a relevant factor in a company's choice of location, whether in terms of the distance from the raw materials or the customer. As the quality of service becomes more important as a way to add value, the speed, reliability and flexibility of delivery takes on greater significance. In these circumstances, being close to your customers or being easy to get to, is a selling point. Infrastructure also means local services such as waste disposal, entertainment, health, education and other public services.

The market

For many small business start-ups, being close to the customer is essential. It is often the reason the business started in the first place. What some entrepreneurs forget is that as they grow their customer base becomes more geographically dispersed, and what seemed like a good location, may quickly become a disadvantage. This factor is more significant for a product that gains weight in the production process as the cost of transporting the finished product is greater than the cost of transporting the raw materials.

The number of competitors in a given market may differ with changing locations. It might be better to locate a new business in a position away from a lot of competition.

Qualitative factors

So far, the factors considered have all been quantitative, but some factors cannot have numerical values attached to them.

For example, the decision to start a business is sometimes determined by a person's desire for a different kind of life. So the quality of life in a location might be a significant factor. The quality of local schools and hospitals, the weather, the local sports facilities or the nightlife might all play a part in the location decision.

Other factors such as local planning laws, local regulations and the availability of land for expansion might be important. The quality of labour, and the ease with which workers can travel to work could be relevant.

In the end, an entrepreneur will have to take a number of quantitative and qualitative factors into account, and the relative importance of each one will depend upon:

- The nature of the product – does it gain or lose weight in the production process.
- Is it a service? – in which case its location is more likely to be influenced by the customers' location needs.
- Do costs, both fixed and variable differ in different locations?

Business in action

Regus

Wouldn't it be great if you could locate your business anywhere? Move it temporarily to suit your needs? Never have to commit to long-term locations?

With Regus, you're free to run your business without the financial or management burden that comes with traditional office rental. That's because we take care of everything – your office is equipped and ready to go. All you need to do is choose the right location and move in. Offices can be chosen from over 1600 locations, each supported by technology and a team of people to help with running the office, greeting visitors or taking calls. Offices can be rented for short periods of time, or for occasional use.

Work your way

Fig. 9.2 *Regus*

■ How limited is the entrepreneur in her/his choice of locations?

■ What qualitative factors, if any, are important?

■ Case study

Xtreem

When Zachary Hardingham decided to start a business, there was only ever going to be one thing he would do, and that was to open a shop selling windsurfing and kitesurfing equipment. The other thing that was certain was the location. 'I've loved West Wittering in Sussex since I was a kid' he said. 'We went to Bognor Regis every year for our holidays, and I loved going to the beach at West Wittering and seeing the windsurfers.' So his decision to locate Xtreem was an easy one for him. It helped that local amenities were good and that the weather was better than most other parts of the UK. There were good business reasons for locating to the Sussex coast as well. For example, windsurfing, sailing and other water sports are very popular in the area, which is a very popular tourist destination in the summer, with tourists spending over £150m annually in the area. Suppliers were close by, and there was a steady supply of people able to teach the visitors the basics of windsurfing.

Zachary and his family had struggled to afford a house in the area, because house prices were 20 per cent above the national average, and he still hadn't managed to employ an office manager. It seemed that salaries for skilled professionals were high as well.

Still, as Zachary headed for the sea for his regular morning session out on the waves, he wasn't worried by this, or by the two other windsurfing shops that had opened nearby this summer.

■ Show the skills

When making location decisions in answer to an examination question, it is important to give reasons why a location might be rejected, as well as why an alternative location might be preferred.

Questions

1. Explain the main factors that influenced Zachary's location for Xtreem. (8 marks)

2. Do you think that Zachary was influenced more by qualitative or quantitative factors? Justify your answer. (10 marks)

3. Analyse the possible problems of the location chosen by Zachary. (8 marks)

4. To what extent is the opening of two other windsurfing shops in the area an opportunity or a threat to the success of Xtreem? (14 marks)

💡📖✔ *In this chapter you will have learned to:*

- describe the main quantitative and qualitative location factors affecting location decisions and appreciate that different factors will have varying importance to different businesses, depending on their particular circumstances

- understand why some entrepreneurs start businesses from home, and understand some of the potential disadvantages of teleworking

- use location factors to make and justify location decisions for particular businesses.

For answers to activities and case study questions see **kerboodle**

10 Employing people

Setting the scene

Part-time and temporary employment in the UK

In December 2012 there were 30 million people in employment in the UK. 8.4 million of these were in part-time employment (usually less than 35 hours per week), and 21.2 million were in full time employment.

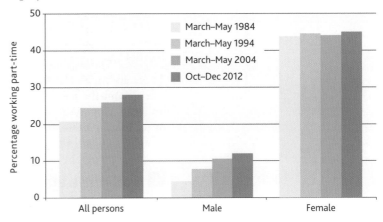

Fig. 10.1 *Percentage of people in employment working part-time: by sex, 1984, 1994, 2004, 2012*

Even though the total number of people employed in the UK in 2012 increased, despite weak economic conditions, most of this increase was a result of more part-time working. The number of people working in temporary jobs also increased and is now estimated to be over 1.6 million.

Many labour market experts have tried to analyse reasons for these trends. Most are agreed that the need for employers to keep labour costs down in tough economic conditions is a major factor. Also, the need to keep a workforce as flexible as possible is becoming more urgent. Businesses want the ability to increase output at short notice if the economy improves but they do not want high numbers of permanent employees.

On average, part-time workers earn a third less per hour than full-time workers. This pay gap has not changed much in 30 years. It helps to explain the difference in average pay between male and female employees. The five highest paid professions in the UK (aircraft pilots, chief executives and directors of advertising, marketing, sales and telecommunication businesses) are all dominated by men and have a tiny proportion of part-time positions.

In contrast, four of the five worst paid occupations (restaurant waiting staff, bar staff, catering assistants and launderers) are dominated by women, and have more part-time posts than full-time ones.

Labour Force Survey and TUC

So far, you have learned about many of the key decisions that an entrepreneur will need to take at the start of a business. Many business textbooks, and most successful business people will say that the most important asset that a business has is its staff. So that means that the most important decision that an entrepreneur can take is employing the right people.

There are many elements to this decision, and in this chapter you will learn about the factors relating to the decision whether to employ people on a full- or part-time basis and whether to employ them on a permanent or temporary basis. In addition, you'll learn about the benefits and drawbacks of using consultants and advisers.

Full-time employees

As the figures above show, full-time employment is by far the most significant part of total employment in the UK. For the entrepreneur starting a business, there are a number of benefits to employing people on a full-time basis.

Benefits

- Higher output may be possible from employees who work full time because they are able to commit to longer hours. Many people choose to work longer hours than they are contracted to because they want to do a good job.
- Full-time employees are available all the time to handle unexpected events.
- Full-time employees might be able to build up better working relationships with each other because they spend a lot of time together.
- Full-time employees might be able to build up good relationships with customers or suppliers. In a competitive market, good customer service may be a key differentiating factor.
- It might be easier for full-time employees to take advantage of training opportunities.

Drawbacks

- High cost of employing people full time, especially if the value of their output falls in times of less than full capacity.
- Full-time employees might not give the business flexibility in terms of an ability to increase capacity or improve the skills base of the business.

Study tip

Despite the benefits of employing people part time, and the trend towards more part-time employees, remember that most employees are full-time. Many businesses employ a combination of full- and part-time employees in order to combine the benefits of having a core of workers full time with the flexibility that a proportion of part-time employees give the business.

Part-time employees

Part-time employment is a relatively small part of the overall labour market in terms of numbers, but it is growing in significance. Examples of part-time arrangements include:

- Term-time workers – some businesses employ people during term time and give unpaid leave during school and college holidays.
- Zero hours contracts – this is an arrangement whereby there is no fixed number of hours that a person is expected to work, but the hours worked changes as the demand for the employee changes.

Benefits

- Flexibility is the key benefit. A small business that wants to operate for longer, or increase output slightly will often do it by employing someone part time to cover the extra work.
- Part-time employees can be used when there are busy periods of trade. For example, hotels, restaurants and supermarkets all use part-time employees to cover peak trading.
- Part-time employees can also be used to extend trading or production periods. For example, a supermarket might employ part-time staff to operate in the evening and at weekend, or a petrol station might extend its night time hours with part-time staff.
- Part-time work allows some people to manage work alongside other commitments, such as family. This means that businesses have access to a wider pool of labour and can employ people who they would not otherwise be able to attract if all they offered was full-time work.

Fig. 10.2 *Most employees in some industries are employed on part-time contracts*

- Some part-time staff job share, allowing a wider range of skills and talents to enter the business.
- If someone cannot or does not want to continue working full time, employing them on a part-time basis means the business retains valuable experienced staff.
- Finally, as a small business just starting out, part-time staff represent a starting point, enabling the business to build itself slowly, as it becomes more established.

Drawbacks

There can be drawbacks to employing people on a part-time basis. However, it is important for an entrepreneur to realise that it is illegal to treat part-time staff less favourably than full-time staff. In particular, employers should be careful not to indirectly discriminate against female employees, many of whom work part time.

- Part-time staff may find it more difficult to be able to access training opportunities to the same extent as full-time staff and special arrangements may need to be made.
- It may be more difficult to communicate with part-time employees.
- Part-time employees may be less able to build close relationships with customers.
- The costs of employing and managing people on a part-time basis may not be much lower than on a full-time basis. For example, it costs as much to administer a part-time salary as it does a full-time one.

Recent legislation has given many employees with children and other dependents the right to request to go from full-time to part-time work, and employers have a legal duty to consider these requests and can only reject them on business grounds.

Study tip

When considering the benefits of employing people part time, don't forget that legislation brought in over the last few years gives part-time workers the same rights as full-time workers. This might act to reduce the flexibility enjoyed by small businesses.

■ Activity

The changing labour market

Look at Figure 10.3 and answer the following questions:

1 Describe the changes in employment in primary and secondary employment between 1978 and 2005.

2 Analyse the possible impact of the changes in tertiary employment between 1978 and 2005 on a small recruitment agency business.

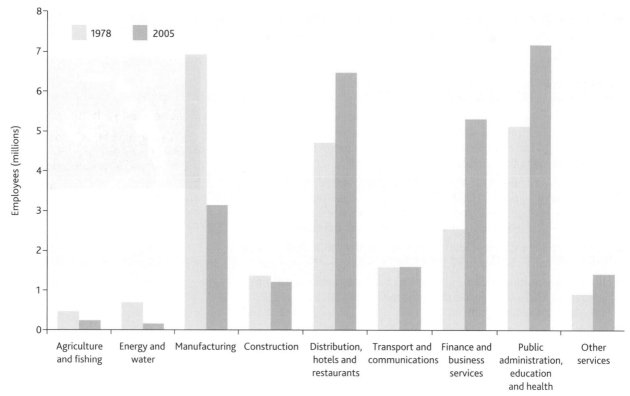

Fig. 10.3 *Employee jobs: by industry 1978 and 2005 (Source: Employee Jobs)*

Another choice that a business has is whether to employ people permanently or on a temporary basis. The majority of employees are permanent. This means that they are employed on an indefinite basis, and will end their employment either by resigning, retiring, by being made redundant or being sacked. An increasing number of businesses are using **temporary employees**.

■ Temporary employees

Benefits

■ If the volume of business may be uneven or uncertain the entrepreneur can keep the level of staffing flexible.

■ There may be specific tasks or jobs that need doing, which may have a finite time period. For instance, a small business might need an IT system designing and installing. This could mean a period of intense work, but only for a period of time.

■ Key terms

Temporary employee: one who is employed for a fixed period or periods of time. Often these workers are seasonal workers and may work full or part time. They rarely have the same benefits as permanent employees such as pensions or health insurance.

- The business may lack certain skills, which are only needed for specific periods of time. For example, a small business may need specialist HR advice as it goes through a period of recruitment or redundancy.
- A small business may wish to make or sell a product or service for a fixed period of time, and therefore has a need for a type of labour for a fixed time period.
- Temporary employees may help a business through a period of short term staff shortage or loss. A common example is maternity cover.
- Temporary workers who prove extremely valuable may eventually become permanent.

Drawbacks

- Temporary employees may not know the workings of the business or its culture.

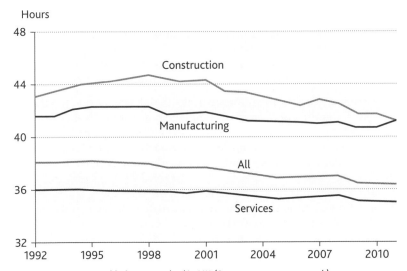

Fig. 10.4 *Average weekly hours worked in UK (Source: www.ons.gov.uk)*

- Temporary employees may not be as motivated as permanent employees.
- Constant changeover of employees may make communication more difficult.
- Customers may not like a constantly changing workforce, particularly if the business is a service business.

■ Consultants and advisers

Finally, some small businesses need very specific help and advice, often about the general running of the business, rather than about particular tasks that need carrying out. In these circumstances, small businesses will sometimes hire **consultants** or advisers.

Benefits

- Small businesses can gain the benefits of specialist skills without having the cost of employing people full-time.
- Entrepreneurs can add to their skills base as and when they need to.
- Business can adjust size of workforce up or down quickly.

■ **Activity**

Falling average hours worked

Look at Fig. 10.4. How can you explain the decline in the average number of hours worked in the UK?

■ Key terms

Consultants: businesses or individuals who provide professional advice or services for a fee. Often the advice is on how to make the small business more successful or to deal with a specific problem.

■ Avoids the need to search for and recruit staff, which can be risky if the wrong people are recruited.

■ Business start-ups can gain the advice of specialists in the early stages of the business. Often this is provided free or at a subsidised rate.

Drawbacks

■ Consultants will not know the business as well as employees.

■ Consultants may not be as motivated to work hard for the business as employees.

■ In some cases, consultants can be expensive.

 Case study

Slivers-of-Time

Slivers-of-Time Working is for anyone with spare hours to sell to local employers.

This new way of working gives individuals immediate cash, all sorts of skills and a verified CV of successful short bookings. Employers get an ultra-flexible, motivated pool of top-up workers who can be booked at short notice. They can be economically trained.

Slivers-of-Time is the ultimate in flexibility. People able to offer small amounts of time flexibly and at short notice for a wide range of jobs are known as 'work seekers' and they offer their time via a website. They do this via an online diary of the hours each particular day they are available for work. For example: *'It's now 5.00 pm, I want to work between 6.00 and 9.00 this evening.'* They also define the types of bookings they will do, how far they'll travel and how their hourly rate is to be calculated for each booking. Businesses looking for workers input their needs, for example *'3 people for 2 hours at lunchtime today'*, they see everyone who wants to do that specific booking ranked by reliability and hourly rate. They can buy instantly.

Table 10.1 *Buyers and sellers of Slivers-of-Time*

Sellers of slivers-of-time	Buyers of slivers-of-time
Parents	Local authorities
Students	Caterers
Newly retired	Retailers
Carers	Manufacturers
Partially employed	Leisure industry
Medically restricted	Hospitality providers
Business starters	Promotions companies
Job-seekers	Logistics providers
Experience seekers	Service companies
Work returners	Care providers

There are a number of benefits to this flexible way of working, and it is clear there is a growing number of people who want to work more flexibly.

■ **Show the skills**

When evaluating the impact of using part-time and temporary workers, it is very important to apply your answer to the business in question. Part-time workers are very commonly found in jobs where the demand for the product is not constant, for example seasonal goods and services. In businesses that want to keep highly qualified workers, for example in micro-chip development, it would be rare for these workers not to be offered full-time contracts.

'Our leaflets are ready. How do I find 10 people to distribute them in today's rush hour?'

'I need a pool of workers we can induct and then hire hour-by-hour as we need them'

'I need 2 extra people for my lunchtime rush hour starting in one hour'

Slivers-of-Time Marketplace

'I want to work around my studying, and the needs of my children'

'Retired shouldn't mean no longer wanting work. I like to do a few hours a week for a bit of cash'

'We want exposure to different employers each week, on our terms. We want variety and skills'

Fig. 10.5 *The Slivers-of-Time marketplace (sliversoftime.com)*

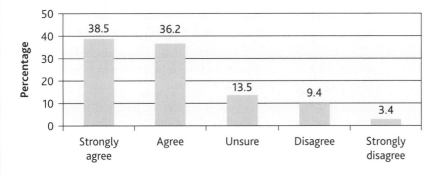

I would rather do different types of work than having to do the same job all the time

Fig. 10.6 *Changing attitudes to flexible working (continued overleaf)*

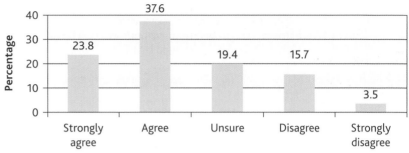

I would rather work at different places on different days than work in the same location all the time

Fig. 10.6 *Continued*

Questions

1 Describe the possible benefits to the employee of the Slivers-of-Time system. (6 marks)

2 Explain the possible disadvantages of the system to a small printing business. (6 marks)

3 Analyse the importance of technology to the Slivers-of-Time system. (6 marks)

4 Evaluate the possible limitations of the Slivers-of-Time system. (10 marks)

5 Research task: Use the Trades Union Congress (TUC) website to investigate the differences in pay levels between full-time and part-time employees, and between male and female employees. Write a brief report on your findings (400 words).

💡✔ *In this chapter you have learned to:*

- understand the benefits and drawbacks of employing workers on a full- and a part-time basis and understand some of the circumstances where part-time employment might be suitable for both employee and employer

- understand that many businesses employ a combination of full and part-time staff in order to enjoy both the benefits of a core of full-time workers with the flexibility that part-time employees give a business

- assess the benefits and drawbacks of temporary as opposed to permanent employment and appreciate the circumstances in which temporary employees might be useful to a business

- evaluate the limitations of part-time and temporary employment, especially in terms of the difficulties of communicating with or maintaining the morale of staff.

For answers to activities and case study questions see **kerboodle**

Practice questions

Chapters 7–10

1 Explain what is meant by the term 'sole trader'. *(2 marks)*

2 Describe TWO possible benefits of forming a partnership, to three school friends who are considering starting a business that designs and builds luxury houses. *(6 marks)*

3 Define the term 'stakeholders'. *(3 marks)*

4 What is the meaning of the term 'unlimited liability'? *(3 marks)*

5 Describe TWO differences between a private and a public limited company. *(4 marks)*

6 Analyse three factors a taxi service should consider before taking out a bank overdraft facility. *(6 marks)*

7 Evaluate THREE ways in which a not-for-profit business might differ from a business that has profit as its main objective. *(8 marks)*

8 Describe TWO disadvantages of using personal sources of finance to start up a bed and breakfast business. *(4 marks)*

9 Nick and Wendy Evans began their organic vegetable business three years ago and have slowly expanded the business by reinvesting profit. They started the business after moving to the Sussex countryside when they left their jobs in London. They now want to expand more quickly so they can supply to a large supermarket. The expansion will need to be financed from sources outside the business. Nick and Wendy are the only shareholders in the business, which is a limited company.

    a) Describe THREE pieces of information that a bank is likely to need before making a decision whether to lend £20,000 to an organic vegetable grower. *(6 marks)*

    b) Define the term 'venture capitalist' and explain the benefits to Nick and Wendy of this source of finance. *(8 marks)*

    c) What is meant by the term 'qualitative location factors' and why might they be important to Nick and Wendy? *(6 marks)*

    d) To what extent is it advisable for Nick and Wendy to grow slowly or more quickly? *(10 marks)*

10 Explain THREE possible location factors relevant to a decision about where to locate an accountant's business. *(6 marks)*

11 Analyse THREE possible drawbacks of an accountant operating her business from home. *(6 marks)*

12 Explain THREE possible benefits to a hotel of employing part time staff. *(6 marks)*

13   Analyse THREE possible difficulties a business growing and selling strawberries to supermarkets might encounter by employing temporary workers. *(8 marks)*

14   Assess the likely problems a dry cleaning business might have when trying to decrease the proportion of part-time and increase the proportion of full-time staff working at its branches. *(6 marks)*

15   Describe THREE ways a house builder might benefit from using a business consultant. *(5 marks)*

16   Gemma Harcourt has run her sports-goods business, Finishing Line UK, as a sole-trading operation, a partnership and a limited company. She started the business in 2000 and the business is currently growing at a rate of over 25 per cent a year. The business grew quickly and soon she needed more space, more money, and some help. She formed a limited company in 2006.

The business still struggles financially, and is currently considering ways to raise finance for the purchase of a new shop in the centre of Manchester. She has looked at a number of possible locations in the city centre, but can't make up her mind as to the best location.

One of the most challenging and rewarding parts of running the business is dealing with staff. Each shop has a full time manager, and four part time sales staff, all of whom have been with the company for a few years now. She can't seem to get the number of staff right. At certain times of the week, staff struggle to find things to do, whilst at other times they are rushed off their feet. The problems are made worse when they suddenly get a large number of orders from the website, which they struggle to process quickly if they come in during a busy part of the week.

a)   Describe THREE possible benefits to Finishing Line UK of incorporation into a limited company. *(6 marks)*

b)   Suggest TWO possible sources of external finance for the purchase of the new Manchester shop. *(2 marks)*

c)   Assess the possible factors likely to influence the location of the Manchester shop. *(8 marks)*

d)   To what extent would the use of temporary employees solve the problems experienced by Finishing Line UK? *(10 marks)*

Introduction

Chapters in this section:

How would you try to calculate the profit made by this market stallholder?

It should be clear by now that setting up a new business is challenging but potentially rewarding. There are so many different issues to consider before a business idea can come to fruition. Yet there is still one vital aspect of entrepreneurship that has not yet been covered – PROFIT!

Most entrepreneurs will be setting up in business with the intention of 'making money'. This may not always be the primary goal, as we will see in Chapter 15 – Assessing business start-ups, page 105, but it is likely to be of some significance to all entrepreneurs. When some business owners say that 'I am not in it for the money' this does not mean that they do not care how much cash the business is creating or how much of a profit or loss it is making. It might suggest, though, that there are personal aims even more important than 'making money'.

However, no matter what these other aims might be, unless a lucky entrepreneur has bottomless pockets, it will be essential for anyone planning to start a business to have a clear idea of the importance of cash and profit to its future survival and success. This section provides a clear explanation of the financial issues and concepts that all budding business owners must be aware of. But the business owners will not be the only group interested in the financial forecasts for costs, revenue and profit (or loss). Investors and banks providing finance will be keenly aware of the need for entrepreneurs to forecast these financial data. They will also want to see records of what actually happens to sales, costs and profit when the business starts trading.

So, financial planning is an essential part of preparing to set up a new business. This section focuses on the key financial concepts that entrepreneurs must understand and apply to their new business plan.

These include business costs and revenue, profit, cash flow, the output level needed to break even and setting financial plans or budgets. Some essential calculations are carefully worked through and explained and the interpretation of these results is made clear.

The section is divided into five chapters.

Chapter 11: Calculating costs, revenues and profits What do we mean by profit and how is it calculated? What is the difference between profit and sales revenue? What are the most likely costs that have to be paid by a small business? If the aim of a new business is to make money for its owner, then understanding the factors that determine profit is essential.

Chapter 12: Using break-even analysis to make decisions How many customers will the business need before it covers all of its costs and starts to make a profit? How could the level of profit be increased by reducing the break-even number of customers? A new business will be required to 'break-even' as soon as possible so that the entrepreneur can start to make a return on the initial investment.

Chapter 13: Using cash flow forecasting What is meant by 'cash flow' and why is cash important to a business? Why is it important to plan for future cash needs and how is this done? What is the typical structure of a cash flow forecast? More small businesses fail due to lack of cash than for any other reason – cash flows must be planned for.

Chapter 14: Setting budgets Making financial plans and trying to keep to them. Which parts of the business need these plans and what are the advantages in setting them? What are the common problems often associated with setting budgets? Target setting is an important part of new business planning – budgets provide a direction for the business and a means of checking progress.

Chapter 15: Assessing business start-ups How can an entrepreneur judge whether the business is a success or not? What are the main risks that confront new business start-ups? What are the most common reasons for the failure of newly formed businesses? Despite the best laid plans of entrepreneurs there are still many risks that await every new business start-up – and these can overwhelm the unprepared.

Calculating costs, revenues and profits

Key terms

Profit: what is left after costs have been deducted from revenue.

Profit = Total revenue – total costs.

Setting the scene

Rashid

Rashid was pleased with himself. In his first month of trading he had sold and fitted 10 car satellite navigation systems, two more than originally forecast in his Business Plan. Rashid's electrical skills and his friendly personality had impressed his customers.

He had purchased the first 50 satellite navigation kits from a website specialising in stock sell-offs from failed businesses. He had paid £100 each. This had swallowed up most of his start-up capital. He rented a small lock up garage for £120 a month. The large sign he fixed to the doors had cost him £120 but attracted lots of attention. Other advertising costs in his first month had been more than expected. The local newspaper had just increased its classified rates – £150 was £30 more than planned. He sold the kits for £275 fully fitted. Rashid could have just sold the kits themselves but he wanted to 'add value' to them by doing the fitting too. Each fitting kit cost Rashid £10. Other costs – such as fixed charges for business rates and electricity – had been paid and these totalled £200 per month, just as predicted. He had already paid an accountant for help with setting up the business and writing the business plan.

Rashid started to work out his profit for the first month. His only real worry was that two of his customers – whom he had known from school days – had asked for some time to pay him. He had agreed as he wanted to make the sale. But when would they pay? Should he include these two kits when working out his first monthly profits?

Discussion points

1. What evidence is there that Rashid had thought about the costs of running his business before he set it up?

2. Do you think he made a profit in his first month of trading? How would you try to work this out?

3. Why would profit be important to Rashid?

4. If you were Rashid, would you have offered the two customers 'credit', i.e. time to pay him back?

The meaning and importance of profit

Profit is a surplus. It is the surplus of the value of sales made by a business over its total costs of production. It is very important to entrepreneurs and small businesses for a number of reasons:

1. Profit is used as a measure of success by the owners of a business who have invested capital into it.

2. Banks and other lenders will be unlikely or unwilling to lend to a business that does not either forecast a profit – or actually make one.

■ Key terms

Revenue: the value of sales made during a trading period.

Total revenue = selling price × number of items sold.

Costs: these are expenditures made by a business as part of its trading operations.

Fixed costs: costs that do not change with the level of output or sales.

Variable costs: costs that change directly with the level of output or sales

Total costs: fixed costs + variable costs.

Study tip

Total revenue includes products sold on credit as well as those sold for cash during the trading period.

3 It is the return or reward to entrepreneurs and business owners for taking risks with their capital. If no profit is made, this will discourage further investment and may lead to business closure.

4 As a surplus, profit provides a source of finance for further expansion of the business.

To understand profit it is essential to understand the relationship between profit, **revenue** and **costs**.

💡 Measuring business costs

Consider Rashid's costs in the case study above. They were typical of the costs faced by most small businesses. Some of them had to be paid before he started trading such as the accountant's fees. These are start-up costs. Others did not vary with the number of kits he fitted. The garage rent and advertising costs would have to be paid even if Rashid did not sell a single kit. These are referred to as **fixed costs**. See Fig. 11.2. Even if Rashid sold a further ten kits the fixed costs of the business would not change. Finally, some costs were only incurred as he sold and fitted the kits. Clearly, the cost of the 'Satnav' kits themselves depended on the number of customers. These are called **variable costs**. See Fig. 11.1. Adding fixed and variable costs together gives a firm's **total costs**.

■ Activity

1 In Rashid's case can you give ONE further example of:
   a a fixed cost, and
   b a variable cost?

2 Calculate the total monthly fixed and variable costs (ignoring start-up costs) for Rashid if he sells and fits 12 units.

3 Explain to Rashid why profit is going to be important to his business.

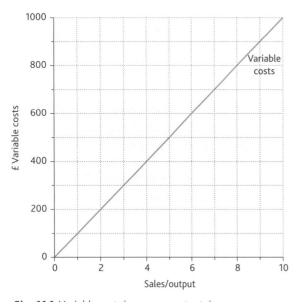

Fig. 11.1 *Variable costs increase as output rises*

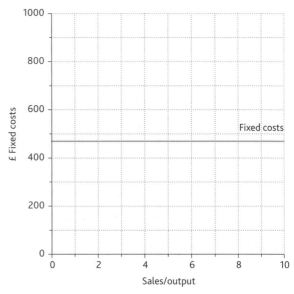

Fig. 11.2 *Fixed costs do not change as output rises*

Why calculate costs of production?

When planning to start a new business, entrepreneurs will need to forecast likely costs. These predictions will allow:

- A forecast of profit or loss to be made – will the business be a viable one?
- Forecasts of the likely break-even level of output – this is explained in the next chapter.
- Cash flow forecasts to be drawn up so that financial planning is undertaken.
- Pricing decisions to be made based on cost data.

Once a new business is up and running why should the owner need to know what costs are being incurred? There are several reasons for this:

- Keeping a check of actual costs against the forecasted costs that were part of the original business plan. Is the firm exceeding these costs and, if so, why?
- Using cost information to help in the pricing decision. In Rashid's case, any substantial increase in either variable or fixed costs may lead him to raising his price to customers.
- Calculating whether costs are greater or less than revenue – is the firm profitable at this level of sales or not?

Measuring sales revenue

Consider Rashid's sales in the case study above. Do you agree that his total revenue for the first month was £2,750? This figure is obtained by multiplying the price of each fitted kit (£275) by the number of kits sold (10). Remember: the sale of the two kits on credit is still included as revenue!

Rashid could try to increase his revenue in month 2 in two ways:

1 Try to sell and fit more than 10 kits this month – increase his sales.
2 Raise the selling price from £275.

If Rashid was absolutely confident that potential customers would pay more than £275 then his revenue would increase with a higher price. But how likely is this in reality? If he raised the price in month 2 to £300 for a fitted kit and customers fell to 8 his total revenue would fall to £2,400. So, entrepreneurs such as Rashid have to be cautious about price changes as they may have a negative impact on total revenue. The ability of any entrepreneur to increase price to gain extra revenue will depend on the level of competition the firm faces and how 'unique' the good or service is.

Making a profit?

Profit = Total revenue – Total costs

Rashid did indeed make a profit not including his start-up costs in his first month – this was a good start to his business. How could he try to increase this level of profit in later months?

The total profit of any business during a trading period depends on two main factors:

Business in action

Calculating costs and comparing these with revenue is important for all businesses. Southdown Infants School in Bath has been operating its own school catering service as a separate business for several years. Variable costs per meal are 90p and the meals are sold for £1.60. The fixed costs make up most of the difference – but that still leaves a healthy profit which is invested back into improving catering facilities.

Study tip

Students often confuse 'cost' with 'price' – the differences should now be clear. Don't think as a consumer all the time – think like an entrepreneur!

Activity

1 Can you suggest two ways Rashid could use to try to sell more kits **without** changing the price of them?

2 What might happen to the number of customers if he raised his selling price?

3 Recalculate Rashid's revenue for month 2 if he reduced the price for a fitted kit to £250 and sold 13 of them.

Link

The relationship between price and revenue is studied in more detail in Chapter 32 – Using the marketing mix: pricing, page 239.

Activity

1 Calculate Rashid's profit from his first month of trading. State any assumptions made.

2 Calculate Rashid's profit in month 2 if he sells and fits 15 systems @ £275 each. State any assumptions made.

Study tip

Never confuse profit with cash. If products are sold on credit, a profit may be recorded but there is no cash to show for it yet!

Fig. 11.3 *Pricing decisions are very important in a competitive market such as pizza restaurants*

Show the skills

The topics of revenue, costs and profit/loss are very common ones for examination questions. Always: state clearly any formulae you use; show your working calculations carefully; be prepared to compare your result with another figure, e.g. the previous year's profit. Being able to handle quantitative data in the form presented in this chapter is an important examination skill.

Profit on each item sold. Rashid makes £100 on each kit sold without fitting (price of £200 less the variable cost of each kit of £100). The profit margin of each fitted kit is

£165 (£275 – {£100 + £10 fitting kit})

The quantity sold in the trading period. If in month 2 he sells 15 fitted kits at the same price as month 1 his total profit will increase.

Case study

Pizza price dispute

It was the first time that the partners had disagreed since setting up Pizza Parlour four months ago. Sales revenue had exceeded forecasts but so had variable costs. Profit was therefore lower than planned. The cost of the 'quality ingredients' which were the original focus of the business had turned out to be much higher than expected.

Figures for the last month had been:

Sales: 1,000 pizzas @ £6 each

Fixed costs: £1,300

Variable costs: £4 per pizza (average)

'This profit is not enough to expand the business and I do not believe it pays us for the risks we are taking' said Markus, one of the two partners. 'I think we should buy cheaper ingredients – say £3 per unit – and cut the price by 50 pence. We would be cheaper than most local competitors and I estimate sales could rise to 1,200 per month'.

'This would hit the image we have worked hard to build up,' said Claire, the other partner. 'I think we should do the reverse. We should sell our pizzas at a 10% higher price and spend another £200 on advertising each month. Judging by our last adverts this could increase sales by 5% per month.'

Questions

1 Using examples from this case distinguish between the following:

a Sales and sales revenue. (4 marks)

b Fixed costs and variable costs. (4 marks)

2 Outline TWO reasons why profit is important to this newly formed business. (4 marks)

3 Analyse the possible drawbacks to this business of buying cheaper ingredients. (6 marks)

4 Which of the two suggestions for increasing profit would you recommend the partners to decide on? You should use calculations of profit before any price changes and forecasted profit after both price changes to support your recommendation. (14 marks)

5 Research task: Assume that you are planning to open a restaurant in your town. Find out in as much detail as you can the likely level of annual fixed costs for this business, assuming the property is to be rented and is to hold around 20 customers and the equipment is to be leased (a form of renting).

☑ *In this chapter you will have learned how to:*

- understand why businesses need to make a profit

- explain the differences between variable and fixed costs

- calculate business costs at different output levels

- calculate revenue at different levels of output

- calculate profit or loss at different levels of output

- discuss different approaches that might be used to increase profit.

For answers to activities and case study questions see

12 Using break-even analysis to make decisions

Setting the scene

Eat-your-fill

'We have been working flat out all month but I don't think we have made any profit yet,' complained Sara. 'I think we set our prices too low which is why we are so busy – but are we making any money, that's what I want to know?' Sara was the co-founder of 'Eat-your-fill' fast food restaurant. She and fellow entrepreneur, Jack, had been surprised by the huge demand from the public for their organic burgers and vegetarian menu options. However, the cost of their food supplies was proving to be higher than forecast due to seasonal shortages and yet the menus with fixed prices had been printed several weeks ago.

'We agreed on an average price of £10 yet the food costs per customer seem to have risen from the £3 forecasted when we drew up the business plan to about £4 now,' explained Jack. 'So we need to serve more customers each week just to cover our fixed weekly costs of £2,800'. 'Either we start looking for other, cheaper, food suppliers or we have to get the menus reprinted showing a 20% price rise – I am not going to exhaust myself for nothing,' warned Sara.

Discussion points

1. Would you classify the food costs as being a fixed or variable cost of this business?

2. Why does the increase in the cost of food supplies mean that the business 'needs to serve more customers each week just to cover fixed weekly costs of £2,800'?

3. What would be the advantages and disadvantages of each of the two proposals Sara made to increase the profitability of 'Eat-your-fill'?

Breaking-even

When a business is said to be 'breaking-even' it is just earning enough sales revenue to pay for all of its total costs. It is not yet making a profit but it is not recording a loss either. For an entrepreneur planning a new business this is a really important situation to aim for. If the business is able to break-even quickly then there should be opportunities to make progress to start earning a profit. Banks and other lenders to the business will be very interested to know whether the business is planned to break-even within one month or one year – the longer the period, the greater the business risk.

For existing businesses, just breaking-even will mean that business managers will need to take important decisions to turn 'breaking-even' into a profit.

How can the break-even level of production be calculated and how can decisions be made to reduce this level of output so that higher profits can be made? Answers to these crucial questions are the focus of this chapter.

■ Contribution and contribution per unit

Contribution is one of the most important financial concepts in Business Studies.

It is not the same as profit as in calculating contribution fixed costs are NOT subtracted. It is the surplus made after all variable costs have been paid for from sales revenue and this surplus goes towards paying for fixed costs. The following diagram helps to explain this relationship.

■ **Key terms**

Contribution: this is the difference between sales revenue and variable costs of production.

Fig. 12.1 *Contribution: how it is earned and what it is used for*

Contribution per unit of output is widely used by entrepreneurs and business managers to assist in taking important decisions. This figure can then be used to calculate the **total contribution**. Profit can then be calculated by using the formula: Total contribution - fixed costs.

■ **Key terms**

Contribution per unit: this is the difference between the selling price of one unit and the variable cost of producing one unit.

Total contribution: unit contribution × no. of units sold.

■ Case study

In the case study on page 80, Sara and Jack originally planned the contribution per customer to be £7 (£10 – £3). If they served 500 customers in one week then the total contribution would have been:

$$500 \times £7 = £3,500$$

This would be used to pay the restaurant's weekly fixed costs and any surplus is profit.

Questions

1 Using this total contribution figure, calculate the weekly profit from the restaurant if 500 customers were served each week. (1 mark)

2 What is the new contribution per unit following the increase in food costs? (1 mark)

3 What is the new total contribution per week if 500 customers are served each week? (1 mark)

4 Is the restaurant now making a weekly profit if 500 customers are served? (2 marks)

Some important points to remember about contribution per unit:

- ■ It can be increased by raising the selling price
- ■ It can be increased by reducing variable costs per unit
- ■ It is not the same as profit per unit as fixed costs are not subtracted
- ■ An increase in contribution per unit raises the potential profit that a business can make.

It is very useful in business decision making, such as in setting prices, and in calculating the break-even level of output.

Study tip

Never make the mistake of describing 'contribution' as being profit – they really are different concepts.

Key terms

Break-even level of output: this is the level of output or the number of customers that earns enough revenue to cover total costs of production.

Calculating the break-even level of output

At the break-even level of output although revenue covers total costs there is no surplus so no profit is yet being earned. Obviously, if a business was **never** able to reach the **break-even level of output** it would never record a profit.

In the previous case study, should Sara and Jack have planned to achieve a high or a low number of customers in order to break-even?

There are obvious benefits from planning to reach a LOW break-even output. This means that all costs are being covered with a small number of customers. Any contribution made after this level of output means profits will now be made. But how is the break-even level of output calculated?

Example 1

If a printing business pays fixed costs of £500 per week and each customer earns the business a contribution of £250, how many customers each week are needed to pay for fixed costs – and therefore break-even? 2 is the answer – but what is the 'formula' used?

$$\text{Break-even output} = \frac{\text{Fixed costs of the business}}{\text{Contribution per unit}}$$

Example 2

A petrol station buys in petrol at 93p per litre. The selling price is 99p per litre. Weekly fixed costs are £1,200. How many litres of petrol does it have to sell to break-even?

$$\text{Break-even output} = \frac{£1,200}{99p - 93p} = 20,000 \text{ litres}$$

Example 3

The petrol station owner has been able to negotiate lower annual electricity charges and weekly fixed costs fall to £1,140. How will this affect the break-even level of output?

$$\text{Break-even output} = \frac{£1,140}{6p} = 19,000 \text{ litres}$$

The results from these examples are important. They show that, if nothing else changes, a **reduction** in contribution per customer or unit will RAISE the break-even level of output. If output does not increase then profits of the business will FALL. So, if one of Sara's two suggestions were put into effect, the increased contribution per customer would reduce the break-even level of output and increase profit – IF nothing else changes!

Calculating break-even output is an easy way of checking the viability of a new business proposal. It does not guarantee profitability or future success, of course, but it does give a really important indicator to the entrepreneur and the bank of the likely number of customers needed before the business can start to cover all of its costs. If this output level seems unreasonably high, then the entrepreneur may have to reconsider the original business plan and look at ways to either reduce fixed costs or raise contribution per unit of output.

Whilst these break-even calculations give a useful guide to the number of units of output or the number of customers needed to cover all costs they do not show how much profit the business could actually make. To be able to do this, we now need to turn to break-even charts.

Activity

1 Calculate the break-even number of customers needed by 'Eat-your-fill' restaurant at:

a the original forecasted variable cost level and

b the actual variable cost level. Comment on your results.

2 Even though Sara's suggestions will increase contribution per customer, why might they NOT lead to higher profits?

💡 Break-even charts

Table 12.1 *Cost and price data for 'Eat-your-fill' restaurant*

Information needed	'Eat-your-fill' data
Weekly fixed costs	£2,800
Variable costs per customer (original forecasted figure)	£3
Average revenue earned per customer	£10
Maximum weekly number of customers – the capacity of the restaurant	600

These are graphs that show the revenue and costs of a business at different levels of output. They can be drawn by following a number of stages. In our example we will be using the 'Eat-your-fill' data in the first case study of this chapter. Here is the essential information that we will need taken from that case study plus some other important data.

You are advised to follow these stages carefully by drawing the chart on graph paper.

Stage 1

Mark out the scales on graph paper. The vertical axis will record weekly costs and revenues in £. The scale will extend from zero at the origin to the maximum revenue that can be earned = 600 customers × £10 each = £6,000. Mark out the scale in squares of £1,000.

The horizontal axis records the number of customers (or units of output). This scale will extend from zero at the origin to a maximum capacity of 600. Mark out the scale in squares of 100.

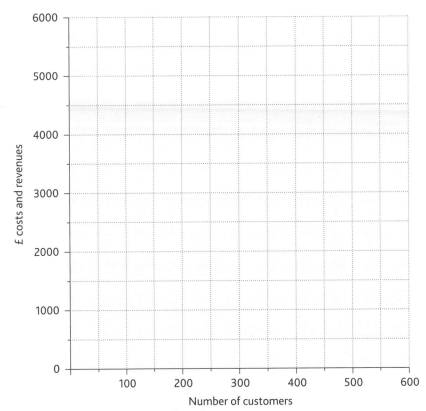

Fig. 12.2 *Mark out the scales as indicated*

Stage 2

Draw in the fixed cost line. Weekly fixed costs are £2,800 and – because they do not vary with the number of customers – this line can be drawn completely horizontal from the point £2,800 on the vertical scale.

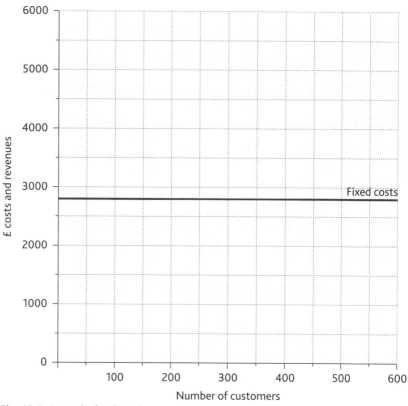

Fig. 12.3 *Draw the fixed cost line*

Stage 3

Draw in the variable cost line. Variable costs per customer were forecast to be £3. Start this line at zero – no customers means no variable costs are used in production. Just one more point is needed to complete the variable cost line. At 600 customers a week, total variable costs will be £1,800 – add this coordinate onto the graph and then join the two points with a straight line from zero to £1,800.

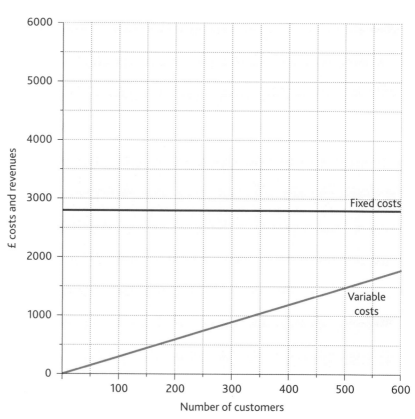

Fig. 12.4 *Draw in the variable cost line between zero and £1,800 (at 600 customers)*

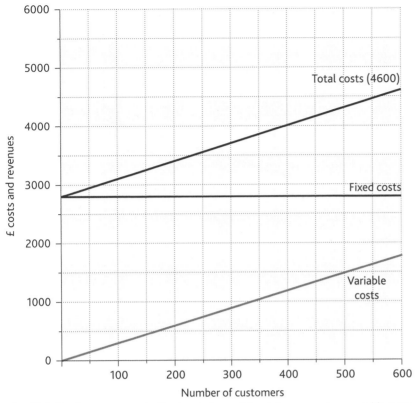

Fig. 12.5 *Total costs start at the fixed costs line and rise at the same rate as variable costs*

Stage 4

Add fixed and variable costs together at all levels of output to give the total weekly costs of the business. This line STARTS at £2,800 because even with no customers, there will be weekly fixed costs of £2,800. The fixed cost line is then drawn parallel to the variable cost line ending it at 600 customers. To check on this – the total costs at 600 customers will = £2,800 + (600 × £3) = £4,600. This coordinate will give you a total cost line parallel to variable costs.

Study tip

You only need two coordinates to draw a straight line – there is no need to plot more than two points.

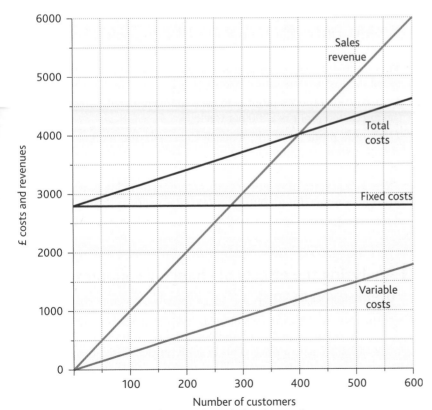

Fig. 12.6 *Adding the revenue line completes the break-even chart*

Stage 5

Add the revenue line to complete the break-even chart. The restaurant's revenue will be zero with no customers so this line starts at the origin. The other coordinate needed will be at maximum sales revenue – 600 customers × £10 = £6,000. Draw a straight line between zero and £6,000 (at 600 customers).

Stage 6

The level of output at which the firm just breaks even can now be shown by drawing a vertical line down to the horizontal axis from where total cost = total revenue.

At 500 customers per week, a profit of £700 is made.

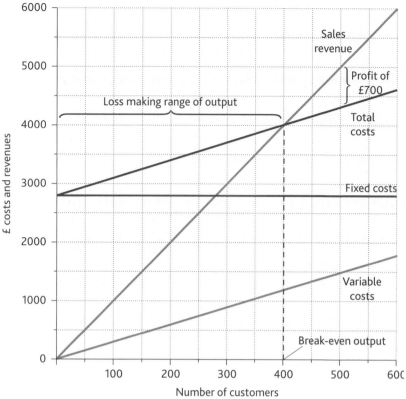

Fig. 12.7 *Draw a vertical line to the horizontal axis to show the break-even point*

■ Key terms

Margin of safety: this is the amount by which the existing level of output is greater than the break-even point.

Activity

1 Read off the forecasted level of profit if 550 customers were served in one week.

2 Calculate the margin of safety at 550 customers per week.

▣ Reading the break-even chart

What does the completed chart show us? Using the chart we are able to tell:

■ The restaurant's original forecasted break-even number of customers = 400.

■ That up to 400 customers a loss is made by the business – this is called the loss making range of output.

■ After 400 customers a profit is made – for example, at 500 customers, the forecasted profit is £700 per week.

■ The largest profit is, clearly, made at the maximum level of capacity of 600 customers and there is a profit making range of output of 200 customers.

■ There is a **margin of safety** of 200 customers from break-even at 400 customers to maximum output at 600 customers, if this is reached.

Read off the forecasted level of profit if 550 customers were served in one week.

▣ Analysing the effects of changing variables on break-even output

One of the most significant uses of break-even analysis is to analyse the impact on the break-even output and potential profit levels of a change in either variable costs or price. This is sometimes referred to as 'what if analysis' because the technique allows managers to answer questions such as: 'What if the price increased, how would this affect the break-even point?' Both the break-even formula and break-even charts can be used for this analysis.

Example 1

Sara and Jack should have considered what would happen to their restaurant's break-even point and profitability if variable costs should rise – as food costs actually did. Using the break-even formula we can confirm the result you may have obtained earlier with variable costs now at £4 per customer:

$$\text{Break-even output} = \frac{\text{Fixed costs}}{\text{Contribution per unit}} = \frac{£2{,}800}{£6} = 467 \text{ customers}$$

Confirm the result in Example 1 by changing your break-even chart showing that variable costs now rise to £2,400 at 600 customers – you will need to increase total costs too. What happens to the restaurant's profits at 550 customers compared to the original forecast? Might this new break-even chart have discouraged Sara and Jack from setting up their new business?

Example 2

The following break-even chart was drawn by Bill Potter who planned to open a sports shoe shop. It was based on the following forecasted data.

Table 12.2 *Bill's cost and price data for the sports shoe shop*

Information needed	Bill Potter's forecasts
Annual fixed costs	£30,000
Variable costs per customer	£45
Selling price per pair of shoes	£105
Expected maximum sales level	2,000 pairs per year

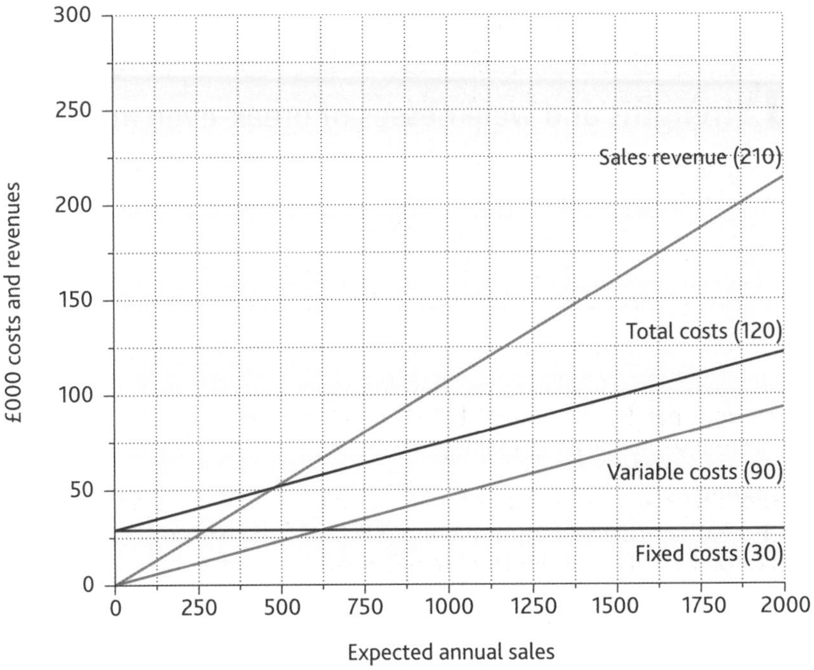

Fig. 12.8 *Bill Potter's break-even chart*

Study tip

Remember that to ***increase*** profit, the break-even level of output should be ***lowered*** by, for example, cutting costs or raising the price.

Bill included this break-even chart into his Business Plan. He was surprised when his bank's Business Development Manager queried the high forecasted selling price. She claimed that she knew the area that Bill was planning to set his shop up in better than he did and she didn't know anybody who would pay £105 for a pair of sports shoes! Bill agreed to revise the chart after he had done more market research.

Following visits to many sports shoe shops he decided that £85 was a more realistic selling price – but that this would mean buying cheaper styles with an average variable cost of £40. He also decided to rent a shop in a slightly better shopping centre costing an extra £20,000 a year. The new break-even chart now looked like this:

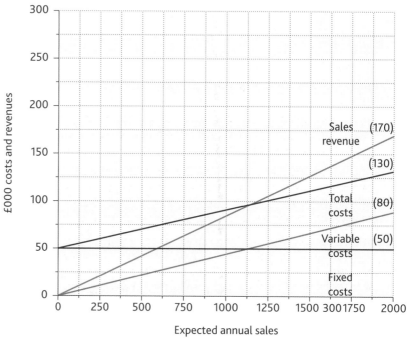

Fig. 12.9 *Bill's break-even chart based on market research evidence*

Activity

Compare Bill Potter's two break-even charts.

1 How has the expected break-even point changed?

2 What has happened to 'maximum' profit assuming 2,000 pairs sold a year?

3 Explain to Bill why his new business proposal is now less viable than with the original forecasts

💡 Strengths and weaknesses of break-even analysis

Strengths

■ It is a relatively simple concept and the formula can be understood and used by most entrepreneurs.

■ The information it provides can be vital when taking a decision whether to go ahead with a business proposal.

■ It is widely used to support applications from entrepreneurs for loans.

■ It can be quickly adapted to allow for many 'what if' situations to be considered and compared. This reinforces the usefulness of the technique for decision making.

Weaknesses

■ It assumes that all output produced is sold – there is no scope for keeping stocks with break-even analysis.

■ It over simplifies business situations. For example, we have assumed above an 'average' customer revenue and 'average' variable cost and in reality there will be considerable variations.

- Many firms sell more than one product – e.g. a range of sports shoes not just one style! Break-even becomes much more difficult to apply in these cases.

- Fixed costs are rarely completely fixed over a wide range of output and variable costs could vary with bulk discounts as the business expands. Break-even analysis assumes 'steady and consistent' increases in variable costs.

- As we saw with Sara and Jack, misleading or inaccurate data leads to incorrect break-even forecasts.

- A break-even chart does not show what **will** definitely happen – it is a planning aid to help business managers consider the impact of various possible decisions.

Business in action

Cheet: Bags of Style

Setting up 'Cheet: Bags of Style' was always going to be a risky enterprise for fashion handbag designer Emily Cheetham (pictured right). To cut start-up costs to a minimum she worked from a room in her flat and used her aunt's sewing machine. She used her wide circle of friends to help promote her products.

The business has recently had some success with made-to-order commissions and trade sales in two independent boutiques and this has increased sales to four bags per week. This means the business is just breaking even with a weekly sales turnover of £1,200.

Emily hopes to keep the business growing so that it becomes profitable but she is determined to continue to keep costs down. She has started to outsource production which gives her more time to design and sell. She is planning a ready-to-sell collection that should 'fly off the shelves' and help the business go beyond break-even and keep a healthy cash flow.

www.cheetlondon.com

Case study

Is it still worthwhile?

The meeting with the bank's Small Business Manager had not gone well. The manager had appreciated the work that Lena and Boris had put into their business plan but the assumptions behind the break-even analysis had been criticised as being too optimistic. The manager had redrawn the break-even chart with new assumptions about contribution per unit and the business seemed much less viable. 'Why should his figures be any more accurate than ours?' moaned Boris. 'That's not the point – he won't lend the money unless we make this business proposal seem more profitable,' explained Lena. 'What we need to do is rethink the figures behind the break-even and see if we can convince him that the business is worth the risk'.

The couple were planning to set up a home fitness business which offered specific, personalised get-fit courses for people who were not keen on traditional gyms. They both intended to keep their own gym jobs going but would employ others to provide the 'home service'. The main variable cost was going to be the employment of hourly paid well qualified fitness instructors. The main fixed costs were the leasing of vans and keep-fit equipment. The bank manager had doubted the low hourly wage rate included in the break-even calculation and the pricing levels forecast by Lena and Boris. 'You need to charge more than that if you expect to make much of a profit,' had been the manager's last comment.

Two weeks later the couple had revised their figures and had redrawn the break-even chart. They were prepared to do battle with the manager once more. The revised data used by Lena and Boris is in the table below – together with the manager's own estimates.

Table 12.3 *Boris and Lena's financial data*

	Bank Manager's estimates	Boris and Lena's revised data
Fixed costs – weekly	£2,100	£1,500
Variable cost per customer hour	£15	£12
Average price to customer	£45	£37
Expected number of customer hours per week	80	80

Boris and Lena had decided they could recruit less well-qualified fitness instructors and lease second-hand not new vans in drawing up their new revised figures.

Questions

1. What do you understand by the terms:
   a contribution per customer, and (2 marks)
   b break-even level of output? (2 marks)

2. Explain TWO benefits to Lena and Boris of undertaking break-even analysis in this case. (4 marks)

3. Analyse the viability of this business proposal by undertaking break-even analysis using either the formula or a chart. Compare the break-even points, the forecasted profit levels and the margins of safety (at assumed expected number of customers) using the data. (8 marks)

4. Using your results and any other information in the case, would you advise Lena and Boris to go ahead with this business proposal? Justify your answer. (10 marks)

5. Research task: Use the BBC business website to research a company that is struggling to meet its break-even point. For example, search for the Boeing 787 Dreamliner.

☑ *In this chapter you have learned to:*

■ explain what contribution and contribution per unit mean

■ explain what 'breaking-even' means and define break-even point

■ use contribution per unit to calculate the break-even point

- draw a break-even chart and identify and explain its main features
- change any of the key variables – price, variable cost and fixed cost – and re-draw a break-even chart or recalculate the break-even level of output
- use the data provided by break-even charts to assist entrepreneurs in decisions about starting a business
- evaluate the usefulness of break-even analysis.

For answers to activities and case study questions see

Practice questions

Chapters 11 & 12

1 Explain why profit is important to any business. *(4 marks)*

2 Explain why the revenue of a business is unlikely to increase by 10% when it raises prices by 10%. *(4 marks)*

3 Identify FOUR costs that will have to be paid by a taxi business – and classify them into either variable or fixed costs. *(8 marks)*

4 A friend of yours plans to set up a specialist online computer magazine. Customers would pay by subscription. Explain the importance to your friend of distinguishing between contribution and profit when starting up his business. *(8 marks)*

5 Distinguish clearly between the break-even level of output and the margin of safety by sketching a typical break-even chart. *(4 marks)*

6 Explain TWO reasons why a new entrepreneur might find break-even analysis useful. *(4 marks)*

7 A garden maintenance business owner finds that she has to work four days a week just to 'break-even'. Analyse TWO steps she could take to reduce this break-even point of production. *(8 marks)*

8 A jewellery retailer finds that its costs of new stock are rising due to increasing gold prices. Analyse TWO steps the business owner might take to maintain total levels of profit from the business. *(8 marks)*

9 Analyse TWO possible reasons why a new business start-up might discover that the original break-even analysis in the Business Plan is very inaccurate. *(8 marks)*

10 Analyse why the owner of a hotel in an area with considerable seasonal demand variations might find it useful to distinguish between the variable and fixed costs of the business. *(8 marks)*

11 Evaluate the usefulness of break-even analysis to this same hotel business. *(10 marks)*

12 The break-even chart below shows the current position for a specialist manufacturer of executive computer desks or work stations. The current level of output is 3,000 per year, although capacity is 5,000 desks. The owner of the business is aiming to increase profitability and is considering the following change: Reducing the price to £450 but increasing output and (hopefully) sales to 4,000 desks.

a)   Mark the new expected sale revenue line on the chart.   *(2 marks)*
b)   Identify the new break-even level of output.   *(1 mark)*
c)   Compare the profitability of the business at 3,000 units @
           £500 and at 4,000 units @ £450.   *(4 marks)*
d)   Do you think the business owner should make this change to
           a lower price? Explain your answer.   *(8 marks)*

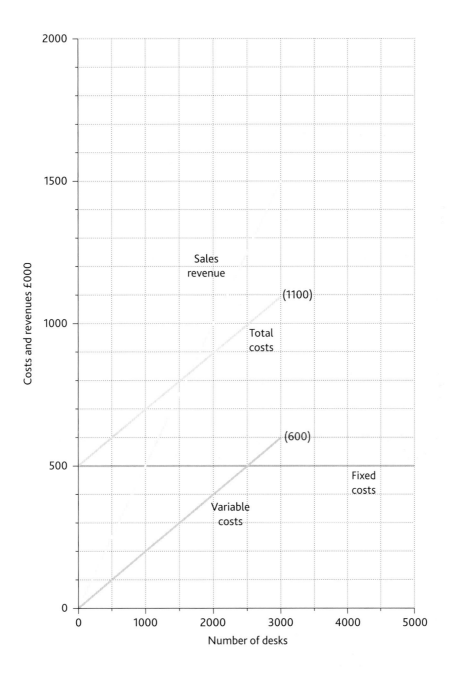

Using cash flow forecasting

Setting the scene

Sun Optical

Sun Optical had been making spectacles for years. The business was in a rut with no sales growth and low profits. The owners agreed to recruit a qualified Managing Director who could give a new direction. Geoff Harding did not take long to make changes. He suggested raising the annual sales revenue from £1 million to £4 million in two years by specialising in fashion sunglasses. New in-house designs were created. Geoff's links with the industry helped him gain big orders from some of the leading names – Dolland and Aitchison and John Lewis, for example. The sunglasses sold for high prices. These large orders were profitable but there was a big problem. The biggest firms were the slowest payers! The big retailers expected several months of credit and such high standards that some production had to be scrapped.

Geoff became concerned about the firm's cash flow. Suppliers were screaming for payment. The bank overdraft had reached record levels. Overtime working by staff to complete orders on time was leaking more cash out of the business. Then Geoff discovered that his bookkeeper had not included VAT or transport costs into the monthly cash flow forecast – they had even less money than they thought! He even asked long-serving staff for cash loans which many agreed to.

Friday the 13th was not lucky for Geoff. A department store buyer was visiting in the morning and the bank manager was due in the afternoon. Mid-way through the day, he learnt that the major 'finishing' machine had broken down and a major supplier had rejected the latest order for materials.

Within weeks, the assets of the business had been sold off and the people and firms owed money by Sun Optical received a fraction of what they were owed.

Discussion points

1. Why did this business fail to survive? Explain the problems the business faced in as much detail as you can.

2. Can you suggest ways in which the business could have overcome its major problems?

3. To what extent was lack of forward planning or forecasting a weakness of the business?

What do you think the term cash flow means?

Cash gives 'immediate spending power'. A firm's cash will be held in its tills and safes but also in current accounts with a bank. A business needs cash to pay bills and expenses such as:

- Rent
- Taxes

- Wages
- Suppliers
- Electricity

Without enough cash, as Sun Optical found out, bills cannot be paid and the firm will be forced out of business. The amount of cash held is never constant – it changes with the payments made and received. These are called **cash flows**.

In this chapter we discover why cash flow is important to all businesses and how cash flows can be forecasted to reduce – but not to eliminate – the risk of running out of cash.

The importance of cash flow

The Sun Optical case study allows us to see the importance of cash flow to all businesses – even those that claim to be making a profit! Profit does not pay the bills and expenses of running a business – but cash does. Of course profit is important – especially in the long term when investors expect rewards and the business needs additional finance for investment. Cash is always important – short- and long-term. Cash flow relates to the timing of payments **to** workers and suppliers and receipts **from** customers. If a business does not manage the timing of these payments and receipts carefully it may run out of cash even though it is operating profitably. If suppliers and creditors are not paid in time they can force the business into **liquidation** of the business's assets as it appears to be **insolvent**.

So, cash flow is certainly important – especially to small business start-ups. Why is cash flow planning so vital for entrepreneurs?

- New business start-ups are often offered much less time to pay suppliers than larger, well-established firms – they are given shorter credit periods.
- Banks and other lenders may not believe the promises of new business owners as they have no trading record. They will expect payment at the agreed time!
- Finance is often very tight at start-up so not planning accurately is of even more significance for new businesses.

How to forecast cash flow

This is one of the most challenging sections in a typical Business Plan. The entrepreneur will have to consider the sources and timing of **cash inflows** and **cash outflows** usually on a month by month basis. Let's take the case of Jim, an entrepreneur planning to open a car valeting service aiming to offer this service to individual customers and owners of car fleets such as taxi firms.

Forecasting cash inflows

Where to start? Jim will probably attempt to forecast cash inflow first. Some of these will be easier to forecast than others. Here are some examples of cash inflows and how they might be forecast:

- Owners own capital injection – easy to forecast as this is under the owner's direct control.
- Bank loans received – easy to forecast if it has been agreed with the bank in advance, both in terms of amount and timing.
- Customers cash purchases – difficult to forecast as it depends on sales. So, a sales forecast will be necessary – but how accurate might this be?

Key terms

Cash flow: the total cash payments (inflows) into a business minus the total cash payments (outflows)

Liquidation: this is turning assets into cash and may be insisted on by courts if suppliers have not been paid.

Insolvent: when a business cannot meet its short-term debts.

Cash inflows: payments in cash received by a business such as those from customers or from the bank e.g. receiving a loan.

Cash outflows: payments in cash made by a business such as those to suppliers and workers.

Study tip

Do not confuse profit with cash flow. Even a profitable business can run out of cash and be forced to close. For example, selling products to customers on credit might be profitable, but it means delaying cash inflows.

■ Key terms

Debtors: these are customers who have bought products on credit and will pay cash at an agreed date in the future.

Credit sales: value of goods sold to customers who do not pay cash immediately.

Study tip

Never fall in to the trap of referring to forecasts as ACTUAL accounts – they are financial planning estimates that are dealing with the future.

■ Link

For further explanation of overdrafts, see Chapter 8 – Raising finance, page 53.

■ Key terms

Cash flow forecast: an estimate of a firm's future cash inflows and outflows.

Net monthly cash flow: the estimated difference between monthly cash inflows and outflows.

Opening balance: cash held by the business at the start of the month.

Closing balance: cash held at the end of the month – becomes next month's opening balance.

■ Activity

Try to think of as many likely cash payments that could be received and made by a business as you can.

■ **Debtors** payments – difficult to forecast as these depend on two unknowns. Firstly, what is the likely level of **credit sales**? Secondly, when will debtors actually pay? One month's credit may have been agreed with them but payment during this period can never be guaranteed.

Forecasting cash outflows

Again, some of these will be much easier to forecast than others. Here are some example cash outflows and how they might be forecast:

■ Lease payment for premises – easy to forecast as this will be in the estate agent's details of the property.

■ Annual rent payment – easy to forecast as this will be fixed and agreed for a certain time period. The landlord may increase the rent after this period, however.

■ Electricity, gas, water and telephone bills – difficult to forecast as these will vary with so many factors such as the number of customers, seasonal weather conditions and energy prices.

■ Labour cost payments – these forecasts will be based largely on demand forecasts and the hourly wage rate that is to be paid. These payments could vary from week to week if demand fluctuates and if staff are on flexible contracts.

■ Variable cost payments such as cleaning materials – the cost of these should vary consistently with demand so revenue forecasts could be used to assess variable costs too. How much credit will be offered by suppliers – the longer the period of credit offered the lower will be the start-up cash needs of the business.

When there appear to be so many uncertainties involved in cash flow forecasting you may start to wonder why firms bother! We will leave this argument to the final section of this chapter. Now we turn to the drawing up of a cash flow forecast.

💡 The structure of cash flow forecasts

A simplified **cash flow forecast** is shown in Table 13.1. It is based on Jim's car valeting service. Although there are different styles of presenting this information, all cash flow forecasts have three basic sections:

Section 1 – Cash inflows. This section records the cash payments to the business including cash sales, payments from debtors and capital inflows.

Section 2 – Cash outflows. This section records the cash payments made by the business including wages, materials, rent and other costs.

Section 3 – **Net monthly cash flow, opening balance** and **closing balance**. This shows the net cash flow for the period and the cash balances at the start and end of the period. It is common to assume that if the closing balance is negative (shown by a figure in brackets) then a bank overdraft will be necessary to finance this.

What does this tell Jim about the prospects for his business? In cash terms, the business appears to be in a good position at the end of four months. This is because:

■ In April the closing cash balance is positive so the bank overdraft has been fully repaid.

■ There was only one month – the first month of operation – in which the monthly net cash flow was negative.

■ The monthly net cash flow is positive from February onwards.

Table 13.1 *Jim's cash flow forecast for the first four months (figures in brackets are negative)*

Cash inflows	All figures in £000	JAN	FEB	MAR	APR
	Owner's capital injection	6	0	0	0
	Cash sales	3	4	6	6
	Payments by debtors	0	2	2	3
	Total cash in	9	6	8	9
Cash outflows					
	Lease	8	0	0	0
	Rent	1	1	1	1
	Materials	0.5	1	3	2
	Labour	1	2	3	3
	Other costs	0.5	1	0.5	1.5
	Total cash out	11	5	7.5	7.5
Net cash flow	**Net monthly cash flow**	(2)	1	0.5	1.5
	Opening balance	0	(2)	(1)	(0.5)
	Closing balance	(2)	(1)	(0.5)	1

BUT – never forget that these are only forecasts and the accuracy of the cash flow forecast will depend greatly on how accurate Jim was in his demand, revenue and material cost forecasts.

Why businesses forecast cash flows

There are several important advantages to cash flow forecasting, especially for new businesses:

- By indicating times of negative cash flow, plans can be put in place to provide additional finance, for example arranging a bank overdraft or preparing to inject more owner's capital.

- If negative cash flows appear to be too great then plans can be made for reducing these, for example by cutting down on the purchase of materials or machinery or by not making sales on credit, only for cash.

- A new business proposal will never progress beyond the initial planning stage unless investors and bankers have access to a cash flow forecast – and the assumptions that lie behind it.

Cash flow forecasting – what are the limitations?

Although an entrepreneur should take every reasonable step to increase the accuracy of the business cash flow forecast – by using relevant market research for example – it would be foolish indeed to assume that it will always be accurate. There are so many factors, either internal to the business or in the external environment, that can change to blow a cash flow forecast off course. This does not make them useless – but, as with any business forecast they must be used with caution and the ways in which the cash flows have been estimated should be understood. Here are the most common limitations of them:

- Mistakes can be made in preparing the revenue and cost forecasts or they may be drawn up by inexperienced staff or entrepreneurs.

Activity

With reference to Table 13.1 draw up a revised cash flow forecast for April assuming:

1. Cash sales are forecast to be £1,000 higher.

2. Materials are forecast to be £500 higher.

3. Other costs were forecast to be £1,000 higher.

Study tip

In Unit 1 you will not be asked questions about how a business might improve its cash flow position – these questions might appear in Unit 2 though.

■ Show the skills

When evaluating the importance of cash flow forecasts, do not forget that even a very detailed cash flow forecast does not guarantee that a new business enterprise will be successful. The cash flow forecast could be inaccurate. Also, other factors such as competitors, management skills and economic factors will all impact on the success of a business.

- Unexpected cost increases can lead to major inaccuracies in forecasts. Fluctuations in oil prices lead to the cash flow forecasts of even major airlines being misleading.
- Wrong assumptions can be made in estimating the sales of the business, perhaps based on poor market research, and this will make the cash inflow forecasts inaccurate.

Case study

Fashion shop forecasts look good

'I have stood outside of some of these fashion shops for hours counting the number of people coming out with their carrier bags and I am convinced my sales forecasts are OK,' announced Sayuri to her business partner, Korede. They were both putting the finishing touches to their business plan for an exclusive 'top brands only' fashion store in the city. Sayuri's primary research was not the only evidence they had used in arriving at the sales forecasts and the cash inflow forecasts. Some desk research on the internet had also revealed the rapid growth of high income consumers spending increasing amounts on expensive clothing.

Cash outflow forecasts had been based on estimates of electricity and telephone usage. Korede had found what he thought was a suitable shop so they knew how much the rent would be. They would pay themselves a salary of £2,000 a month each initially. Other labour costs were less certain. Should they employ full-time salaried staff or part-time hourly wage employees? The cost of buying the clothes was also uncertain. There would be no problem if they sold all the suits and dresses that they bought in – but how likely was that? And what would happen to cash flow forecasts if stock was left unsold and huge price reductions had to be advertised? Whatever the uncertainties, both Sayuri and Korede realised why they had to construct a cash flow forecast for their business plan. The almost completed forecast is shown opposite:

Questions

1 Complete the cash flow forecast shown in Table 13.2 by inserting values for x, y and z. (3 marks)

2 Analyse TWO problems of drawing up a cash flow forecast Sayuri and Korede may have experienced. (6 marks)

3 The first three months actual trading was poor and cash sales were 20% below forecast. Draw up a new cash flow forecast for July assuming 20% lower cash sales, 20% lower clothes purchases, an opening cash balance of £2,000 and all other factors remaining unchanged. (8 marks)

4 To what extent would drawing up a cash flow forecast increase the chances of this business being successful? (14 marks)

5 Research task: Visit a bank branch and ask for a pack of information for starting up a new business. This pack will almost certainly contain a pro-forma cash flow forecast. Comment on any differences between this format and the one used in this chapter.

Table 13.2 *Sayuri's and Korede's cash flow forecast for the first four months of trading (all figures in £000)*

Cash inflows	All figures in £000	APRIL	MAY	JUNE	JULY
	Owners' capital injection	28	0	0	0
	Cash sales	6	8	12	9
	Payments by debtors (e.g. credit card companies)	0	2	2	3
	Total cash in	34	10	14	12
Cash outflows					
	Lease	18	0	0	0
	Rent	2	2	2	2
	Clothes purchases	6	4	3	4
	Labour	3	3	4	3
	Other costs	6.5	2	2.5	1.5
	Total cash out	35.5	11	11.5	y
Net cash flow	Net monthly cash flow	x	(1)	2.5	z
	Opening balance	0	(1.5)	(2.5)	0
	Closing balance	(1.5)	(2.5)	0	1.5

☑ *In this chapter you will have learned to:*

■ explain the difference between cash and profit

■ understand how a profitable business can run out of cash

■ analyse the most likely sources of data for cash flow forecasts

■ understand the structure of a typical cash flow forecast

■ change a cash flow forecast on the basis of new information

■ evaluate the usefulness of cash flow forecasts.

For answers to activities and case study questions see **kerboodle**

Setting budgets

■ Setting the scene

ChipRepair fails to meet targets

ChipRepair was set up six months ago by two school leavers with a passion for computers, especially taking them to bits! Andy and Kate decided during their A2 year that their business would specialise in fault finding, repair and servicing of home computers. They would travel to clients' houses as they could not afford their own premises. Limited market research had been undertaken, mainly questionnaires to the parents of school friends. They found out that, especially amongst the older generation, there was a lot of ignorance about computer problems, loading of new software and ways of updating existing hardware. The survey suggested that many people were prepared to pay for specialist computer help at home. This suggested a market opportunity!

In planning the business, the couple planned to aim for eight clients a week. They thought of charging £30 an hour, about £5 less than three competitors in their town. They estimated that each job would take two hours on average. So, the sales revenue target was £1,920 per month. Transport costs were difficult to predict – how far should they be prepared to travel for new business? Eventually, in the business plan they forecasted £200 per month each as the likely expenditure on travel. Promotion costs they estimated to be £100 a month – mainly on newspaper and magazine adverts. Finally, after considering other costs as well, they predicted that they would make a profit of around £500 per month.

After the first six months Andy and Kate had a reality check. Actual revenue was 50% less than target – new customers were harder to come by than predicted. As a result, they had travelled much further for new business than planned and this had increased transport costs. They had doubled their advertising limit to appeal to more potential customers. Over this period the couple only just broke even – they were so disappointed.

Discussion points

1. Why do you think Andy and Kate decided to set targets for income and spending for their new business?

2. Suggest several factors that could make these targets unreliable.

3. If you were advising Andy and Kate, how would you recommend them to make more reliable targets?

■ Key terms

Budgets: financial targets for the future covering revenue (income) and expenditure over a certain time period.

■ The importance of budgets

Perhaps, they did not realise it but Andy and Kate were setting **budgets** for their business. This is a very important part of financial planning and control.

What was the purpose of setting these financial targets? How did they help the two owners set up and control their business in its first few months of operation? There are a number of key benefits to a business – especially a new one such as ChipRepair – from planning future expenditure and income using budgets:

- **Expenditure budgets** (or cost budgets) set spending limits for a business and separate departments or individuals within a business. If every employee or **budget holder** was able to make sure that their own spending budget was not exceeded then the costs of the entire business should not get out of control.

- **Income budgets** (or revenue budgets) can be a motivating factor for those given the target. If these budgets are reasonable and realistic then employees will often want to do their best to ensure that they are achieved. By having a system of **delegated budgets**, most employees can be given some financial responsibility. A manager's performance can be measured by comparing targets with actual results.

- New businesses need budgets to be included in the business plan. With these it will be easier to judge whether the business idea is viable – and lenders can assess if it is worthwhile investing in the business.

- **Profit budgets** not only provide clear goals and targets that motivate people to perform well but also allow quick monitoring of performance against actual profits made.

Setting budgets – how is it done?

- This is not an easy task as so many of a firm's budgets will depend on accurate sales forecasts.
- *Stage 1*. Set clear objectives for the firm for the coming year. For example, if the aim is to increase sales and/or market share then this must be reflected in the sales budget.
- *Stage 2*. Gather information, for example undertake market research to provide information to base sales on.
- *Stage 3*. Construct a sales budget showing target revenues from each product and region.
- *Stage 4*. Based on this sales budget, set budgets for major cost areas such as labour, material costs, energy costs, promotional spending.
- *Stage 5*. Set a profit target based on the sales and cost budgets already established.

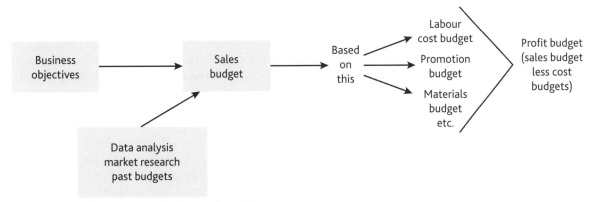

Fig. 14.1 *The budgeting process for the next financial year*

■ Link

For more information on budgets, see Chapter 16 – Using budgets, page 114.

Setting budgets for new businesses

This is even more difficult because there is no past data to act as a guide – as Andy and Kate found out! Where did they go so wrong in setting their targets?

If they had followed a few basic rules or guidelines for entrepreneurs setting their first budgets they might have been more accurate with their targets.

1 Use spreadsheet software and keep updating records regularly – don't wait until the end of six months to be surprised by lack of progress!

2 Set budgets for at least 12 months as most new businesses will be expected to make a loss in the first few months. But is this loss still expected at the end of the first year?

3 Give great importance to monthly sales forecasts – this is the key factor, as explained above. Andy and Kate should have undertaken more detailed and extensive market research and sales forecasting.

4 Make sure ALL of the costs of operation involved in producing and delivering the product to customers are included in the budget.

5 Keep a cumulative, month by month total of profits or losses – this would have shown Andy and Kate the trends over the first six months and when the business actually broke even.

6 Monitor each major budget monthly and take corrective action as soon as possible. Perhaps ChipRepair could have seen the problem of transport costs much earlier.

💡 Monitoring budgets

Monitoring budgets is a vital part of the budgetary process. It attempts to make sure that:

▪ Money from each expenditure budget is being spent on the correct items and not being misallocated.

▪ All costs are being accounted for – an accurate record is being kept.

▪ Major cost 'excesses' are being reported to senior managers before the expenditure is agreed.

▪ Revenue and profits are meeting target levels – and senior managers informed if this is not the case.

■ Problems of setting budgets

Some of these must be making themselves clear already. The future can never be certain and no matter how much time and effort goes into forecasting and target setting, budgets can still turn out to be very different from the actual business performance. Apart from changes to the external environment which can make budgets inaccurate – such as an economic recession, technological change or inflation in raw material prices – numerous other factors can make the budgeting process less effective than it should be. This list gives an insight into just some of the main ones:

▪ Managers with delegated authority may try to persuade their bosses to set spending budgets higher than they really need to be. If they are successful, then these managers are much more likely to reach other targets set for them – such as a budgeted level of sales.

▪ Inaccurate budgets which may have been set by senior managers with no input from 'people on the ground' might be very demotivating for the manager and the department trying to keep to these inappropriate targets.

- Short-term decisions to keep to rigid budgets, e.g. using cheaper production materials, might damage the business's longer term reputation.

- Budgets that are too easy to achieve will not promote the motivational incentives that more challenging targets would.

- Most importantly though – and this applies to new businesses in particular – the key sales revenue budget is subject to so many constraints outside of the business's control that the process of planning for a certain sales level is very difficult indeed.

Despite all of these potential problems, virtually every business will undertake budget setting and will monitor performance against budget. As was stated at the beginning of the chapter setting budgets is a key part of financial planning.

Fig. 14.2 *London 2012 Olympic logo. The original cost budgets for the Olympics were inaccurate. (www.london2012.com)*

Case study

ChipRepair: two years on

After their initial disappointment over the first six months trading, Andy and Kate set more realistic budgets for the following year based on the experience they had gained. The business proved to be increasingly successful. Two years from starting out, the owners had saved enough capital to allow them to plan for opening their own computer shop. This would not compete with the big multiple stores by selling mass market computers. It would focus on stocking specialist programs, upgrade equipment and peripherals that would appeal to computer 'buffs'. It would also offer on-site diagnosis and repair of computer problems.

The couple had found a suitable location – a former TV shop that had ceased trading. They were also lucky enough to recruit an ex-manager, Omar, from Dixons who wanted to work more independently and concentrate on computing rather than other electrical goods. He would run the ChipShop and the store's repair facilities. Andy and Kate would continue to expand the existing ChipRepair business.

The owners were keen to set clear monthly income and expenditure budgets for the shop and to monitor these carefully. They wanted to make sure that Omar was running the shop in the way they wanted. The targets for the first three months are given below.

Activity

Analyse THREE problems that your school or college might have in setting subject department spending budgets for the next financial year.

Table 14.1

ChipShop budgets (£000)	April	May	June
Income: Sales revenue (sale of items from shop)	2	2	5
Repair revenue	1	2	2
Expenditure: Overheads	1	1	1
Labour costs (Omar's salary plus wage costs for an assistant)	2	2	3
Cost of items sold and materials used	1	1	2
Profit/(loss) budget	(1)	0	1

The **actual** losses of the shop in the first three months totalled £4,000. The owners found that Omar had spent more on staffing than targeted – but less on advertising. He seemed not to be working in the shop himself but spending all day on dismantling customers' computers – his own real interest. Repair revenue was slightly higher than expected – but shop sales were much lower. They talked to Omar about this three monthly poor performance. His response was clear:

'If you had told me what the shop sales budget was I would have known how unrealistic this was. We need to staff the shop all day as I am busier than expected repairing computers. I can't do two things at once. Your budgets need to be discussed with me in future then we can monitor progress more accurately.'

■ Show the skills

When analysing the usefulness of budgets and budgeting, do not forget that you could make a link with other sections of the specification. For example, the setting of budgets as targets for departments or teams of employees could prove to be motivating and might encourage hard work to meet them – as long as the budgets are realistic.

Questions

1 What do you understand by the terms:
  a Income budget   (2 marks)
  b Profit budget?   (2 marks)

2 The actual results were used in setting the budget for July. Draw up a July budget, based on that for June, with:
  a Shop revenue down 20%, repair revenue up 20%;
  b All costs up 20%.   (6 marks)

3 Analyse TWO problems of setting budgets for a new business, such as the ChipShop.   (6 marks)

4 Discuss ways in which the two owners could set more realistic and useful budgets for the ChipShop.   (14 marks)

✓ *In this chapter you will have learned to:*

- understand what budgets are
- explain how budgeting aids financial planning, especially for new businesses
- differentiate between income, expenditure and profit budgets and explain how these can be set
- understand why the monitoring of budgets is an important part of budgetary control
- discuss the problems of setting budgets.

For answers to activities and case study questions see

In this chapter you will learn to:

- compare different objectives for different start-ups

- assess the performance of business start-ups with original objectives

- analyse the strengths and weaknesses of a business idea and/or plan

- analyse the risks faced by new businesses

- evaluate the main causes of new business failures.

Setting the scene

A tale of three entrepreneurs

People start their own business for very different reasons. **Robert Braithwaite** established Sunseeker power boats in 1968 with a team of seven staff. It now employs 1,200 people and makes millions in profit each year. 'I was always a person with enormous ambition,' said Mr. Braithwaite after being awarded a prestigious prize for his entrepreneurship by Ernst and Young Accountants. He plans to increase sales and profits of Sunseeker each year and his aim is to make Sunseeker such a well-known brand that when people 'think power boats they will think Sunseeker'.

Chrissie Townsend heads an action group which has a clear objective: 'My aim is to break down social barriers on a crime ridden housing estate.' She set up a bus route which provided the first bus link to the estate and allowed people to have access to other areas.

Tony Cesay, a former boxer, uses sport and nutrition to build self-esteem in marginalised inner city kids. His enterprise is called 'Kid Gloves'. These are just two examples of entrepreneurs who have set up not-for-profit business ventures as a form of social enterprise. Tony said: 'The big problem with gaining finance is that councils and other bodies just do not understand if what you are proposing does not have profit as a clear objective.'

Business and social entrepreneurs have a lot in common. They build something out of nothing. They are ambitious to achieve. They set objectives – but not necessarily the same ones. They are creative and not afraid to make mistakes.

Discussion points

1. Do you think it is important for all entrepreneurs to have clear objectives for their enterprise? List as many advantages as you can for an entrepreneur having clear objectives.

2. Why will different entrepreneurs often have different objectives?

3. Is profit the only objective owners of new businesses should have and the only way to assess success?

Fig. 15.1 *A Sunseeker boat*

💡 Objectives of business start-ups

No two entrepreneurs are the same. They may be from different social groups and have had different personal and employment experiences. Their reasons for starting their own business might be very different too. In a recent survey by accountants Coopers and Lybrand, entrepreneurs were asked for the main driving factors in setting up their own business:

- 65% said because of a sense of personal satisfaction from being independent.

■ 43% liked the idea of doing things their way.

■ 37% said they were looking for profits and capital growth.

■ 16% said they wanted to pass something on to their children.

Different personal ambitions will lead to different **business objectives**. Here are just a few possible objectives that might be set for a new business:

Profit maximisation

Trying to earn as much profit as possible – but this might conflict with other objectives. For example, attempting to increase sales by cutting prices for long-term growth could damage short-term profits.

A certain rate or level of profit

Most entrepreneurs need income and capital growth to lead to a desired lifestyle – but profit may not be a realistic short-term aim for some slow developing businesses. When this profit objective is just enough to give owners a 'comfortable' lifestyle without working too many hours or without danger of losing control it is often called **profit satisficing**.

Survival

This is likely to be a primary objective in the first few years of any new business. It may also become a primary objective for any business that enters a crisis stage in its development.

Sales growth

The owners try to make as many sales as possible. This may be because they believe that sheer size is the best chance of business survival. Larger businesses can also benefit from economies of scale.

Social objectives

In the case of social entrepreneurs, the main objective will be to correct one of society's problems but there may be a financial requirement to at least break-even too.

Why set objectives for a new business?

These are the key benefits from setting objectives:

■ Give direction and focus to the owners and the people who work in the business.

■ Create a well-defined target so the owners can make appropriate plans to achieve these targets.

■ Inform lenders and investors of the aims of the business.

■ Give a guideline for assessing the performance of the business over time.

The most effective objectives that a business might establish should meet the following criteria:

S

Specific – Clearly related to only that business, for example, a restaurant might aim to serve an average of 35 customers per night.

M

Measurable – Putting a value to an objective helps when assessing performance, for example to achieve sales of £500 per month.

A

Agreed – By all of those involved in trying to achieve the objective. This will increase the motivational impact of the objective.

R

Realistic – Objectives should be challenging but not impossible! This would demotivate the staff involved.

T

Time specific – Objectives should have a time limit so that performance can be assessed effectively. Setting an aim of reaching profits of £10,000 has little meaning unless a time period is specified, for example in the first year of trading.

Study tip

Remember that the most effective objectives should be 'S.M.A.R.T.'

How to assess the 'success' of a business idea

Just as business objectives can be very different so success or failure will be assessed in different ways. When judging the success of a new business it is essential to begin with the original objectives. If the main aim is sales growth then sales data must be referred to. Profit levels must be compared with the profit target if this was the primary initial objective. Business enterprises that have an initial objective of survival will be judged as failures if they do not exist 12 months after start-up!

There is little point in using an inappropriate measure of 'success'. In the 'setting the scene' case study, assessing the success of a social enterprise by means of profits or sales would be completely inappropriate. Instead social value indicators should be used, for example, how many poor children have been directly helped or how many unemployed have been taken on as workers. It is estimated that each social enterprise creates an average of five jobs and that £10,000 to train a social entrepreneur can lead to £100,000 of benefits to society. This benefit is not the same as 'business profits'.

What are the risks of business start-ups?

Entrepreneurs take risks – this is an unavoidable fact. Investing time and money into a new business idea can lead to failure for many reasons. Risks of business activity can be assessed and steps taken to reduce some of these but uncertainty will never be completely removed. What are the main risks that entrepreneurs face?

Lack of business and management skills

Many entrepreneurs, especially young ones, have no or few management skills and they may have little experience of business. This increases the chance of failure as lack of action when a crisis develops, due to inexperience, could lead to failure of the enterprise.

Activity

A Beauty Clinic has been operating for two years. It is owned and managed by a sole entrepreneur.

1. What evidence or data would you need to be able to assess the success of this clinic?

2. Why would it be important to know what the objectives of this entrepreneur were before assessing the success of the clinic?

Possible ways to reduce risk: Attend training courses in entrepreneurship; business advice from experienced consultants.

Lack of knowledge of legal requirements

The laws may be very detailed and complex for certain business ventures, such as those handling and selling food or when using machinery to make goods.

Possible ways to reduce risk: Training courses, specialist legal advice, take a partner with a legal background.

Competition

Unless the entrepreneur has come up with a really unique idea, there are likely to be close competitors who may have more experience and greater financial resources than a new start-up. Competitors may take actions to make it very difficult for the new business to survive.

Possible ways to reduce risk: Closely monitor the decisions and actions of key rivals, offer a better customer service than competitors.

Increased taxes or interest rates

As the finances for new businesses are often very limited at the best of times, any negative change in economic policy by the government could lead to increased outflows of cash from a small business with weak financial foundations.

Possible ways to reduce risk: Plan ahead as much as possible, cash flow forecasting essential.

Changes in consumer tastes

This is a potential risk for all businesses, not just new ones. The major difficulty for most business start-ups is that they tend to be focused on just one product – and if consumer demand switches away from this then the entrepreneur may have no other products to 'fall back on'.

Possible ways to reduce risks: Keep in close contact with customers – feedback from these would be very helpful.

Technology

New technology creates business opportunities AND risks for existing businesses. How many people now buy floppy disks or VHS tapes? Small businesses with creative entrepreneurs are often ahead of larger businesses in the application of new technological possibilities. 'Facebook' started as a single person operation. However, changes in IT can quickly wipe out a competitive advantage of a new business.

Possible ways to reduce risks: Training course, accept change positively and stay ahead of changes if possible.

Why new businesses fail

Fail they certainly do. Statistics from the Small Business Association show that nearly 60 per cent of new start-ups fail within four years of being established. These are the most common reasons for new business failures:

Activity

A chef with years of experience in running large, busy kitchens invests her savings in her own specialist 'sushi' style restaurant.

1. What are the biggest risks that she could experience in setting up this business?

2. Explain how any two of these risks might be reduced.

3. Would the profit (or loss) made at the end of the first year be the best way to assess the success of this business? Explain your answer.

Study tip

You will be expected to be able to discuss the chances of success or failure of new business start-ups operating in different markets/ industries.

1 Insufficient capital

This is a common mistake – underestimating the amount of money needed both to start the business and keep it going during the first few years. This problem is often made worse by overestimating the income of the business in these crucial years. By assuming a low break-even point and a rapid payback of initial loans many entrepreneurs mislead themselves and when reality strikes, the shortage of capital forces the business into insolvency.

2 Poor management skills

By not having enough experience in the areas of finance, record keeping, purchasing, selling, hiring and managing employees, entrepreneurs are starting business life with a huge handicap. Sometimes sheer enthusiasm and energy will pull the business through but unless owners quickly recognise what they do not do well and seek help, the business may soon face disaster.

3 Poor location

This is a common problem for new business dealing directly or selling to the public. By not being able to afford prime sites, entrepreneurs have to be imaginative in the ways they use to attract potential customers. A good location can often allow a struggling business to survive – but a poor location may spell the end of even an effective new business idea and a well-organised owner.

4 Lack of planning

Failure to make realistic plans based on accurate, current information will often lead to the collapse of a business. Managing the business on a day by day basis – perhaps because the entrepreneur is so busy – does not allow for long-term decision making and planning for future problems. Planning should be a continuous feature of a start-up – and it will always require regular study of market research and customer data.

5 Over-expansion

New business owners often confuse success with how fast they can expand the business. However, rapid expansion requires injections of capital and management expertise. Trying to handle rapid growth with no assistance or with inadequate capital may lead to excess stress and insolvency.

6 External factors

Unexpected changes in demand, sharp increases in costs or the unavailability of essential supplies are all factors beyond a new business's control and they could all cause it to fail. Interest rate increases, oil price rises and the failure of a supplying business are events that are difficult to predict and plan for. The lack of finance and the high dependency on borrowed capital makes start-up businesses particularly vulnerable to these factors.

Activity

If you were planning to start up a business importing specialist food products from Europe, discuss **four** of the most important steps you might take to reduce the chances of failure.

Fig. 15.2 *Levi Roots, founder of Reggae Reggae Sauce*

Case study

The difference between success and failure

Music Zone collapsed in 2007 with the closure of over 100 branches. Started by entrepreneur Russ Grainger in 1984 with just one market stall, the business grew into the UK's third largest high street retailer of CDs and DVDs. He sold his stake in the business for £12 million in 2005. It was bought by a team of the existing managers. They had to borrow heavily to buy Russ out. The outlook for the business suddenly worsened in 2006. Interest rates started to rise, the business had over-expanded with borrowed capital and technological advances in downloading greatly reduced the demand for CDs and DVDs.

Levi Roots and his Reggae Reggae Sauce has been one of the great success stories of Dragons' Den. This BBC programme gave Levi the opportunity to gain £50,000 of funding from experienced entrepreneurs in exchange for giving up 40 per cent of his venture. He has now obtained huge orders from Sainsbury's and other supermarkets for his unique sauce. One business consultant said: 'Levi had a clear sense of what he wanted to achieve – rapid sales growth. He obtained finance which was not borrowed and the support and advice of two experienced business managers. With Levi's skill in dealing with the media and marketing his unique product with his own music, I can't see how this new start-up can fail.'

www.leviroots.com

Show the skills

If the question asks you to 'assess the success of this business start-up', you must compare the performance of the business against the original objectives for it. You might also want to question whether these objectives were realistic in the first place.

Questions

1. List THREE different objectives that an entrepreneur might set for a new business.   (3 marks)

2. Outline TWO reasons why Music Zone failed.   (4 marks)

3. Analyse TWO reasons for the initial success of Reggae Reggae Sauce. (6 marks)

4. Evaluate the chances of Levi's business continuing to be successful over the next five years.   (10 marks)

5. Research task: Use the internet to research the reasons for the success or failure of any recently established business or well-known entrepreneur.

✔ *In this chapter you will have learned to:*

- understand why new businesses need clear objectives
- analyse why different entrepreneurs will establish different objectives for their businesses
- assess the risks that business start-ups experience and the reasons why a high proportion fail.

For answers to activities and case study questions see

Practice questions

Chapters 13–15

1   List THREE likely sources of cash inflows for a business selling petrol with both cash and credit sales. *(3 marks)*

2   **a)**   How would you attempt to forecast the cash inflows for an entrepreneur setting up a wedding photography business? *(4 marks)*

      b)   How could you forecast the cash outflows for the same business? *(4 marks)*

3   Would you advise an entrepreneur, who is very busy in planning the setting up of a new sports clothing shop, to spend time on creating a cash flow forecast? Explain your reasons. *(6 marks)*

4   Explain the difference between these two terms: Total monthly cash inflow and monthly net cash flow. *(4 marks)*

5   Explain why the cash inflows of a business selling goods on credit will be more difficult to forecast than for a business just selling for cash payment. *(4 marks)*

6   **a)**   Explain to an entrepreneur setting up a hairdressing salon for both men and women the importance of setting budgets for the business. *(6 marks)*

      b)   Analyse THREE reasons why the income budget for this business might not be achieved. *(6 marks)*

      c)   What do you understand by the term 'monitoring budgets' and why would this be important for the entrepreneur running this business? *(4 marks)*

      d)   Explain why the sales budget is so vital in the overall budgeting process of this hairdressing business. *(4 marks)*

7   **a)**   If you were an entrepreneur about to start a business developing computer games, what objectives might you set for this business, and why? *(4 marks)*

      b)   How would you assess whether, after two years, your business had been successful? *(4 marks)*

      c)   What are the risks in setting up a business developing computer games? *(4 marks)*

      d)   Explain THREE measures you could take to reduce the chances of this business failing. *(6 marks)*

Introduction

i

HMV issued profits warnings. What could directors have done to improve liquidity and profitability?

Setting up a business can be hard work and very risky. Once the firm is established and operating the hard work is not over! Entrepreneurs and managers need to continually monitor business performance, plan financial needs and take measures to improve cash flow and profitability.

The focus of this section is on improving the financial performance of **existing** businesses. This contrasts with Unit 1 which focused on planning for businesses yet to be established. All business enterprises whether they are recently established small firms or much larger, possibly famous enterprises that have been trading for many years, need to assess their financial performance regularly.

Decisions can then be taken to try to improve:

▨ Performance compared to original budgets.
▨ Cash flow to ensure adequate flows of cash are available to meet all likely future needs.
▨ Profitability.

All three chapters in this section use financial measures to indicate how well a business is being managed. Each chapter also considers actions that managers and business owners can take to improve financial performance. Some calculations are included in this section as they will help to assess profitability and performance but each process is clearly explained and illustrated by examples.

This section builds on Financial planning in Unit 1 Section 2 so it is a good idea to re-read Chapters 11–15 to confirm your understanding of the concepts covered in this Unit.

Chapter 16: Using budgets This builds upon Chapter 14 – Setting budgets, page 100. It deals in detail with the comparison of budgeted and actual business performance. This information can then be used to inform decision making by managers.

Chapter 17: Improving cash flow Chapter 13 – Using cash flow forecasting, page 94, introduced the concept of cash flow forecasting. The ways in which a business can improve its cash flow – and the possible limitations of these ways – are considered in this section.

Chapter 18: Measuring and increasing profit The key importance of profit and how it was calculated was explained in Chapter 11 – Calculating costs, revenues and profits, page 75. Building upon this understanding Chapter 18 introduces the concept of net profit margin and return on capital as important measures of business efficiency. The methods managers can use to try to increase profitability are explained and evaluated.

Key terms

Expenditure budget: is a plan of the future expenses of a business or cost centre.

Cost centre: is a section of a business which incurs expenses.

Profit centre: is a section of a business which incurs expenses and generates revenue so the profit of it can be calculated and a profit budget set.

Delegated budget: is given to a specific manager to manage and control. The manager can also be involved in helping to determine the size of the budget.

Setting the scene

Missing the targets at XL Foods

'You are the only divisional manager who failed to meet their budgets over the last 12 months. I think you have some explaining to do.' Mick knew that the interview with the Chief Executive was going to be tough – but this was not a good start.

'I know the profit figures are below budget but this is only half the story,' began Mick in reply. 'Firstly, I argued for a higher budget for promotion spending for my frozen food division – but other managers got in first! This explains why sales are less than expected. Also, the unforeseen increase in petrol prices hit my division hardest as we have to transport goods the furthest – our biggest customer is in Eastern Europe. So our costs were higher than forecast. In all other cost areas I met the budget very closely so the differences are not that great.' Mick was relieved when the CE agreed after looking at the detailed figures Mick had prepared.

Discussion points

1. Can you identify one problem of setting budgets from this case?

2. Why is it important to compare 'budgets' with 'actual' figures?

3. How might the differences between budgets and actual figures be used by managers?

The benefits of using budgets

Why do firms use budgets and budgetary control?

1 Controlling finances

Expenditure budgets reduce the risk of a business over-spending. If every person in an organisation responsible for a budget – all budget holders – ensures that their own section or department does not exceed budget, the business will meet its overall expenditure plan.

A budgetary system allows more money to be allocated to 'problem' or under-performing departments or products. If a firm has one product that is failing to meet sales targets, then an increase in the promotional spending budget might be needed.

2 Improving employee performance

Most employees respond well to being given reasonable and agreed objectives in the form of budgets. Budgets can be used as a financial objective for a **cost centre** or **profit centre** of a business. Managers can benefit in particular from **delegated budgets**. This means being involved in helping to set budgets, and given responsibility for managing and controlling them. This increases the status of the managers involved, and provides a powerful motivational element to their work.

The potential drawbacks of using budgets

1 Conflicts can arise in two main ways

First, departments may compete with each other for a larger slice of the expenditure funds available in the business. A strong manager or a skilled negotiator may gain a large budget for the department they are responsible for – at the expense of other sections which might actually have needed the resources more urgently.

Secondly, short-term budget cuts, for example in promotion, to meet strict targets might lead to long-term problems for the business if sales fall as a result. Those setting budgets should not just consider the immediate financial issues facing the business.

2 The motivating impact of budgets can fail to be achieved for two reasons

First, if very ambitious targets are set then these might be considered virtually impossible to achieve by the budget holder. These budgets will then fail to motivate and could instead disillusion those responsible for meeting them.

Secondly, target setting is likely to have most motivational effect when the people with the responsibility of meeting the targets are able to participate in the setting of them. If budgets are just 'handed down from higher management' with no input or discussion from budget holders then they will lose most of their potential for increasing motivation.

The calculation and interpretation of variances

We have identified that one of the main benefits of using budgets is to make comparisons between the original target and the actual figure. For example, comparing the budgeted sales figure set for a business 12 months ago with the actual sales value that was achieved. Any difference between these two figures is called a **variance**.

The purpose of **variance analysis** is to highlight and pinpoint areas of poor performance over a certain time period – as well as indicating areas where performance has been good.

There are two distinct types of variances – we will look first at **favourable variances**.

Favourable variances occur for two reasons. Either actual sales revenue was higher than budget or actual costs/expenditure levels were lower than budget.

Key terms

Variance: the difference between a budgeted figure and the actual figure achieved.

Variance analysis: is the comparison by an organisation of its actual performance with its expected budgeted performance over a certain time period.

Favourable variance: this is a change from a budgeted figure that leads to higher than expected profits.

Table 16.1

	Budget	Actual	Favourable variance
Sales revenue	£50,000	£60,000	£10,000
Fixed costs	£15,000	£13,000	£2,000
Labour costs	£20,000	£17,000	£3,000

Assuming these were the only costs and revenues for this business the actual profit is £15,000 greater than budgeted due to these favourable variances.

■ Key terms

Adverse variance: this is a change from a budgeted figure that leads to lower than expected profits.

Study tip

Do not assume that an adverse variance is always 'bad' – or a favourable one always 'good'! If costs are lower than budgeted due to cheaper materials being purchased this will cause a favourable variance – but could these cheaper materials lead to poorer quality and more wasted output?

The second type of variance is called an **adverse variance**.

Clearly, these arise either because sales revenue was *below* budget or actual costs/expenditure levels *exceeded* the budgeted figures.

Table 16.2

	Budget	Actual	Adverse variance
Sales revenue	£75,000	£71,000	£4,000
Fixed costs	£32,000	£33,000	£1,000
Labour costs	£18,000	£21,000	£3,000

Assuming these were the only costs and revenues for this business the actual profit is £8,000 less than budgeted due to these adverse variances.

In practice a business is likely to be faced with a combination of both favourable and adverse variances.

■ Case study

Table 16.3

	Budget	Actual	Variance
Sales revenue	£650,000	£645,000	V
Fixed costs	£46,000	£44,000	W
Labour costs	£230,000	£256,000	X
Material cost	£98,000	£94,000	Y
Profit	£276,000	U	£25,000 adverse

Questions

Copy out Table 16.3.

1. Calculate the actual profit and insert it in cell U. (2 marks)

2. Calculate all of the variances V–Y and indicate whether they are favourable or adverse. (4 marks)

3. Suggest TWO possible reasons for:

   a the sales revenue variance and

   b the labour cost variance. (4 marks)

Study tip

Do not confuse the terms favourable and adverse with positive and negative – as we have seen it is the impact on PROFIT that makes a variance either favourable or adverse NOT whether it is positive or negative.

🔍 Using variance analysis to inform decision making

Managers can use variance information to improve decision making and planning for the future. This is most effectively done not just at the *end* of the budget period (often one year) but on a *monthly* basis. This will allow managers to take corrective action during the year and avoid the risk of a large adverse variance just at the end of it. To undertake variance analysis effectively, it is essential for managers to be able to identify the main possible *causes* of variances:

Possible causes of favourable variances:

■ Lower interest rates lead to a higher than expected increase in sales.

■ Bad publicity for a competitor's products boost sales above target levels.

- Unions agree to a wage settlement below the rate of inflation that was budgeted for.
- Higher £ exchange rate makes imported components cheaper than forecast.

Possible causes of adverse variances:

- Competitors offer special price deals that lead to lower sales for our business.
- Staff efficiency falls and this leads to higher wage costs for each unit produced or sold.
- Oil price increase raises energy costs.
- Rent increases forced through by property owner are higher than expected.

Having established the most likely causes of the variances, how will variance analysis affect managers' decisions? We will consider two examples.

1 One of the most frequent management problems highlighted by variance analysis is sales revenue falling below budget.

Table 16.4 *Adverse sales revenue variance*

Possible management decisions	Potential drawbacks of decision
1 Lower prices to increase sales and market competitiveness	Are consumers sensitive to price changes? Could this start a price war with rivals? Might perceived quality image be hit?
2 Increase promotional spending	This will affect the promotion budget Rivals might spend even more Will impact just be short-term?
3 Update the product range	How long will this take? Will new products be successful? New product development budget must be increased
4 Look for new markets, e.g. new segments or new countries	Market research costs will increase Will products need to be adapted to meet new market needs?

2 The second example concerns adverse production cost variances. If they were caused by higher production levels resulting from increased sales this would not be a problem. So, the first task of management would be to pinpoint the exact cause of these variances – were they caused by higher material costs, higher production levels or higher labour costs – or a combination of these?

Table 16.5 *Adverse production cost variance*

Possible management decisions	Potential drawbacks of decision
1 Obtain cheaper supplies of materials and components	Will quality and reliability be reduced? Will new suppliers be as reliable?
2 Cut wages	Impact on motivation levels? Could lead to disruptive industrial action
3 Increase labour productivity to reduce labour cost per unit	May need new machinery and staff training – adding to costs in the short term
4 Reduce waste levels	May need a change in working practices or a new recycling policy – short-term benefits may be limited

Case study

Variance analysis highlights problems at Highcroft

For the second month running, Highcroft Hotels had recorded lower profits than expected. The variance analysis is shown below:

Table 16.6

	Jan			Feb		
	Budget	Actual	Variance	Budget	Actual	Variance
Sales revenue	85	80	5 A	105	95	10 A
Food/drink costs	36	34	2 F	42	43	1 A
Labour costs	12	15	3 A	13	16	X
Fixed costs	16	18	2 A	16	15	Y
Profit	21	13	8 A			Z

The management of the hotel were particularly concerned about two of these variances. The sales revenue was substantially below budget – yet the number of guests staying at the hotel was almost exactly as they had originally forecast. Also, the adverse food and drink variance in February was a concern. With the guests spending less than budgeted, how had food and drink costs risen above budget?

The managing director of the hotel was relieved that these problems had been spotted early in the year. She was determined to take action which should solve these adverse variances in the months to come.

Show the skills

When answering questions which require you to analyse budgets, it is important to get the figures right – and to understand what favourable and adverse variances mean. The evaluation of the budgeting system can consider whether or not managers allowed any involvement in budget setting. It is much less motivating to have a budget 'handed down' from managers than to be involved in setting one.

Questions

1. Calculate values for X, Y and Z in Table 16.6 and indicate whether the variances are adverse or favourable. (6 marks)

2. Explain the importance to the hotel of using monthly variance analysis – even though budgets are set for the whole year. (4 marks)

3. Analyse possible reasons for:
   a. the sales revenue adverse variance and (4 marks)
   b. the food and drink adverse variance in February. (4 marks)

4. Evaluate how the Managing Director of the hotel might overcome these adverse variances in the coming months of the year. (14 marks)

5. Research task: Access the BusinessLink government sponsored website, aimed at small businesses, to find out more about: 'Using your budget to measure business performance'.

In this chapter you will have learned to:

- explain the benefits and drawbacks of using budgets
- calculate and interpret both favourable and adverse variances
- use the results of variance analysis to assist managers in taking decisions.

For answers to activities and case study questions see

17   Improving cash flow

Setting the scene

Insolvency administrators take over company

About 200 jobs are under threat after Scott and Docherty, a Leeds based engineering firm set up in 1898, called in insolvency administrators. The company has, quite simply, run out of cash. Despite having record order books for its aircraft landing gear, the company has not been able to pay its suppliers for three months. The creditors called in administrators: either to run the business and make more cash from it or sell the assets to pay the bills.

How could an expanding business with an international reputation reach this position? Regular cash flow forecasts had been drawn up and they had suggested a cash flow problem for several months – but not a crisis like this.

Managers believe that the company was hit by a combination of factors that contributed to the cash flow problem. Prices of titanium and other specialist metals, the firm's main raw materials, have increased by 100 per cent in recent months, driven up by demand from China. An important computer-controlled machine broke down and was replaced by a much more expensive version – this had not been predicted in the cash flow forecasts. Finally, the company has expanded so quickly by trying to attract extra orders from Boeing and Airbus that the three monthly credit terms it offered for new orders could just not be afforded. The bank took fright at the ballooning overdraft and finally refused any more finance.

Discussion points

1. How useful had cash flow forecasts been to Scott and Docherty?

2. Explain how the company had 'quite simply run out of cash'.

3. How might the company have prevented this cash flow crisis and the collapse of the business?

What is a cash flow problem?

Just to say 'when there is not enough money' is too simplistic. Firstly, most of us could use more money most of the time! Secondly, it does not recognise the different degrees of 'problems' that can result from inadequate cash flow. The following two examples illustrate this.

Example 1

Firm A realises that its cash flow forecast was too optimistic. It assumed that debtors would pay after one month. In fact, they are taking two months to pay, on average. This is a problem as the firm has to increase its bank overdraft and this bears a high interest rate.

Expensive yes, but this problem does not threaten the survival of this business. After several weeks it is able to get debtors to pay more promptly and the business repays the overdraft.

This is a short-term cash flow problem.

Example 2

Firm B has reached its overdraft limit. It believes it can just survive until it receives cash from the sale of surplus land. Before this deal can be completed, a supplier suddenly insists on cash payment for all further deliveries. This cannot be afforded. Production stops, customers are disappointed and the cash inflows dry up. The firm is forced into insolvency by **creditors** who want all assets sold to be able to get back some of the money owed to them.

This is a long-term – and lethal – cash flow problem!

So, we can state that a cash flow problem occurs when a business is forced to take action that has negative short- or long-term effects because cash inflows are insufficient.

The causes of cash flow problems

Lack of planning

Chapter 13 – Using cash flow forecasting (page 94), covered how to construct cash flow forecasts and the importance of them. This form of financial planning can be used to predict potential cash flow problems so that business managers can take action to overcome it in plenty of time. A lack of such planning can make cash flow problems more likely.

Poor credit control

The credit control department of a business keeps a check on all customers' accounts, who has paid, who is keeping to agreed credit terms – and which customers are not paying on time. If this **credit control** is inefficient and badly managed then debtors will not be 'chased up' for payment and potential **bad debts** will not be identified.

Allowing customers too long to pay debts

In many trading situations businesses will have to offer trade credit to customers in order to be competitive. Assume a customer has a choice between two suppliers selling very similar products. If one insists on cash payment 'on delivery' and the other allows two months trade credit then customers will go for credit terms because it improves *their* cash flow. However, allowing customers too long to pay means reducing short-term cash inflows which could lead to cash flow difficulties.

Overtrading

Overtrading is when a business expands rapidly and has to pay for the expansion and for increased wages and materials months before it receives cash from additional sales. This can lead to serious cash flow shortages – even though the business is successful and expanding!

Unexpected events

A cash flow forecast can never be guaranteed to be 100 per cent accurate. Unforeseen increases in costs – a breakdown of a delivery van that needs to be replaced, or a dip in predicted sales income, or a competitor lowers prices unexpectedly – could lead to negative net monthly cash flows.

Study tip

Cash flow forecasts do not solve cash flow problems by themselves – but they are an essential part of financial planning which can help prevent cash flow problems from developing.

Key terms

Creditors: suppliers owed money by the business – purchases have been made on credit.

Credit control: the monitoring of debts to ensure that credit periods are not exceeded.

Bad debt: unpaid customer bills that are now very unlikely to ever be paid.

Overtrading: expanding a business rapidly without obtaining all of the necessary finance so that a cash flow shortage develops.

Activity

Using your knowledge of finance from Chapter 8 what sources of finance could a small business with ambitious expansion plans use to prevent cash flow problems arising?

Ways to improve cash flow

There are two main ways to improve net cash flow:

1 Increase cash inflows
2 Reduce cash outflows

Care needs to be taken here – the aim is to improve the cash position of the business *not* sales revenue or profits. These are different concepts. For example, a decision to advertise more in order to increase sales, which will eventually lead to increased cash flows, will *worsen* the short-term cash position as the advertising has to be paid for.

Activity

How would the following events affect the cash flow of a bus operating company:

- increase in oil prices
- increased unemployment
- lower train fares?

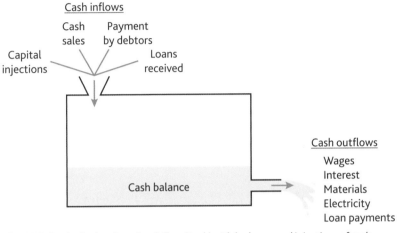

Fig. 17.1 *Symbolic drawing of cash flow 'tank' with leakages and injections of cash*

Table 17.1 *Increasing cash inflows*

Method	How it works	Possible drawbacks
Overdraft	Arranging a flexible loan on which the business can draw as necessary up to an agreed limit	High rates of interest. There may be an overdraft arrangement fee Can be withdrawn by the bank and this often causes insolvency
Short-term loan	Fixed amount borrowed for agreed length of time	Interest costs Must be repaid by the due date
Sale of assets	Cash receipts from selling off redundant assets will boost cash inflow	Selling assets quickly can result in low price The assets might be required at a later date for expansion The assets could have been used as collateral for future loans
Sale and leaseback	Selling an asset, e.g. to a finance company, but continuing to use the asset. An annual leasing charge is paid to the new owner	Leasing costs add to annual overheads Loss of potential profit if the asset rises in price The assets could have been used as collateral for future loans
Reduce credit terms to customers	Cash flow will be brought forward by reducing credit terms from, say two months to one month	Customers may purchase products from firms that offer extended credit terms
Debt factoring	Debt factoring companies buy the customer bills from a business and offer immediate cash. This reduces risk of bad debts too	Only about 90–95% of the debt will now be paid by the debt factoring company – reducing profit The customer has the debt collected by the finance company – does this suggest that your business is in trouble?

Table 17.2 *Reducing cash outflows*

Method	How it works	Possible drawbacks
Delay payments to suppliers (creditors)	Cash outflows will fall in the short term if bills are paid after, say, three months instead of two months	Suppliers may reduce any discount offered with the purchase Suppliers can either insist on cash on delivery or refuse to supply at all if they believe the risk of never being paid is too great
Delay spending on capital equipment	By not buying equipment, vehicles, etc. cash will not have to be paid to suppliers	The efficiency of the business may fall if outdated and inefficient equipment is not replaced Expansion becomes very difficult
Use leasing not outright purchase of capital equipment	The leasing company owns the asset and no large cash outlay is required	The asset is not owned by the business Leasing charges include an interest cost and add to annual overheads
Cut overhead spending that does not directly affect output, e.g. promotion costs	These costs will not reduce production capacity and cash payments will be reduced	Future demand may be reduced by failing to promote the products effectively

■ Business in action

Cosy Cottages

Cosy Cottages makes luxury playhouses for children. Graeme Bird, the owner, insists that all customer orders include a one third payment 'up front' so that 'if something goes wrong with the deal at least we won't be out of pocket for materials,' he said.

Study tip

Remember: Just writing 'the firm should increase sales to improve cash flow' is NOT showing true understanding of the difference between sales revenue and cash flow!

If you suggest 'cutting staff and material purchases' this may reduce cash outflows but what will be the negative impact on output, sales and future cash inflows? This suggestion will nearly always be inappropriate for an examination question on improving cash flow.

■ Case study

It doesn't grow on trees

The violent storms in the autumn brought down thousands of trees and damaged millions of others. Some experts had estimated that it would take the 'tree surgery' industry several years to fell dangerous trees and trim others to make them safe. All councils and businesses were conscious of the huge liabilities they would face if one of their trees injured a member of the public. 'The good times have finally arrived,' said Damien to Gill, co-owners of Tree Trimmers Ltd.

Within days of the biggest storm, the company had been contacted by no fewer than 560 businesses and home owners concerned about the state of their trees. Damien ordered two new pick-up trucks, more chainsaws and employed two full-time staff – who insisted on 50 per cent higher wages than was typical in 'normal' times in the industry. The company recruited a full-time office administrator and took a mortgage out on a larger, more impressive office and yard.

Three months later, Damien and Gill were pleading with the bank manager for more time and a higher overdraft to save their business. 'I know we should have chased up our customers to pay on time and I am sorry about the bad debts, but this is still a growth industry,' pleaded Damien. 'How did we know the government was going to give grants to local councils to set up their own tree clearance teams?' explained Gill. 'Perhaps we could sell and lease back some of our new equipment.' 'You should probably have rented all of this extra equipment rather than buying it outright,' said the bank manager. 'We can offer our factoring service but with your bad debt collection record from customers, we could only offer around 80 per cent of invoice value.'

Questions

1. What do you understand by the term 'cash flow problem'? (3 marks)

2. Outline TWO reasons why Tree Trimmers Ltd had cash flow problems. (4 marks)

3. Analyse the consequences to Tree Trimmers of not taking urgent action to solve its cash flow problems. (8 marks)

4. Evaluate TWO ways, suggested in the case study, in which the business could reduce its cash flow problems. (14 marks)

5. Research task: Investigate how different firms approach the problems of late payment from customers.

6. Research task: Use the following link to watch a short film clip on how to avoid cash flow problems:
https://www.gov.uk/avoid-business-cashflow-problems

Show the skills

Remember that if the question asks you to 'discuss', 'assess' or 'evaluate' ways of improving cash flow, you must explain HOW your suggestions could improve cash flow as well as explaining what the ADVERSE consequences on the business could be from adopting them.

In this chapter you will have learned to:

- explain what is meant by cash flow problems
- analyse the most likely causes of business cash flow problems
- evaluate the methods that businesses can use to overcome cash flow problems.

For answers to activities and case study questions see **kerboodle**

18 Measuring and increasing profit

In this chapter you will learn to:

- calculate and understand the net profit margin
- calculate and understand return on capital
- analyse different methods a business could use to increase its profits
- evaluate the possible impact of these different methods
- explain the difference between a firm's cash flow and its profit.

Setting the scene

Game profitability 'under threat'

Computer games developers are unlikely to make a profit on new titles until at least a year after launch. They are being trapped between rising development costs and increasing price competition. A report by media analyst Screen Digest said that the complexity of next generation games made it hard for publishers to cover production costs. Long development times and large production teams also affected profitability, the report found.

Games publishers which try to spread the appeal of their games across many different hardware platforms are also facing increasing price competition. With so many games to choose from, and rising numbers of publishers setting up in Asia, established producers are making less profit on each game sold.

Microsoft has adopted a different approach and is basing its strategy on exclusivity. It is encouraging some games publishers to produce games **only** for Xbox 360 which allows higher prices to be charged to Xbox users. It seems this strategy is beginning to pay off with the success of exclusive titles such as Epic's *Gears of War*.

Wii Nintendo is focusing on the strategy of game play innovation to attract a wide range of consumers willing to pay high prices. Some industry analysts think this is the best way to increase profitability. One said, 'This market is all about changing technology and games that reflect the latest technology will make the highest profits.'

Discussion points

1. Why is profitability so important for games developers?
2. Why is the profitability of some games developers likely to decline?
3. One strategy to increase profitability is to make technologically advanced, exclusive products. Would this be a good idea for games developers?
4. Suggest others ways a UK based games developer could try to increase profits.

Profit and profit margins

In Chapter 11 – Calculating costs, revenues and profits, page 75, the profit formula was given as:

$$\text{Profit} = \text{Total revenue} - \text{Total costs}$$

This formula gives the total level of profits made by a business in a given time period. It was also explained that total profits could be increased in two ways:

1. Increasing the number of units sold with the same price and cost per unit

If price = £10 and total cost per unit = £4, total profit = £6,000 if 1,000 units are sold. If sales rise to 1,200, total profit also increases, to £7,200.

2 Increasing the profit 'made on each unit'. This can be done by increasing price or reducing cost per unit or a combination of the two. See the next section for more detail.

If price is now increased to £11 and total cost per unit cut to £3, then if sales remain constant (a big IF perhaps?) then profit rises to £8,000 at the original sales level.

Using this second strategy increases the 'profit made per £ of sales'. This is called the **profit margin**. Profit margins are an important measure of business performance.

💡 Measuring profitability 1

Calculating and understanding the net profit margin

Do you recall the difference between fixed and variable costs that was explained in Chapter 11? This distinction is essential for understanding two different measures of profit: **gross profit** and **net profit**.

Gross profit = Sales revenue – Variable costs

Net profit = Sales revenue – Total costs

There is a clear link between these two profit measures. If a firm's gross profit increases AND there is no increase in fixed costs then net profit will increase too.

It is now possible to calculate the gross profit margin and net profit margin – these will provide an even clearer measure of the firm's performance.

$$\text{Gross profit margin (\%)} = \frac{\text{Gross profit}}{\text{Sales revenue}} \times 100$$

$$\text{Net profit margin (\%)} = \frac{\text{Net profit}}{\text{Sales revenue}} \times 100$$

Using these two formulae, we can work out the gross and net profit margins for T-Design:

Gross profit margin (%)

$$\frac{\text{Gross profit}}{\text{Sales revenue}} \times 100 = \frac{£150,000}{£250,000} \times 100 = 60\%$$

This means that on each £ of sales, T-Design makes 60 pence gross profit. Another way of putting it is that on each T-shirt sold, a gross profit of 67% is made.

Net profit margin (%)

$$\frac{\text{Net profit}}{\text{Sales revenue}} \times 100 = \frac{£70,000}{£250,000} \times 100 = 28\%$$

This means that on each £ of sales T-Design makes 28 pence net profit or, on each T-shirt sold, a net profit of 28% is made.

■ **Key terms**

Profit margin: the profit made as a proportion of sales revenue.

Gross profit: this is calculated by subtracting only variable costs from sales revenue, ignoring fixed costs.

Net profit: this is calculated by subtracting total costs from sales revenue.

■ **Activity**

A T-shirt retailer, T-Design, sells 50,000 units in 1 year at £5 each. Each T-shirt is purchased by the shop for £2.00 each. Annual fixed costs are £80,000.

Calculate:

a Gross profit and

b Net profit.

Study tip

Although no questions will be set on the gross profit margin on AQA examination papers, it aids students understanding of why net profit margins may be rising or falling.

Net profit margin will always be less than gross profit margin as every business will have some fixed costs.

The following year the shop again sells 50,000 T-shirts for £5 each but gross profit increases to £160,000 and net profit to £90,000.

1 Calculate the new:
   a gross profit margin and
   b net profit margin.

2 Suggest two reasons for the improvement in the net profit margin.

Key terms

Return on capital: the proportion that the net profit is of the capital invested in the business or project.

Return on capital (%)

$$= \frac{\text{Net profit}}{\text{Capital invested}} \times 100$$

Activity

An entrepreneur plans to invest £12,000 in a new business. She has budgeted net profit of £3,000 for the first year of operation.

1 Calculate the expected return on capital.

2 Why should she be worried if another similar business is making a return on capital of 20 per cent each year?

Study tip

Many examination questions will ask for methods of increasing the profitability of a business. If the question needs an evaluative answer it is very important that you consider at least ONE reason why your suggestion might not be effective.

Measuring profitability 2

Return on capital

Another way of measuring the profitability of a business or a new business project is to compare the profit made with the value of the capital invested. This gives the **return on capital**.

The higher the result of this ratio the more profitable the investment has been – and it could also indicate the efficiency of the management in managing the investment.

The result of this formula could be compared with other businesses in the same industry or other investment projects. The usefulness of the return on capital ratio is increased by making these comparisons. If a business needs to choose between two new projects it may choose the one with the higher return on capital. When rival companies are making a higher return on capital then this indicates that profitability is falling behind that of competitors.

The return on capital on a project or a new business proposal could be increased by either:

a Trying to increase profitability without investing any more capital.

b Attempting to make the same level of profit but with less capital expenditure.

Methods of increasing profit

Increasing profitability is the primary long-term objective of most businesses. There are four main methods businesses can use which might lead to an increase in profits:

1 Increase sales – without reducing the net profit margin.
2 Increase net profit margin by reducing variable costs per unit.
3 Increase net profit margin by increasing price.
4 Increase net profit margin by reducing fixed costs.

It sounds easy, doesn't it! But all four methods have potential limitations which can result in lower profitability in future or which have a negative impact on other objectives of the business. Table 18.1 explains how these four methods could be put into effect – and evaluates their possible impact.

The distinction between cash flow and profit

To many failed entrepreneurs there was no difference between cash and profit – which is why their new business collapsed so soon after start-up! All successful entrepreneurs, in contrast, understand that these two financial concepts do not have the same meaning or significance for a business – especially a newly formed one. It is very common for profitable businesses to run short of cash. On the other hand, loss-making businesses can have high cash inflows in the short term.

The essential difference between cash and profit can be explained with three business examples:

Table 18.1 *Methods of increasing profits*

Method of increasing profits	Examples	Possible limitations
1 Increase sales without reducing net profit margin	1 Introducing new products, e.g. latest version of Sony Playstation 2 Increasing promotion of existing products, e.g. Nescafé TV adverts 3 Selling existing products in new markets, e.g. Tesco opening stores in Thailand	1 It's expensive to develop and launch new products, they are not always successful and it may take several years for sales to increase sufficiently to pay back costs 2 Adds to fixed costs so may reduce net profit margin, it may lead to competitors increasing their promotion too 3 Can be very expensive and fixed costs will increase. The culture and consumer tastes of new markets may be very different
2 Increase net profit margin by reducing variable costs	1 Using cheaper materials, e.g. rubber not leather soles on shoes 2 Cutting labour costs, e.g. relocating production to low labour cost countries such as Dyson making cleaners in Malaysia 3 Cutting labour costs by increasing automation in production, e.g. the Mini production line uses some of the most labour saving robots in the world	1 Consumers' perception of quality may be damaged and this could hit the product's reputation. Consumers may expect lower prices – which may cut the net profit margin 2 Quality may be at risk, communication problems with distant factories 3 Purchasing machinery will increase fixed costs, remaining staff will need retraining – short-term profits may be cut due to these costs
3 Increase net profit margin by increasing price	Raising the price of the product with no significant increase in variable costs, e.g. BT raising the price of its broadband connections	Total profit could fall if too many consumers switch to competitors – this links to Chapter 32 and price elasticity Consumers may consider this to be a 'profiteering' decision and the long-term image of the business may be damaged
4 Increase net profit margin by reducing fixed costs	Cutting any fixed costs, such as rent, promotion costs or management costs but maintaining sales levels, e.g. moving to a cheaper head office location	1 Lower rental costs could mean moving to a cheaper area which could damage image, e.g. for a restaurant 2 Cutting promotion costs could cut sales by more than fixed costs 3 Fewer managers – or lower salaries – could reduce the efficient operation of the business

Example 1

Joe buys fresh fish from a market every day. He pays cash to the traders and gets a good deal because of this. He sells all of his stock on a High Street stall to shoppers who also pay him cash. In a typical week Joe buys fish costing £1,000 and sells it for £2,000.

Q: Ignoring all other costs, how much profit does he make in a typical week?
A: £1,000

Q: What was the difference between his cash inflows and outflows in a typical week?
A: £1,000 – as all purchases and sales were in cash.

In this very simplified example, CASH = PROFIT at the end of the week (but we have ignored other expenses too!)

Study tip

When given the opportunity, emphasise the importance of a business having enough cash in the short term. Profit can wait – but cash payments are always being made.

■ Activity

In month 1, a business buys in 500 items for £5 each. It pays half the cost in cash and the other half is purchased on two months credit. The business sells all items for £10 each in month 1. Ignoring all other costs and payments:

1. How much profit did the business make on these 500 items?

2. What was its net cash flow in month 1?

Example 2

Shula owns Fine Foods, a specialist delicatessen. Last month she bought £500 of fresh goods from a supplier who offers one month's credit. The goods sold very slowly during the month and she was forced to cut her prices several times. Eventually she sold them all for only £300, paid in cash by her customers.

Q: What was her profit or loss, ignoring all other costs?
A: A loss of £200 – because even though she has not yet paid for the goods they are still recorded as a cost.

Q: What was the difference between her cash inflow and outflow?
A: A positive £300 – because she has not paid the supplier yet. So Shula has a positive cash flow from these goods this month even though she made a loss on them.

CASH was not the same as PROFIT for this business.

Example 3

Sanjit is concerned about competition for his jewellery shop. He buys most of his stock over the internet for cash – but has decided to increase the credit terms he gives to his customers to two months. Last month he bought some rings for £3,000 and paid in cash. He sold them all in the same month for £7,000– yet will not receive payment until two months time.

Q: How much profit did he make on these rings?
A: £4,000 – the rings have been sold and revenue recorded from the sale even though no cash payment has been made.

Q: What was Sanjit's cash flow position from these deals?
A: A negative outflow of £3,000 – he may be very short of cash until he receives payment from his customers.

CASH was not the same as PROFIT for this business – and there is a real danger that it could run out of cash to pay its everyday costs such as wages and rent.

So, profitable businesses can fail if they do not have sufficient cash to continue operations. The importance of cash flow forecasting, as explained in Chapters 13 and 17, is just as great for profitable businesses as those making a loss.

◰ Case study

Tesco and Sainsbury's – which supermarket is more profitable?

Bitter rivals for many decades, these two giant retailers have both made big profits in recent years. However, Tesco has grown much more rapidly and now has total sales twice that of Sainsbury's. By looking at the published accounts of both companies the following sales revenue figures can be compared:

Table 18.2

Sales revenue (all figs in £m)	2011	2012
Tesco	60,455	64,539
Sainsbury's	22,943	24,511

Sales are important, of course, but which of these two rivals is more profitable? We will now compare net profit:

Table 18.3

Net profit (all figs in £m)	2011	2012
Tesco	3,641	3,835
Sainsbury's	665	712

Fig. 18.1 *Total sales revenue for Tesco was more than double that of Sainsbury's in 2012*

Sainsbury's has made lower profits in each of the years being considered. But, is this just because its sales are lower? Or could it be that the business is less profitable than Tesco because it also has lower net profit margins?

Questions

1. Explain the term 'net profit margin'. (2 marks)

2. Calculate the net profit margin for both companies for 2011 and 2012. (4 marks)

3. Analyse TWO possible reasons for Sainsbury's lower net profit margin. (8 marks)

4. Evaluate any TWO decisions the management of Sainsbury's could take to increase the profitability of the business. (10 marks)

5. Research task: Use the internet or copies of these two companies' published accounts to discover the following data for the latest year possible: sales revenue and net profit (also known as profit before tax). Calculate net profit margins for both companies and compare with your previous results. Which company has improved profitability most?

☑ *In this chapter you will have learned to:*

- explain the difference between gross and net profit
- calculate and understand the importance of net profit margin
- calculate and understand the importance of return on capital
- analyse different methods businesses can use to increase profits and profitability
- evaluate the impact of these methods on business
- differentiate between cash flow and profit.

For answers to activities and case study questions see **kerboodle**

Show the skills

When comparing the profitability of two or more companies, it is also important to consider the overall objectives of each business (short-term profits might not be a priority), and also the number of years the businesses have been trading. The profitability of a recently established business might be lower than long-standing ones if it is keeping profit margins low to attract new customers.

Practice questions

Chapters 16–18

1   Explain TWO advantages to a furniture manufacturing business from using a budget system. *(4 marks)*

2   Explain TWO problems this business might face when setting budgets. *(4 marks)*

3   Distinguish, with the aid of examples, between 'favourable cost variances' and 'adverse cost variances'. *(6 marks)*

4   Distinguish, with the aid of examples, the difference between a 'favourable revenue variance' and an 'adverse revenue variance'. *(4 marks)*

5   The following variance data has been produced for 'Value Furniture Ltd'.

Item	Budget (£)	Actual (£)	Variance
Sales revenue	960,000	1,200,000	Favourable £240,000
Labour costs	275,000	360,000	X
Rent and business rates	190,000	170,000	Y
Raw materials	230,000	320,000	Z

    a)   Calculate the variances X, Y and Z and indicate whether they are favourable or adverse. *(6 marks)*

    b)   Identify and explain the possible causes of the sales revenue and labour cost variances. *(6 marks)*

    c)   Assess the value of variance analysis to this business. *(8 marks)*

6   Outline TWO possible actions a business might take in response to an adverse sales revenue budget. *(6 marks)*

7   Outline TWO factors that might lead to a car retailing business experiencing cash flow problems. *(6 marks)*

8   Explain TWO ways that an entrepreneur might use to try to avoid cash flow problems. *(4 marks)*

9   A TV retailing business is experiencing a cash flow crisis. Explain and evaluate two ways in which the business might overcome this cash flow problem. *(10 marks)*

10   Explain, with a worked example, the meaning of the net profit margin. *(4 marks)*

11   Explain how a firm might be experiencing an increase in gross profit but a fall in its net profit. *(3 marks)*

12 A clothing manufacturer, Barca Designs, produces most of its products in Spain. It sells to European retailers which operate in a competitive market segment for smart, high priced clothing. Consumer incomes have been rising in recent months and sales of up-market clothing retailers have been reported as reaching record levels. Many of these firms sell very up to date fashions and are increasingly importing their clothing from manufacturers in low wage countries.

Profit, sales and capital invested data over the last two years for Barca Designs is shown in the following table:

	2011 (£m)	2012 (£m)
Sales revenue	35	42
Gross profit	7	8
Net profit	4	3
Capital invested	25	25

a) Calculate the following ratios for both years:

　　i) Net profit margin   *(2 marks)*

　　ii) Return on capital   *(2 marks)*

b) Analyse possible reasons for the trend in the net profit margin ratio.   *(8 marks)*

c) Explain why the return on capital result is important to this business.   *(3 marks)*

d) The business has an opportunity to invest capital in a new Spanish factory project costing £5m. The expected annual net profit from the project is £2m. Explain, with calculations, whether this project would improve the company's overall return on capital.   *(6 marks)*

e) Evaluate TWO further ways that this business might use to attempt to increase its profitability.   *(8 marks)*

People in business

Introduction

This section continues to develop the theme of improving the effectiveness of a business. The growth of many small firms happens in a very haphazard and unstructured way and this can lead to unnecessary inefficiency. At some point the manager must face the issues that are bound to emerge as the workforce increases in size and complexity.

Entrepreneurs generally start by doing all the important jobs in the business themselves, and it is difficult for them to let go of some of the responsibility for tactical decision making, and pass it on to other members of the workforce. This process can influence how the structure of the organisation evolves. If the founder(s) want to retain as much control as possible, the decision making will be contained within a small group of powerful people at the centre of the organisation. However, while this approach may be very successful when the business is small, it is not an efficient way to run a larger business, and at some point decisions must be taken as to the best ways to improve the organisational structure.

In Chapter 10 we saw that small businesses employ a range of workers and make use of specialist advisers and consultants. As firms grow, the need for such specialist skills, and for a stable workforce increase. This may mean that instead of using outside agencies, the firm needs to recruit specialists to work within the business full time. This section looks at the options available to businesses so that they can develop an effective workforce to meet the needs of the market. This includes the recruitment and selection process and a life-long learning approach to developing existing employees who may need to be retrained due to new technology, products and customer demands.

Once an effective workforce has been recruited and trained, how can it been retained? There is always the possibility that a rival business will tempt the best employees away with attractive financial rewards and the promise of better promotion prospects. For growing businesses, there is a need to ensure that the money spent on recruiting and training the workforce is not wasted. This section looks at the range of motivational techniques that can be used to ensure that the effectiveness of the workforce is not diminished by rising absenteeism and falling productivity.

This section is divided into four chapters. The key issues covered by each chapter are:

Chapter 19: Improving organisational structures What are the key elements of organisational structures? How important are the issues of levels of hierarchy/spans of control, work loads, job allocation and delegation? What are the workforce roles within a business, and how can organisational structure affect business performance? To what extent does the quality of internal business communication impact on the effectiveness of businesses?

Chapter 20: Measuring the effectiveness of the workforce This chapter looks at how those involved in decision making can make better judgements about the contribution made by employees to the success of the business. What is labour productivity and how is it calculated? What is the calculation for labour turnover? Is absenteeism from work a serious problem for businesses and how does a firm know what the rate of absenteeism is?

Chapter 21: Developing an effective workforce: recruitment, selection and training Here we investigate the process of creating the best possible workforce. What types of recruitment are there? What are the stages in the recruitment process from identifying the vacancy to receipt of applications? Which method of selection is most appropriate for choosing the best employees? How can recruitment and selection improve the workforce? What methods of training are available to small to medium-sized businesses?

Chapter 22: Developing and retaining an effective workforce: motivating employees This chapter looks at the options available to businesses to ensure that they get the very best out of their most important asset – their employees. Which financial methods can be used to motivate? How can improving job design motivate workers? Is empowering employees effective and can team working be used in small businesses? What are the main motivational theories? What is the link between the organisational structure and the motivational techniques available to managers? How would you select the best candidate for this job?

In this chapter you will learn to:

- explain the different ways in which organisations can be structured

- apply effective organisational structures to different scenarios

- explain workforce roles within a business

- analyse how organisational structure affects business performance

- analyse the importance of issues such as levels of hierarchy/spans of control, work loads, job allocation and delegation

- evaluate the extent to which the quality of internal business communication can impact on the effectiveness of businesses.

Fig. 19.1 *YogaBugs Logo*
(www.yogabugs.com)

Key terms

Organisational structure: the way the jobs, responsibilities and power within a business are organised.

Setting the scene

Family business

It surprises a lot of people that 75 per cent of businesses in the UK are family run: most people cannot imagine anything worse! YogaBugs Ltd, the brainchild of Fenella Lindsell and her sister-in-law Lara Goodbody, was launched in 2003. 'I should say I can see problems with working with family but I can't,' Lindsell says. 'I feel very privileged to work with Lara. We have different strengths – she's a figures girl, better at all the accounting and she gets things done very quickly, but I think I'm better at writing and taking care of the intellectual property.'

Bringing your work home can even have its advantages: 'We have a hell of a time. My husband is in brand licensing, and my brother works for a marketing agency and they're always happy to help. No money changes hands; they come up with ideas then we all talk about them. There are lots of conversations in the kitchen and in the car; we even go on holiday together!'

YogaBugs' initial aim, tapping into the government initiative to get children more active, was to train people to teach children yoga. Soon demand for their teachers outstripped supply and they started franchising. As the business has expanded, they have taken on other members of staff. Is there friction between outsiders and those in the family? 'We've got two other people on staff who are fabulous, so luckily there is no conflict. We all work hard, and keep everything professional, but I think we strike a good balance.'

Guardian *Sept 2006*

Discussion points

1. Given their personal strengths, how might Fenella and Lara have organised YogaBugs when they first launched the company?

2. Fenella and Lara decided to franchise their business idea (see Chapter 2 – Generating and Protecting Business Ideas, page 9) and have appointed an Operations Manager to support this method of expansion. Will it be easy for them to trust someone outside the family with such an important job?

3. 'The quality of internal communication can be vital to the success of a small business as it expands.' To what extent do you think this is true of YogaBugs?

Organisational structure

In any organisation, the allocation of jobs is necessary to ensure that the business operates as efficiently as possible. In its simplest form, an **organisational structure** may only involve two or three people; however, as the firm becomes more successful and employs more staff, the need to make individual roles and responsibilities clear becomes ever more important. An **organisational chart** can be used to illustrate the structure in place or proposed, and should include the following features:

■ Where the responsibility and authority for decision making lies within the business.

■ The job titles and roles of positions in the business (and the name of the person currently holding that position).

■ The lines of authority which show who each employee is accountable to and who they are responsible for.

■ The lines of communication through the business.

Small and medium-sized businesses, especially those that are growing quickly, are likely to change the organisational structure quite regularly. In the early stages of any firm's life, the entrepreneur is likely to take a very 'hands-on' approach, but this becomes less practical as the business becomes bigger, and gradually many of the day-to-day decisions are passed on to other trusted members of the team. The way in which the organisational structure is developed by a business's owners may take into account a number of factors:

■ The business environment – is the market very competitive and does the business need to keep costs low and be as up-to-date as possible?

■ The skills of the employees – if the business is made up of a small number of highly trained professionals, the organisational structure may be very different to a firm employing a larger number of unskilled or semi-skilled workers.

■ The culture of the organisation – if the business has gained its market share based on originality, cutting-edge design and flair, the organisational structure must not restrict creativity. However, the firm may have developed its place in the market because of an emphasis on traditional values, with consistency being very important. In this case, the structure is likely to be formal and each position within the organisation clearly defined.

Key elements of an organisational structure

When deciding on how to develop the most effective structure in a small or growing business, there are several key elements that the entrepreneur should consider.

■ **Key terms**

Organisational chart: a diagram showing job titles, lines of communication and responsibility within a business.

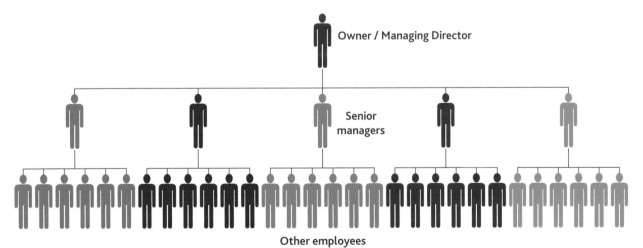

Fig. 19.2 *Diagram showing three levels of hierarchy*

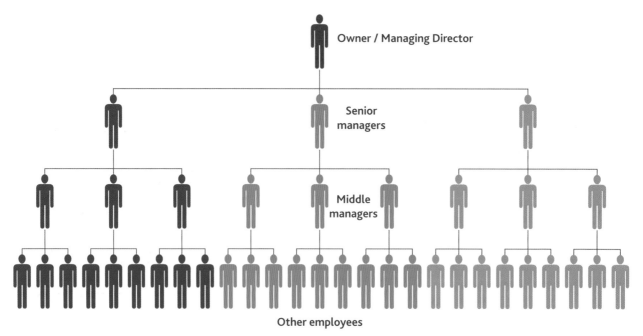

Owner / Managing Director

Senior managers

Middle managers

Other employees

Fig. 19.3 *Diagram showing four levels of hierarchy*

Levels of hierarchy

Levels of hierarchy refer to the number of layers within an organisation, with each layer representing a level of authority. All employees have a clearly defined role and their relationship with every other post holder in the business is established. This approach is usually based on departments such as finance and marketing. It is a formal approach to organisational structure, favoured by more traditional businesses. The more layers that exist in the hierarchy, the longer the **chain of command** from those at the top to those at the bottom of the organisation. This structure can lead to communication problems because the **lines of communication** are stretched, which can slow down the movement of important information. This can cause particular difficulties for smaller businesses that have to stay in touch with market conditions if they are to maintain their market share.

As you can see, in Figures 19.2 and 19.3, these two firms are run by the owner. The structure of the organisation is very different, with the second business having one more level in the hierarchy.

Span of control

This is also illustrated in Figures 19.2 and 19.3. In Figure 19.2, each member of the senior team has a wide **span of control** because he/she is responsible for six members of their department. In Figure 19.3, the span of control is much narrower: each manager is responsible for three people. A narrow span of control allows for close supervision of the work of employees, whereas a wider span gives subordinates the chance for more independence.

Work load and job allocation

As small businesses grow, one of the reasons why a structure emerges is because the **work load** for individual employees becomes too great, and some of their tasks are passed to other, probably new workers. When a structure is being designed and improved, the question of work load must be considered. In Figures 19.2 and 19.3, the work load of the managers in the first organisation is likely to be greater than that for the managers and supervisors in the second, because they have a wider span of control, that is they are responsible for more subordinates. The importance of work load should not be underestimated, because an employee feeling that they have too much work to do is likely to be unhappy and this can cause problems for the business (Chapters 20 and 22 – Measuring the effectiveness of the workforce and Developing and retaining an effective workforce, pages 143 and 160).

The way in which **job roles** are allocated within a business can also have an impact on the structure which develops. In traditional organisations, jobs are grouped by function, for example marketing, finance, human resources and operations. However, in many small firms, a task-based approach is taken where jobs are grouped around the completion of a particular task or project, for example opening a new office or completing a contract for a specific client.

Delegation

Delegation means passing the authority to perform tasks or take decisions to other people in the organisation. Why is this necessary as a business expands? The owners of successful businesses can become overwhelmed by workload and the number of decisions to be made. By appointing employees who are willing and able to accept authority, business owners can delegate tasks and some decision making. This will leave the owners more time to focus on the bigger strategic decisions affecting the business. Delegation is very important not just for the business owner and senior managers, but also the 'delegates' – the employees who are given the delegated authority. It can improve their motivation as they consider themselves trusted employees. One very important principle of effective delegation is that the final responsibility for a decision still remains with the delegator – the person who delegated the authority.

Communication flows

Organisation charts show the formal lines of communication. These are the ways in which communication is passed through an organisation. In a small business, most **communication flows** are likely to involve face-to-face meetings which can be quick and direct. As a business grows, it may not be possible for all messages to be communicated in this way. Also, some messages have to be written, such as a contract of employment. Effective communication flows must be maintained if a business is to perform well. This is particularly true when a business grows geographically with, perhaps, its head office in one region but factories or shops in other regions. IT-based methods are increasingly used for internal communication. These can be quick and they leave a written record, but they reduce the amount of face-to-face contact in an organisation, and too many messages (emails, for example) can lead to communication overload.

Organisational structure affects communication flows. A tall structure with many levels of hierarchy can experience poor communication. The chain of command is long and messages may have to pass through several layers of management before reaching the employees on the final level of hierarchy. This is one of the reasons why most businesses use a wide organisational structure with few levels of hierarchy.

Why are good internal communications important?

Efficient internal communications can have the following benefits for growing businesses:

■ All managers and employees should be aware of the objectives of the business. This will provide focus and motivation. Decisions will be made that aim to increase the chances of achieving these objectives.

■ Customer needs can be met: market research, after-sales service and increasingly business 'blogs' are used to gather information about customer satisfaction, which must be communicated to the appropriate department so changes can be made.

■ **Key terms**

Job role: the tasks involved in a particular job.

Delegation: passing the authority to make specific decisions to somebody further down the organisational hierarchy.

Communication flows: how information is passed around an organisation including downwards, upwards, sideways and through the grapevine or gossip network.

■ Link

For more information on Human Resources training see Chapter 21 – Developing an effective workforce: recruitment, selection and training, page 149.

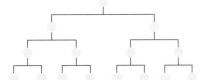

Fig. 19.4 *Hierarchical structure*

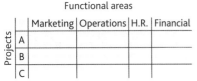

Fig. 19.5 *Matrix structure*

Fig. 19.6 *Entrepreneurial structure*

- Decision-makers are aware of ideas and improvements for the business: in a competitive market, this could mean the difference between success and failure for a small or growing firm. Listening to the opinions of employees can be a cheap and effective way to improve the quality of goods and services provided.

- Decision-makers are aware promptly of changes in the business environment: this could be a new competitor entering the local market or a change in tastes and fashion. As a business grows, how can the entrepreneur ensure that he/she does not lose touch with the dynamics of the market? The answer is to ensure that up-to-date information is available to the tactical decision-makers. Communications should flow in all directions, not just downwards. However, the lines of communication need to be organised rather than chaotic and haphazard.

■ Types of organisational structures

There are a variety of structures that small and growing businesses can use, which may depend on the personality of the founder of the organisation as much as any other factor such as the business environment and the skills of the employees.

Hierarchical structures

Hierarchical structures, such as those illustrated in Figures 19.2, 19.3 and 19.4, allow specialist functional job roles to develop in a business, which can be very useful for employees who can see the promotional opportunities available within their area. The work load for managers and supervisors may be determined by their span of control: a narrow span reducing the work load, and a wider span of control having the opposite effect. A possible disadvantage of an increasingly hierarchical structure is that communication can slow down, and this may hamper decision making.

Matrix structures

Matrix structures are based around tasks or projects and involve the creation of teams that include all the necessary functional specialists. Employees are encouraged to use their individual talents and skills and their job roles are likely to be much more varied. Teamworking in a matrix structure can be very motivating. However, the work load may be unevenly spread amongst the members of the team, which can cause resentment. Each team member may have loyalties to both the team and his/her department.

Entrepreneurial structures

Entrepreneurial structures are usually found in small businesses in very competitive markets, where quick decision making is important to maintain and increase market share. A core team of decision makers, the founder(s) and a small number of trusted colleagues with or without specific job roles are supported by a number of general employees with little or no decision-making power. This approach can only really work in a small business situation, because as an organisation grows, the increasing work load makes it impossible for such a small number of employees to be effective.

Informal structures

These exist where there is no obvious need for any formal structure. In a firm of professional specialists such as doctors or solicitors, everyone works as part of one team, with perhaps centralised administrative support. If a business decision needs to be taken, a meeting of all members of staff will be arranged.

Workforce roles

There are some key **workforce roles** within any organisation. The people in the following positions can have a direct impact on the motivation of employees and the efficiency of communication flows throughout the firm.

Supervisors

People who are directly responsible for one or more subordinate, depending on whether the organisational structure is tall (narrow span of control) or flat (wide span of control). All the employees within their area of responsibility will have a work load to fulfil and the amount of delegation will depend on the management style adopted by the supervisor (see Chapter 22, page 160). Essentially, the role of the supervisor is to allocate jobs to subordinates and ensure that tasks are carried out to a satisfactory standard.

Team leaders

Employees who facilitate the functioning of a group of employees within the organisation. This role fits best with a matrix structure, but a team approach to working can function within a hierarchical structure as well. Rather than allocating jobs, the team leader ensures that the work load is spread fairly between team members, that the resources required by the team are available, and that deadlines are met.

Managers

Employees who oversee the operation of a specific area of a business. This involves not only the staff within their area, but also resources such as stock, materials and equipment. Managers will delegate to subordinates such as supervisors and team leaders, if that is their style. However, they retain responsibility for decisions made and need to have confidence in their team/department.

Directors

Appointed by the shareholders to oversee the running of the business. They usually take responsibility for a particular function/area of the organisation. However, they do not generally get involved in the day-to-day running of larger organisations, but are likely to be very hands-on in new and small to medium-sized businesses.

Improving the organisational structure to enhance business performance

There is no single organisational structure that suits all businesses at all stages of their development. It is often necessary to adapt and improve the organisational structure to enhance business performance.

Cutting overhead costs

A business is facing increased price competition and needs to reduce overhead costs. In this case it might be that a level in the hierarchy is removed. This may significantly reduce fixed costs, but it will increase

Key terms

Workforce role: the tasks involved in a particular level or grade of job within an organisation.

Link

For more on team working see Chapter 22 – Developing and retaining an effective workforce: motivating employees, page 160.

Link

For more information on reducing costs see Chapter 11 – Calculating costs, revenues and profits, page 75.

Activity

1. Construct an argument to support using supervisors in a clothes retailing business with several branches rather than team leaders.

2. Prepare the counter-argument that suggests team leaders would be better.

3. Finally, make a judgement about which argument is stronger in this scenario incorporating the phrase 'it depends on'.

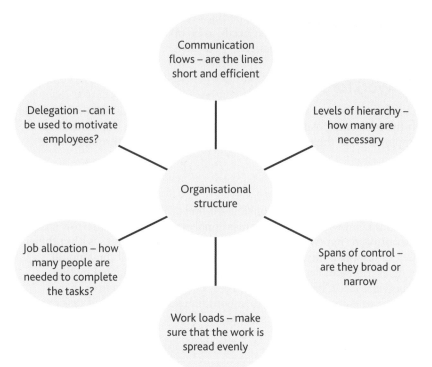

Fig. 19.7 *Diagram to show the influences on an effective organisational structure*

the span of control of the remaining managers. Care must be taken otherwise the additional work load could be de-motivating. However, the lines of communication will be shortened, which should be an advantage to the firm.

Revising workloads

Business expansion can result in greatly increased work loads for some managers. For example, as employee numbers expand, the Human Resources manager may struggle to cope with recruitment, selection, appraisal and other duties related to employment. An additional role, or level of hierarchy, may need to be created in the Human Resources department. This would then allow the manager to delegate certain duties and decisions to this additional person to revise work loads.

The growth of the business

If the firm has grown in an informal, haphazard way, does the structure need to become more formal, and roles more clearly defined? How will this affect the communication flow and the motivation of employees? By making adjustments to the structure, the business can operate more efficiently, perhaps changing from an entrepreneurial structure to a hierarchical structure with a few levels in the hierarchy.

Responding to market conditions

Have new competitors entered the market, forcing prices down and increasing the need for financial efficiency? Can changes in the organisation of the business, such as creating a flatter, less hierarchical structure help to achieve this? With shorter lines of communication the business may be more responsive to changes in the market which could give it an edge over more bureaucratic rivals.

Ownership changes

Does a change from sole trader to partnership or to private limited company (Chapter 7, pages 44–8) present an opportunity to improve the business's organisational structure? What workforce roles can be created and how involved are the new partners or shareholders going to be?

Customers' needs

Are the requirements of individual clients so specific that introducing an organisational matrix structure would be best, or should a project-based approach be confined to the operations and sales departments? An alternative might be to organise the structure of the business into customer types rather than functional areas.

The entrepreneurial culture within the company

Are creativity and risk taking being stifled by the formal organisational structure that has developed? How could a change in the way the business is organised ensure that an entrepreneurial culture is retained? The business could be organised into product areas which could encourage specialist teams. On the other hand, is it time for the firm to create a more stable, formal structure because the potential costs of failure have become too great, and new ideas need more careful consideration?

Factors such as these can be the basis for an evaluation of proposed changes to an organisational structure. Use your judgement to assess the extent to which improving the structure might increase the effectiveness of the organisation.

Study tip

Most organisations use some sort of hierarchical structure because this identifies job roles and responsibilities within the business. However, this does not mean that they do not use a matrix structure within the organisation: a project-based approach may be the most appropriate for research and development, IT and marketing.

Case study

Charlie Bigham's

Charlie Bigham's is a private limited company creating hand-made ready meals using fresh ingredients every day. The business was started in 1996 by Charlie Bigham and now employs 300 staff. There are very few levels of hierarchy in the firm. Charlie takes a hands-on approach to running the business and is directly involved in all the key decision making. No recipe hits the supermarket shelves without Charlie's sign off. However, he has delegated some responsibility to specialists who run various functional areas within the business including: kitchen production, sales, marketing, finance, operations, purchasing, health and safety and human resources. Each of these managers is responsible for all employees working in that area.

Charlie and the team are very keen that customers give their feedback on the meals. They encourage customers to give feedback via email, telephone or by writing in. Charlie's chefs also run 'Chef Academy' whereby junior members of the team are taught to cook a wide variety of dishes and learn new kitchen skills. There is a strong culture of in-house staff training and promoting from within.

www.bighams.com

■ Show the skills

Questions may be directed towards asking how the organisational structure of a business affects its performance. Always apply your answer to the business in the case study. For example, comment on the number of levels of hierarchy or the size of the spans of control. If the business is growing rapidly, perhaps by opening branches in different locations, then the structure will need to allow for good lines of communication and effective delegation.

Questions

1. Explain the following terms in the context of Bighams:
   a levels of hierarchy (2 marks)
   b delegation. (2 marks)

2. Explain why Charlie had to delegate some decision making to experts in different functional areas of the business. (8 marks)

3. Assess ways in which the senior management at Bighams could adapt the organisational structure of the growing business to enhance its performance. (14 marks)

4. To what extent will the quality of internal communications impact upon the continued success of Bighams? (14 marks)

5. Research task: Go to the Bighams website to look in more detail at the organisational structure and job roles of people in the organisation.

💡✅ *In this chapter you will have learned to:*

- explain the different ways in which organisations can be structured as they grow in size

- describe important workforce roles: supervisors, team leaders, managers and directors

- analyse the importance of issues such as levels of hierarchy/spans of control, work loads, job allocation and delegation

- discuss the impact the key elements of organisational structure can have on the effectiveness of a business

- discuss the extent to which the quality of internal business communication can impact on the effectiveness of businesses.

For answers to activities and case study questions see **kerboodle**

Measuring the effectiveness of the workforce

In this chapter you will learn to:

- calculate methods of measuring workforce performance

- interpret and analyse measures of workforce performance.

Key terms

Workforce performance: methods of measuring the effectiveness of employees including labour productivity, staff turnover and absenteeism.

Labour turnover: percentage of the total workforce who leave in any given time period (e.g. one year).

▮ Setting the scene

UK labour productivity

Since 2008 and the start of the global financial crisis and the UK recession, output per worker (labour productivity) has fallen by 3% in the UK. This has occurred because, despite national output falling over the last five years, the total number employed has risen. One reason for this could be the big shift towards part-time work. The average numbers of hours worked per employee has fallen in the UK since 2008. Also, it is recognised that some employers 'hoard' labour during a recession for fear that they will not be able to recruit well-qualified employees when the economic upturn starts.

Whatever the cause, the increasing productivity gap between the UK and its main competitors, such as USA, France and Germany, is worrying. In 2004, the average US worker added 34% more value per hour than the average UK worker. Since then, this gap has increased by a further 9 percentage points.

Productivity is falling in all UK industry sectors. In Quarter 4 of 2012, manufacturing productivity fell by 0.8%, and productivity in the service industries fell by 0.5%.

Discussion points

1. What does labour productivity measure?
2. Why should UK businesses be concerned if the labour productivity in the UK is less than in other industrialised countries?
3. Can all businesses measure labour productivity?
4. How else might the performance of the workforce be measured?

💡 Measuring the efficiency of an organisation

The question of the efficient use of resources is considered in the Operations Management section of this book. In the same way that machinery and vehicles must be used rather than standing idle, it is possible to measure the **workforce performance**, and make a judgement about whether or not it is efficient. The aim is to reduce unnecessary costs to the business thereby improving efficiency.

Labour turnover

This refers to the number of employees who leave and join an organisation over a specified time period, for example one year. **Labour turnover** can be classified into two types:

- **Voluntary** – when the employee leaves for their own reasons. This is usually unplanned as far as the organisation is concerned, and is most likely to happen in the first few months of employment.
- **Involuntary** – refers to dismissal or redundancy.

Normally voluntary turnover is much higher than involuntary and is calculated using the following formula:

$$\text{Labour turnover} = \frac{\text{Number of leavers per year}}{\text{Average number of employees per year}} \times 100$$

In the UK the average is currently between 16 and 18 per cent.

Why should labour turnover be calculated?

Obviously a lot will depend on the type of business, and a low percentage can cause problems such as stagnation with a lack of new ideas coming into the firm. However, most businesses would be concerned if the rate of labour turnover was rising, because that would suggest that a growing number of employees were dissatisfied with their current position. According to the Human Resource Management Guide, the cost of labour turnover is about £8,200 per employee, which rises to £12,000 for professionals and managers. The calculation of labour turnover may encourage employers to investigate the causes and find solutions which will save money and may have a longer-term benefit in terms of improved recruitment, selection and training (Chapter 21, page 149) and the motivation of employees (Chapter 22, page 160).

Link

For more information on recruitment, selection and training of employees, see Chapter 21 – Developing an effective workforce, page 149.

Theories of motivation are discussed in detail in Chapter 22 – Developing and retaining an effective workforce, page 160.

Case study

Calculating labour turnover

Here are the details of a medium-sized double glazing company which operates throughout Scotland. A new training programme and bonus scheme was introduced in Year 2.

Table 20.1

	Year 1	Year 2	Year 3	Year 4
Average number of employees	42	41	42	43
Number of leavers	3	6	2	2

Questions

1 Calculate the labour turnover rate for years 2, 3 and 4 (year 1 is shown below). **(3 marks)**

   Year 1:   3/42 × 100 = 7.14%

2 What do the figures suggest about the introduction of the new training programme and bonus scheme? **(6 marks)**

3 Make a list of what the costs of labour turnover might be. **(4 marks)**

Labour productivity

Labour productivity is most commonly measured by:

Output per employee

In some companies this may be quite straightforward, for example the number of zips sewn into pairs of jeans per hour. But where jobs are more complex, a better measure is the total output generated by the employees of the business which can then be turned into an average as follows:

$$\frac{\text{Total output in a given time period}}{\text{Total number of employees}}$$

Key terms

Labour productivity: the output per employee over a given time period. It is calculated by:

$$\frac{\text{Total output in given period}}{\text{Number of employees}}$$

Labour cost per unit of output

One of the most important consequences of labour productivity is the impact it has on 'labour cost per unit of output'. Other things being equal, high labour productivity reduces the labour cost of making each unit. This helps to make a business more competitive.

$$\frac{\text{Total labour costs}}{\text{Total output in a certain time period}}$$

UK productivity

This is the measure the government uses to compare productivity with international rivals. It gives a measure of average output by value per hour worked. This is the measure used in the 'Setting the scene' case study which indicated that the UK is losing ground to major competing countries.

$$\frac{\text{Total value of UK output}}{\text{Total number of hours worked}}$$

▪ Case study

VisGlass

VisGlass produces windscreens for vehicles. It operates in a very competitive market. The management at VisGlass has made great efforts in recent years to increase labour productivity. They believe that increasing productivity is the key to reducing labour costs per unit, which should improve competitiveness.

Table 20.2
Output and employment data at VisGlass from the last four years

	2009	2010	2011	2012
Total output	550,000	500,000	600,000	750,000
Number of production employees	100	95	110	125
Average annual salary per production employee £000	25	25	26	27

Labour productivity 2009:

$$\frac{550,000}{100} = 5,500 \text{ screens per worker per year}$$

Unit labour cost 2009:

$$\frac{£25,000 \times 100}{\text{Total output}} = £4.55$$

Questions

1. Calculate labour productivity per employee for 2010, 2011 and 2012. (6 marks)
2. Calculate the unit labour cost for 2010, 2011 and 2012. (6 marks)
3. Comment on your results to Questions 1 and 2. (6 marks)
4. Assess the importance of these results to measuring the effectiveness of VisGlass's workforce. (10 marks)

Why should labour productivity be calculated?

In a competitive market, any business needs to be sure that it is using its resources efficiently. If the output per employee is falling, this suggests that there is room to improve efficiency. Again, the figures do not provide a solution to any underlying problem, but can be the basis for an investigation into possible causes within the business which can then be remedied. It could be that employees need specific training, or that the payment system needs to be revised in order to improve motivation (Chapter 22, page 160).

Absenteeism

Absenteeism is seen as a good indicator of satisfaction at work and can be calculated using the following formula:

$$\frac{\text{Average number of staff absent on one day}}{\text{Total number of staff}} \times 100$$

Case study

Calculating absenteeism

Here are even more details of the medium-sized double glazing company which operates throughout Scotland. A new training programme and bonus scheme was introduced in Year 2.

Table 20.3

	Year 1	Year 2	Year 3	Year 4
Average number of employees per year	42	41	42	43
Number of leavers	3	6	2	2
Turnover/value of output (£)	1,500,000	1,300,000	1,600,000	1,800,000
Total labour costs	948,600	951,200	948,600	962,400
Average number of staff absent on one day	5	6	2	1

Questions

1 Calculate the percentage absenteeism rate for years 2–4 (year 1 is shown below).   (1 mark)

   Year 1: 5/42 × 100 = 11.9%

2 Describe the trend you observe from the answers. How might you explain this?   (4 marks)

Absenteeism costs the UK £11.6bn a year according to the Confederation of British Industry (CBI). This organisation believes that high absenteeism levels are the main reason why UK productivity is much lower than the US and some other parts of Europe. On average, absenteeism costs UK industry 2.9% of total costs but for British Airways it is 15%.

Key terms

Absenteeism: The number of working days lost as a result of an employee's deliberate or habitual absence from work.

Activity

Explain the costs of absenteeism to a business.

Study tip

You should memorise the formulas for labour turnover and productivity. Remember that all the information you need will be provided, even if you have to do some work to find it! Start your calculations by writing down the formula – it will help you to focus on the information you need – and get you marks for knowledge.

Business in action

Invesco

For most adults at work having one day off sick is not a crime, but it is a major headache for UK industry. According to healthcare consultancy IHC, 40 million days are lost each year in the UK to workplace absenteeism.

93 per cent of employees blame absence on flu; however IHC says that at least 50 per cent of absence is not about health, it is because of bullying at work, family responsibility, job demotivation, low pay, or a hangover.

Ill health can still be caused by someone's job: IHC estimates that 13.4 million working days a year are lost to stress, anxiety and depression, and 12.3 million to back and upper limb problems. This costs UK industry £11.5bn in wages to absent employees, additional overtime and payments to temporary staff.

One firm that decided to tackle the problem is investment management company Invesco, where they calculated that absenteeism cost about £38,000 a year. Invesco overhauled its staff's health provision offering their staff a private GP, physiotherapist, workstation assessments, free health tests, counselling and a non-contributory private medical insurance scheme. One-day sickness absences fell by 6%, saving 60 working days per year. 'It has helped us raise staff morale and increase general health, while reducing down-time in the office and improve productivity' said a spokeswoman.

Why should absenteeism be calculated?

As with the other measures of workforce effectiveness, high or rising absenteeism represents a cost to the business, and as such should be investigated. Some firms take a very heavy-handed approach to this issue, implying that employees are faking illness. However, it might be more appropriate to look in more depth at the possible causes, and find a solution which suits everyone within the firm. That way motivation might increase which may have a positive impact on the quality and quantity of output.

The importance of workforce measures

For any organisation it is important to monitor changes over time so that efficiency and effectiveness can be evaluated. The information gathered about employees can be compared to data from previous years and other businesses or sectors to judge whether or not policies and procedures are working. The questions posed throughout this chapter make it clear that the calculations may not provide the answers to problems within a business. However, they can highlight issues which should be addressed. Chapters 21 and 22 – Developing an effective workforce: recruitment, selection and training and Developing and retaining an effective workforce: motivating employees, pages 149 and 160, contain details of some of the possible solutions available to firms who find that their workforce is becoming less effective.

Case study

The White Hart Hotel

The White Hart Hotel is a great success as it has an excellent reputation and is very profitable. The hotel is well known for great comfort, fine service and exceptional food. Gill and Savan bought the property in the south-west of England six years ago after studying hotel management and catering in Switzerland. Gill manages the staff fairly but firmly. She believes that there is little scope for employee participation in this industry. Until recently, she has been rewarded with excellent employee performance but the latest data suggested some staff discontent (Table 20.4). One employee was overheard to say: 'This hotel is making so much money, why shouldn't we be offered a share of the profits as well as our wages?'

Table 20.4 *Summary of employee performance at the White Hart Hotel*

	6 months ending 31 December 2011	6 months ending 30 June 2012
Average staff employed (full-time equivalent)	42	40
Staff leaving	7	4
Reason most often given for leaving	'Lack of promotion prospects'	'No opportunity for participation'
Absenteeism rate	8%	6%
Serious customer complaints	155	40
Number of customer nights spent in hotel	12,500	11,500

Show the skills

When a question asks you to 'evaluate the effectiveness of the workforce', it is very important to consider what type of business it is. It may be difficult to assess labour productivity in some occupations and businesses. Labour productivity measures need to be compared to previous time periods for *similar* businesses – not businesses in completely different industries. Labour turnover varies greatly between industries – it tends to be highest in those that are well-known for employing temporary workers. Labour absenteeism is likely to be relatively high in businesses that recruit many part-time and seasonal workers, who may have little loyalty to the organisation.

Questions

1. Calculate the difference in the rate of labour turnover between the two six-monthly periods referred to in Table 20.4. (6 marks)

2. Explain what the term 'absenteeism rate' means, and why it is calculated (8 marks)

3. Use the information provided and your own knowledge to analyse the strengths and weaknesses of Gill's approach to her staff. (8 marks)

4. To what extent is high labour turnover and above average absenteeism inevitable in the hotel industry? (14 marks)

5. Research task: Although it is difficult to get exact figures for particular industries, there is a lot of information about general trends on the government's National Statistics website. Make sure that you are familiar with the current situation with regard to the effectiveness of the UK workforce.

✔ *In this chapter you will have learned to:*

- calculate methods of measuring workforce performance including labour turnover, labour productivity and absenteeism

- discuss measures of workforce performance such as the costs to the business of high labour turnover and absenteeism, and the benefits of improved labour productivity.

For answers to activities and case study questions see **kerboodle**

Developing an effective workforce: recruitment, selection and training

In this chapter you will learn to:

- describe the recruitment process
- analyse the benefits and drawbacks of internal and external recruitment
- explain the options which can be used in the selection process
- evaluate the importance of induction training to smaller businesses
- explain the purpose of training and the variety of methods available to businesses
- analyse the benefits and drawbacks of training methods applied to a given business and training need
- evaluate the extent to which recruitment, selection and training can help in the development of an effective workforce.

Key terms

Recruitment and selection process: how a business chooses the best candidate for a vacancy it has identified.

Setting the scene

Catering Associates

Catering Associates provides temporary and permanent catering staff to businesses in Manchester. Their clients include leading sports teams in the region.

They ran a successful in-house training programme which equipped recruits with all the vocational skills they needed. However, many candidates lacked basic maths and English skills. Catering Associates firmly believed that these people had a lot to offer as employees if only they had the relevant skills.

The solution came through the Learning and Skills Council who introduced them to the Train to Gain service. A Skills for Life training provider, WEA North West, came in and shadowed Catering Associates' own training and assessed how to embed the new programme as effectively as possible. They then ran the training at the Catering Associates' on-site learning centre. Initially the programme was piloted with 6–12 learners, but the plan is to make it available to any employee who needs it.

As a result Catering Associates are now able to offer a greater range of services to their clients, which makes the business, as well as their employees, more effective.

Discussion points

1. Why does Catering Associates need to train its employees?

2. Catering Associates now claims to offer its employees more challenging opportunities which helps them realise their true potential. How is Catering Associates benefiting from this development?

3. Releasing staff for training is a cost to Catering Associates. Are there any other solutions to the recruitment problem they faced?

The recruitment process

When a vacancy is identified in an established small to medium-sized business, the **recruitment and selection process** provides an opportunity for the firm to develop a more effective workforce, that is, make the best use of the people it has employed. The recruitment process begins with an analysis of the job itself. It would be a mistake to assume, for instance, that when an employee leaves, the replacement has to have exactly the same job. It could be that the business has grown and the role has changed. For those involved in the recruitment process, the first question should be 'what do we want the new employee to do?' This can lead to improvements in the organisational structure by clarifying job roles and work loads. Similarly, with a completely new role, created by the expansion of the business, the opportunity to reconsider levels of hierarchy, spans of control and work loads within the firm should not be missed.

Identify the vacancy

↓

Write a job description
and
person specification

↓

Advertise the position
internally and/or
externally

↓

Receive and
process applications

Figure 21.1 *The steps in the recruitment process*

■ Key terms

Job description: a summary of the main duties and responsibilities associated with an identified job.

Person specification: identifies the skills, knowledge and experience a successful applicant is likely to have.

Internal recruitment: candidates selected from inside the organisation.

External recruitment: candidates selected from outside the organisation.

■ Link

For more information on levels of hierarchy, see Chapter 19 – Improving organisational structures, page 134.

■ Activity

At Gilds Associates did they seem more interested in the Job description or the Person Specification when recruiting new employees?

Fig. 21.2 *Using personal networks is one way of recruiting employees www.gilds.co.uk*

Once the role is clear, a **job description** can be written. This should include:

- the job title
- the position in the business including the job title of the person the employee reports to and of those who report to them, if any
- the location of the job
- a summary of the general nature and objectives of the job
- a list of the main duties or tasks of the employee

From this description, a **person specification** can be drawn up. This should include the qualities required in a person likely to fill the vacancy.

- Knowledge: the level of education and/or of a more job-specific nature.
- Experience of the type of work involved.
- Skills: practical, interpersonal, managerial, etc.

These can be separated into those which are essential for the job and those which are not essential, but would be helpful.

Why might job vacancies occur in a business?

1. Promotion – the post-holder gets a job higher up the organisational structure (**internal recruitment**) or with another organisation (**external recruitment**).
2. Expansion – creating new jobs which did not exist before.
3. Natural wastage – the post-holder might retire, move away or retrain for another career.

How might a business recruit the best employee for a job vacancy?

Job vacancies may be filled internally or externally, and the choice may be influenced by factors such as available finance and time constraints.

Internal recruitment

1 Promotion/transfer

Somebody who already works for the organisation and has the potential to do a different, or more demanding job. This may come out of a performance management interview.

Jobster
Schedules & Engages

JAN — Who do you know that would be great to work here?

APR — We're looking for a new Marketing manager. Know of anyone?

JUL — Invite the people from your professional training to join our network.

OCT — Our IT development is growing. Do you know any engineers?

Table 21.1 *The benefits and drawbacks of internal and external recruitment*

Internal recruitment	External recruitment
Benefits	**Benefits**
■ Cheapest option: very low advertising cost, and limited time taken to complete the process ■ Promotion/varied job opportunities can be used to motivate employees (see Chapter 22)	■ A bigger choice of alternative candidates, making it more likely that the best person will be selected to meet the specifications of the post ■ New ideas and perspectives may be brought to the business
Drawbacks	**Drawbacks**
■ Another vacancy may be created as a result which may then require external recruitment ■ Ideas generation may stagnate due to lack of 'new blood' in the organisation. Employees staying too long can be as much of a problem as staff leaving too quickly	■ Can be a very expensive and time-consuming process, particularly for a small business. The use of recruitment consultants is very expensive ■ Induction training will be needed for employees new to the company which is an additional cost

2 Internal advertisement

Job vacancies can be advertised in the organisation's newsletter, magazine, on notice boards or via the company intranet.

3 Personal recommendation

Managers, team leaders and supervisors may see potential in a member of their team or department and suggest their suitability for a different post.

External recruitment

1 Job advertisements

Local and national newspapers, recruitment fairs, notice boards at the place of work and increasingly, the internet: both the company website and specific job vacancy websites.

2 Recruitment agencies

Act on behalf of the employer in the process and for a fee will find a candidate with the most appropriate qualifications. They often specialise in particular areas of employment, for example medical, financial, IT.

Business in action

Online recruitment

Although a study found that many organisations were trying to save money by shifting the bulk of their recruitment activity from printed material to online media, substantial numbers have been spurred on by budget pressures to review the whole of their hiring process. The report found that moves to make greater use of online recruitment were both the most widespread change, introduced by 44 per cent of organisations, as well as being the most effective. Two other changes that had been widely adopted were the appointment of a dedicated recruitment manager or recruitment team (used by 42 per cent of organisations) and a greater use of internal recruitment (used by 44 per cent of employers). One in four organisations (25 per cent) that took part in the survey had also introduced a bonus scheme for employees who referred successful candidates to the company.

3 Personal recommendation

Friend or family of an existing employee. This is becoming increasingly popular in small-scale businesses. Employees may be given financial rewards if the person they recommend stays with the company and

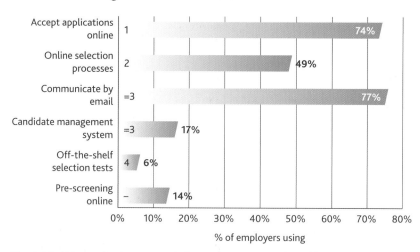

Most effective changes in online recruitment

Fig. 21.3 *Using technology to cut their recruitment costs adapted from www.personneltoday.com*

Activity

Which methods of recruitment do you think would be most effective for Gilds Associates to use and why?

Study tip

Many students don't apply their knowledge of recruitment to the scenario given and just write a general answer about the options available to all businesses. It is very important to think from the point of view of the organisation in the case study: try to imagine that you are the person actually making the decision, it is your business!

Key terms

Methods of selection: ways in which businesses recruit the best candidate for an identified vacancy. These can be internal or external to the organisation and will depend upon the time available, the budget available and the specialist skills available in the organisation.

proves to be a valuable addition to the workforce. An assessment of the applicant's capabilities will still be required of course.

4 Job centres

Designed to get the unemployed into work by advertising vacancies.

Which method is best?

The decision about which method(s) of recruitment to choose will be different for every business. The best alternative may be influenced by circumstances such as the available budget, or the location of the firm. If there is very little money available, because the business is new or expanding, then the cost of each option becomes very important. The availability of a suitable workforce in the local area, perhaps as a result of the closure of a large company nearby, will probably result in a different choice from that where there is a skill shortage and full employment in the region.

■ The selection process

Once applications have been received for a job, the process of selecting the best candidate can begin. Again, this represents an opportunity for the organisation to improve the workforce by choosing the most appropriate **method of selection**, so that the successful candidate meets the needs of the business. The quality of the job description and person specification will have a significant impact on the success of the selection process. If these documents are vague and general, then it is more difficult to prepare appropriate interview questions, or select the best methods of testing, to discover the most suitable candidate.

Methods of selection

There are a number of ways in which candidates can be selected from those who apply. Some businesses may only use one option, but increasingly a range of methods of selection are employed. Selection can be carried out within the business, but for many small and medium-sized firms, the specialist skills required mean that this work may be sub-contracted out to a specialist recruitment agency.

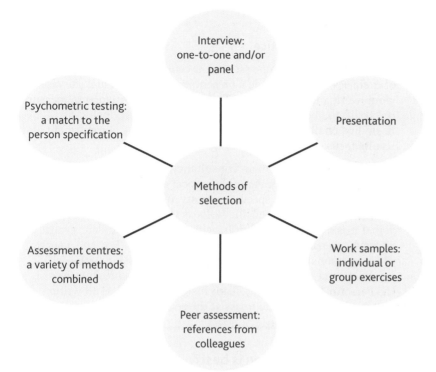

Fig. 21.4 *The main methods of selection*

Interview

The most common method of selection which can range from an informal chat over lunch, to a telephone interview or a formal panel interview. The principle is to ask all candidates the same questions and make a judgement about suitability for a job based on their responses.

Presentations

Candidates are given a subject related to the job or career and are asked to prepare and give a presentation of between five and fifteen minutes to an audience of one or more people.

Work samples

Involve an individual or group of candidates completing exercises that they would be required to undertake as part of the job they have applied for.

Peer assessment

A candidate's colleagues predict how the candidate will respond if placed in a particular work situation or role. This may take the form of a questionnaire sent to current co-workers.

Assessment centres

Assessment centres are used mostly for large-scale recruitment because they are complicated and costly to organise and run. A typical assessment may take two days and could include interviews, written tests, group exercises and individual tasks. Trained assessors collect evidence and present a final collective decision.

Psychometric tests

These are administered by trained professionals and can be used at all levels in an organisation to indicate candidates whose characteristics match those required for a particular job, as described in the Person Specification.

 Activity

Use the internet to complete a variety of online application forms for jobs in your area. You don't need to press the send button. The aim is to note the similarities and differences between the recruitment processes used by a range of businesses.

Activity

Explain why the most effective recruitment and selection process for Catering Associates is likely to be different to that of a solicitors' firm.

Business in action

Recruitment in practice

The Co-operative Group assessment centre consists of a number of exercises, which include a presentation, an individual exercise, group work and an interview. The exercises are designed to measure the skills and behaviours required to be successful, including flexibility, challenge, customer focus, co-operative commitment and results focus.

Team Insight, a recruitment consultancy, helped with the selection of a new Head of Town Planning in local government. The Person Specification was very specific: honesty, integrity, leadership skills, strategic thinking, influencing skills as well as superior number and verbal reasoning skills. Team Insight gave each candidate a range of psychometric tests including a Verbal Analysis Test and a survey of Interpersonal Values. Following a feedback session with each candidate and a formal interview alongside two representatives of the Personnel Department, Team Insight produced a full written report on each candidate to assist the selection process.

Activity

Which factors do you think Catering Associates may consider to be the most important?

Which method of selection is best?

As you will have gathered by now, there is no method of selection which is suitable for all types of job. There is evidence that firms are moving away from the traditional one-to-one interview, but for small or medium-sized businesses the issue may be that there is nobody within the organisation with the skills to carry out other types of selection. This means that the process could be external to the business – sub-contracted to a specialist consultancy firm. This is likely to be a very expensive option in the short term, but if the best candidate is selected, will save money in the longer term because the employee is more likely to be happy. This should mean a better standard of work, and they are less likely to leave or take days off for stress at work.

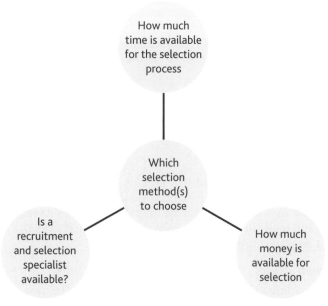

Fig. 21.5 *Factors to take into consideration when deciding which method(s) of selection to use*

How recruitment and selection can improve the workforce

It should be clear by now, that the recruitment and selection process can be used to improve the quality of the workforce. The starting point must be an assessment of the future needs of the business by answering the following questions:

- What quantity of labour, with which skills are needed in the near future? (Discovered from sales forecasts).
- What is the labour turnover rate for the business?
- Trends in wage increases – is the cost of labour rising rapidly or is it stable?
- Are current training programmes likely to lead to increases in productivity?
- Will changes in technology alter the skills needed by employees in the future?

This assessment can then be developed further by an audit of the skills of the existing workforce to identify the abilities of current employees. This process may inform the decision as to whether to recruit internally or externally. When all these questions have been answered, a plan to improve the performance of the workforce, by recruiting people with the required skills from outside the organisation, and training existing employees can be put into action.

An essential element of putting the plan into action is the drawing up of accurate job descriptions and person specifications. If these documents are thought through very carefully, then it should be possible to identify the best candidate for a job. If either one is vague or misleading, the job may turn out to be very different to what the candidate was expecting, which could lead to dissatisfaction and frustration for the employer and employee.

Training

Once a new recruit has been appointed to the business, it is important that they become part of the team as quickly as possible. Furthermore, no firm stays the same for ever, and organisations should try to keep up with developments that affect their industry. This means that **training** should be an on-going process. The skills and qualifications that a new employee brings to the business may not be what are required in one or two years time, so successful firms, and their workforce, will see training as a process of lifelong learning.

Induction training

Good **induction training** means that new starters settle in quickly and happily to a productive role within an organisation and are less likely to leave after the first week! It is the first impression a new employee gets of the business and it needs to be organised and professional. A good induction programme helps with questions about routines, lunch facilities, parking and all the other things that most employees take for granted. It also provides a perfect opportunity for the values and expectations of the business to be made clear to the new employee. Legally, there is also a requirement on employers to ensure that new starters are aware of all issues relating to Health and Safety at work.

The success of any business will depend upon its employees. There are very few firms that do not exist in a competitive environment. Whether it

Link

For more information on the labour turnover rate and productivity, see Chapter 20 – Measuring the effectiveness of the workforce, page 143.

Study tip

To make a judgement about how well the recruitment and selection process is being used to improve the workforce, think about what the firm is trying to achieve by the process, for example more highly skilled employees. You can then decide whether or not they are likely to achieve this outcome and why.

Key terms

Training: giving employees the knowledge, skills and techniques necessary to fulfil the requirements of a job.

Induction training: is given as an initial preparation upon taking up a post. Its goal is to help new employees reach the level of performance expected from an experienced worker.

Activities

1 Ask family and friends who have a job of any kind about the induction process they experienced. Find out as much as you can about the programme content, how long the training lasted and how useful it was.

2 Why is a good induction programme important to a firm like Catering Associates?

is the level of skill employees have or the professional way in which they work, the training provided can make all the difference to the on-going success of a business.

Business in action

Center Parcs

Center Parcs, with its head office in Newark, Nottinghamshire, operates four holiday villages in the UK. Each is set in a forest environment offering sports and leisure facilities plus numerous restaurants, bars and retail outlets. All new employees have the opportunity to find out more about Center Parcs either through its newly launched training website or are invited to spend a day in a Village and experience life as a guest. This is followed by a 'Welcome Workshop' which is an induction to the company and guest care training.

Types of training

There are two types of training available to businesses:

Off-the-job training

Key terms

Off-the-job training: away from the place of work, for example at a training centre or college.

Off-the-job training takes place away from the workplace. This could be at the firm's training centre, as is the case with Catering Associates. Other firms encourage employees to complete courses provided by local colleges on a day-release scheme or distance learning/evening classes. Another alternative is to take advantage of courses provided by specialist firms including management training, financial management and marketing.

There are several advantages to off-the-job training:

- The use of specialist trainers and accommodation. This would not be financially viable for smaller businesses to provide in-house.
- Employees can focus on the training and not be distracted by work. This is particularly true at management or supervisory level, where the temptation to check on how things are going without you, might be too much for some.
- The opportunity to mix with employees from other businesses can be a great support for those who might have sole responsibility for a particular area in their place of work.

There are also disadvantages to off-the-job training:

Activity

Why might Catering Associates use off-the-job training for their employees?

- Employees need to be motivated to learn, particularly if the training is undertaken in their own time.
- It may not be directly relevant to the employee's job because the training may have to cover a wide range of jobs – it may be too general.
- Costs (transport, course fees, examination fees, materials, accommodation) can make off-the-job training beyond the financial resources of smaller businesses.

On-the-job training

Key terms

On-the-job training: learning by doing the job, under the guidance of an experienced member of staff or external trainer.

On-the-job training is given in-house by an experienced member of staff or external trainer to an employee as they are doing their work. It is based on the principle of learning by doing. Ideally, a structured approach should include learning and procedures guides, a form of assessment (formal or informal), and be integrated into the organisation's induction, probation and performance programme. On-the-job training should be monitored by an appropriate supervisor who shows a good example of the processes and procedures being learned. Trainees should have a learning plan that details the what, how, when and where of the structured training programme. This learning plan should have a checklist or diary in which the activities to be learned are listed and may be endorsed when each step is mastered. This gives a sense of achievement to trainees and also provides evidence to managers and supervisors that trainees have mastered their work.

There are advantages to on-the-job training:

- Training an employee in their own working environment, with equipment they are familiar with and people they know can help them gain direct experience to a standard approved by the employer.
- Employees may find that they have more confidence to use the equipment if they are supervised and guided as they feel they are doing the job right.
- Employees may feel more at ease being taught or supervised by people they know rather than complete strangers.
- Managers or supervisors can assess improvement and progress over a period of time and this makes it easier to identify a problem, to intervene and resolve problems quickly.
- This type of training is also productive, as the employee is still working as they are learning.
- As training progresses and the employee begins to feel more confident, this confidence would allow them to work at a higher standard and ultimately be more productive.
- Training 'on-the-job' would also prove an opportunity to get to know staff they might not normally talk to.
- It can be much more cost effective than off-the-job training because it is very specific to the requirements of one job.

There are also disadvantages to on-the-job training:

- Training a person requires skill and knowledge, without which the training may not be done to a sufficient standard.

Business in action
Apex Radio Systems

Fig. 21.6
www.apexradio.co.uk/

Apex Radio Systems is based in Newcastle upon Tyne and specialises in the hire and sale of two-way communications equipment to the retail, leisure and construction industries. It is a fairly small company and employs twenty-two people. Three of these have recently completed *NVQ level 2 in Information Technology*, delivered by Newcastle College, through the Train to Gain scheme.

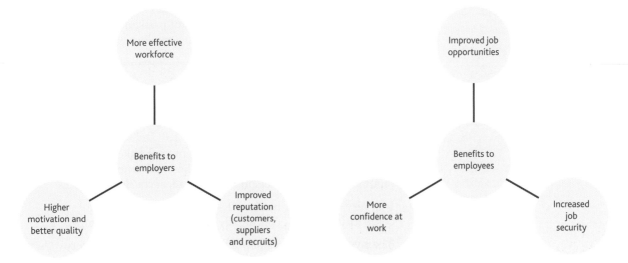

Fig. 21.7 *Benefits of training to employers*

Fig. 21.8 *Benefits of training to employees*

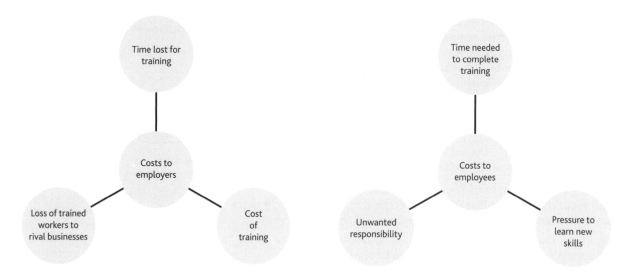

Fig. 21.9 *Costs of training to employers*

Fig. 21.10 *Costs of training to employees*

■ The trainer may not be given the time to spend with the employee to teach them properly, which may lead to substandard training.

■ The trainers may possess bad habits and pass these on to the employee being trained.

■ If a trainer has been brought into the company externally they might not be familiar with the equipment, or layout of the firm, and this could waste time.

Is training important?

Training is often seen by businesses as a luxury, and this is particularly true in smaller firms where the costs involved outweigh the perceived benefits. This is partly because it can be difficult to measure the outcome of training and its impact on the effectiveness of the workforce. It could also be that the directors of the firm think that once trained, their employees will leave to work for a rival business, or to set up in competition with their current employers. Furthermore, many employers may not be familiar with the latest qualifications on offer at local colleges. That is one of the reasons why the Train to Gain scheme was set up to encourage businesses of all sizes, but particularly smaller firms, to see the competitive advantages of training employees throughout their working life.

■ Case study

Simpson's Bakery

Simpson's Bakery is a large independent craft bakery business in the north of England. It has 71 branches, 560 employees and a reputation across the region for its bread, savouries and cakes.

It is very successful, but knows that to stay ahead of the competition it must continually train and develop its staff.

The hygiene operatives play a key role in keeping the bakery scrupulously clean and need to keep up-to-date with changing legislation and health and safety issues.

The newly-built state-of-the-art bakery means that they now use a very high-tech approach to everything they do and so staff need to have highly developed skills to match.

All staff should see how their job role fits into the overall success of the business and understand the company's procedures in more depth.

Options:

1 Hygiene Operatives to attend a local tertiary college on a day-release basis (it will take several years for them all to achieve Level 2 NVQ in Cleaning and Support Services).

2 Hygiene Operatives to be trained in the evenings by a distance learning programme to achieve Level 2 NVQ in Cleaning and Support services.

3 Two days off-the-job training for all department supervisors on new technology used at the bakery.

4 On-the-job training for all operatives (this can be completed over a one month period).

5 Closing the bakery for one week's intensive training for all staff to update skills required.

Questions

1 Use an example from the case study to explain the term 'off-the-job training'. (4 marks)

2 Explain TWO reasons why Simpson's Bakery needs to train its staff? (6 marks)

3 Analyse the arguments for and against closing the bakers for one week to update the skills of the staff at Simpson's Bakery. (8 marks)

4 To what extent can Simpson's Bakery use recruitment, selection and training to help in the development of an effective workforce? (14 marks)

5 Research task: Investigate a local employer in your area (try not to use a national organisation). Find out how they recruit and select employees at two different levels of entry. Do they offer training and if so, what is it?

Show the skills

When answering questions on recruitment and training, you might be able to make the LINK between these aspects of human resource management and employee performance. Recruiting the wrong type of people and not training them effectively is likely to lead to poor performance!

In this chapter you will have learned to:

- describe the stages of the recruitment and selection process
- discuss the benefits and drawbacks of internal and external recruitment
- consider the factors affecting the method(s) of selection chosen by a business
- discuss meaning and importance of induction training
- explain the purpose of training, and the training methods available to a business
- analyse the benefits and drawbacks of off-the-job and on-the job training to businesses
- evaluate the extent to which recruitment, selection and training can help with the development of an effective workforce.

For answers to activities and case study questions see **kerboodle**

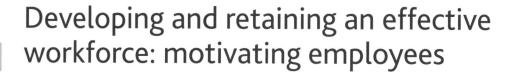

22 Developing and retaining an effective workforce: motivating employees

Setting the scene

Motivating employees at Google

High technology companies such as Google and Cisco are constantly looking for new ways to retain and motivate employees with talent for maximum output. Google has restructured management to give its employees freedom to create ideas to produce blockbuster new products. Workers are rewarded with perks such as onsite pools, child care and free food. A relaxed working environment encourages employees to operate in teams. Free-thinking group work is a particular characteristic of the Google approach. Small individual entrepreneurial groups reject the tightly managed structure of traditional companies. Employees benefit from intrinsic rewards such as freedom, trust and respect. They are empowered to work towards the company's common goal and to control their own work.

Discussion points

1. Why is a highly motivated workforce important to companies such as Google and Cisco?

2. Why do you think the management style and team working used within Google are effective in motivating employees?

3. Would these methods of motivating employees work effectively in much smaller businesses?

Key terms

Motivation: the factors that inspire an employee to complete a task at work.

The meaning and importance of motivation

Motivation is what makes a person do something. Motivation at work is employees performing their tasks to the best of their ability. In business, every employee, whatever their status in the organisation is motivated by their own personal needs and it would be a mistake to assume that there is any one method of increasing motivation which will work for everybody. Motivation is not static: people's lives and priorities change, so do their needs and their motivation. What motivates somebody when they join a firm may not be the same two, five or ten years later.

Motivation is important because it affects the efficiency of a business both in terms of quantity and quality.

Quantity

This refers to the productivity of an employee – output per person. If each employee produces more items for the same level of pay, the labour costs per unit go down, which means that the business is using its resources more efficiently. The Government prefer to use the calculation of UK productivity as a measure of business efficiency. This shows the total output achieved by the UK divided by the total number of hours worked. If the same level of output can be achieved in less time then productivity has increased. Many employees do not produce easily quantifiable output, but the calculation can still be made using turnover and workforce figures. The question for any business is 'how can we achieve greater employee productivity?'

Link

For more information on calculating output and productivity, see Chapter 20 – Measuring the effectiveness of the workforce, page 143.

Quality

This refers to how well the work is done. If there are a lot of complaints, repeat business is low, or wastage rates are high or rising, then this suggests that the quality of work is not of an acceptable standard. In a competitive market, customers will judge a firm on the value for money they receive, which is largely based on product quality (see Chapter 24) and customer service (Chapter 25). Motivated employees are more likely to care about the impact of their work on the success of the business.

 ## Financial methods of motivation: payment systems, bonus systems

Using monetary reward to motivate employees can have significant short-term benefits particularly when the quantity of output or sales is important. The use of these techniques will depend upon particular circumstances. For example, if a business needs to employ additional workers to meet a seasonal increase in demand, they may well use a high rate of pay to attract enough people. Similarly, firms who employ temporary staff to cover for absent employees (holiday, illness, maternity leave) may offer a higher hourly rate than that given to those on a full-time permanent contract. However, they won't have the same terms of employment such as paid holidays or sick pay.

Business in action

John Lewis

John Lewis employees - or partners as they are known - shared out a massive £210 million in 2013 as their bonus, based on a share of the profits, was raised to 17% of salaries. This is almost equal to 9 weeks' pay for all eligible partners. John Lewis, which operates Waitrose supermarkets and John Lewis department stores, made pre-tax profits of £409 million. Many business analysts put the huge success of the business down to the fact that employees are part-owners of the business, so they have a much stronger vested interest in 'going the extra mile' than employees of traditionally owned public limited companies.

Activity

Is the quality of service more important than the quantity of programs produced by a computer gaming business?

Fig. 22.1 *All employees of John Lewis receive a share of the profits*

Table 22.1 *Advantages and disadvantages of payment systems and bonus schemes*

Method	Advantage to the business	Disadvantage to the business
Piece rate: paying employees based on the number of units they produce	Increase in output per person. Particularly useful when production is running below the required level	Quality may drop which can have a knock-on effect on future orders or the price that can be charged for the product
Commission: payment based on the number of units sold	Increased sales and therefore revenue	Employees may be tempted to use unethical techniques which could lead to customer-relations problems
Fringe benefits: options include a company car, private medical insurance or a subsidised canteen	Often valued more highly than increased wages by employees and cheaper to provide	Represent a long-term commitment by the company so reduce flexibility
Profit-sharing scheme: a percentage of the company's profits are distributed to employees	Individual employees see that their effort can make a difference: encourages team working	Divisive if some members of the team do not work as hard as others, but get the same reward
Quality-related bonus schemes: salary is reviewed based on the contribution made in terms of the standards achieved	Employees are motivated to work to the highest possible standard to gain an increase in pay	Difficult to judge quality objectively in the service sector. which can lead to discontent

Which financial and non-financial methods of motivation do you think would be most effective for these groups of people at Wollaton Dental Care:

1 Dentists

2 Administrative staff

Non-financial methods of motivation: improving job design

There is a lot of research to suggest that people perform better at work if their job is more interesting and rewarding. A person who carries out exactly the same tasks, every day, with no variation, is likely to lose interest in their work, and the quality may fall. Motivational theorists suggest that changing the job may increase motivation, or at least reduce boredom and dissatisfaction at work. **Job design** is about looking at the tasks involved in a person's role and trying to make them more interesting and rewarding.

Table 22.2 *Methods of improving job design – advantages and disadvantages*

Method of improving job design	Advantage to the business	Disadvantage to the business
Job enlargement: including a wider variety of tasks within a job description. This is sometimes called horizontal loading and involves giving people more jobs to do that require the same level of skill	Fewer problems with boredom, so mistakes are less likely, which reduces costs	There will be training costs involved and employees may expect more pay
Job rotation: movement between different jobs. Leads to multi-skilling. The ability to carry out several different jobs	Multi-skilling benefits the employer because staff shortages can be covered more easily	This system can be very complicated to organise, and the skill level achieved by an employee may not be the same for each job, causing variations in quality
Job enrichment: increasing the depth of the job by increasing the amount of discretion and authority for decision-making the job holder has	It allows employees to test and develop their managerial skills, which can lead to an increase in internal recruitment opportunities	High training costs: it may be difficult for the employee to balance new responsibilities with their existing work load

Key terms

Job design: changing the nature of a job role in order to increase motivation or reduce dissatisfaction at work.

Empowerment: giving employees the *power* to do their job: trusting them, giving them the *authority* to make decisions and encouraging feedback from them.

Job rotation: varying an employee's job on a regular basis.

Job enlargement: expanding the number of tasks completed by an employee.

Organisational design and methods of motivation

One of the principles behind many of the non-financial motivation methods is **empowerment.** This is based on the observations of theorists who came to the conclusion that employees work best when they have some control over their jobs, rather than simply following a detailed set of instructions, and being closely supervised. With the introduction of any new system to a business, the design of the organisation can have a big impact on the likelihood of success. Human nature tends to lead people to want to protect their position and one way to do this is to retain as much control and power as possible, making employee empowerment difficult to achieve in practice.

Motivational techniques

In a small business the entrepreneur may try to retain control over all aspects of the business, thus making it difficult to use a wide range of methods of motivation.

In Figure 22.2, all the decisions are taken by the Entrepreneur who communicates in one way (downward) with the employees (see Chapter 19). This may be a good way to start a business so that everybody involved is clear about the aims of the business. The methods of motivation available in such circumstances are likely to be financial: saying 'thank you' for increasing output or sales, or benevolent: showing how valued employees are by giving fringe benefits. Non-financial methods of motivation are likely to be limited to **job rotation** and **job enlargement** because there is no loss of control for the entrepreneur. Although this approach can be very successful, because decision making is not delegated by the entrepreneur, the employees are not empowered. It will become frustrating for staff after a while, and can lead to inefficiency, particularly as the business starts to grow and the quantity of decisions to be taken, increases.

Fig. 22.2 *A basic top-down organisation structure*

Delegation and empowerment

An alternative structure which encourages delegation and empowerment might look like this.

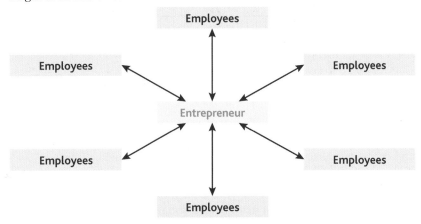

Fig. 22.3 *Organisational structure encouraging delegation and empowerment*

Here the lines of communication are two-way and the employees will be able to contribute to the decision making. In these circumstances, both financial and non-financial methods of motivation are available to the entrepreneur, including **job enrichment** which empowers employees.

Delegating authority to subordinates can be seen as threatening at any level in the organisation, and as a business grows many managers, having been given authority to make decisions, may resist further empowerment of subordinates – they have responsibility for the decision made after all. This is most likely in a traditional hierarchical organisational structure, where job roles are clearly defined and therefore delegation is limited.

Functional structures

A business may develop a functional structure as it grows, as in Figure 22.4, with a clear distinction between marketing, operations, finance and human resources. In this case, all types of motivation are available, although methods such as piece rate are only appropriate for jobs where output per person can be measured. In reality, this traditional approach to organisational design may not encourage empowerment, particularly if the structure becomes increasingly hierarchical as the business expands. Narrow spans of control and long lines of communication do not encourage delegation (Chapter 19).

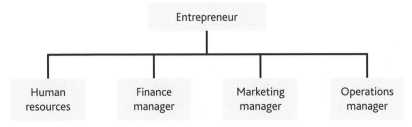

Fig. 22.4 *Organisational structure based on functional areas*

Divisional structures

However, an alternative model is based on the observation that most of the important decisions in a growing business are likely to be about products or customers. By organising the firm into divisions, it is possible to empower more employees which may have a positive impact on

> **Key terms**
>
> **Job enrichment**: increase the level of responsibility within a job to make work more challenging and rewarding.

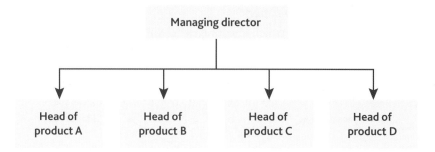

Fig. 22.5 *Divisional organisational structure*

motivation. Within each division, there is marketing, production, finance and other specialist staff who work together, and they will all have to make a contribution to decisions taken about their product.

In Figure 22.5, the entrepreneur runs a business with four different products, each one having a team of functional experts. Each division can set targets and employees are likely to feel a strong sense of belonging to the team, because their contribution can be clearly identified. Financial motivators are likely to be profit-sharing, and fringe benefits because others that reward the output of individuals rather than the group would work against this structure. Non-financial methods can include job enlargement and job enrichment.

Structure by customer type

In Figure 22.6, the business has designed its organisation by dividing its customers into different types, for example, commercial local, commercial national, private local and private national. The firm does not have to be very large, but the employees working in each section have very clear responsibilities, and their success can be measured quite easily. Again the emphasis is on the team sharing responsibility and specialist skills can be developed to suit the needs of the customers. Financial motivators can reward those who increase sales such as commission, profit-sharing, and quality-related bonuses, however, care needs to be taken to ensure that the scheme is not divisive, with individual members of a team competing against each other. Non-financial motivators may include all types of job design including job enrichment, which means that employees throughout the organisation can be empowered.

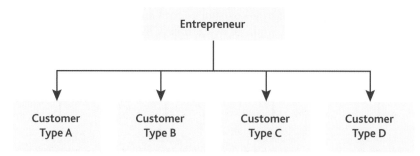

Fig. 22.6 *Organisational structure by customer type*

Does empowering employees benefit a business?

For empowerment to be effective in any business, it needs the support of the most senior staff. Secondly, the objectives of the organisation should be very clear to all employees, so they have a reference point for decision making. Neither of these prerequisites should be difficult to achieve in a small to medium-sized business.

Advantages of empowerment can be:

- It enhances motivation.
- It increases employee commitment, thereby reducing labour turnover and absenteeism.
- It increases team spirit and a goal-orientated approach to working.
- It frees the time of senior management so they can focus on more strategic decisions.

Disadvantages of empowerment can be:

- Employees may need to be trained and educated in decision making, which can take time and money.
- Processes cannot be standardised so there may be wide variations in the effectiveness of individual employees and how they respond to empowerment.
- The role of the manager becomes less clear which can lead to different motivational problems.

For empowerment to be successful within a business there needs to be a balance between the role of the individual employee and a more traditional managerial approach to running an organisation. It certainly fits into a flat organisational structure with a wide span of control, rather than a tall hierarchical structure.

Working in teams

The use of teams is common in business, and can be applied to most organisational structures. As shown in Chapter 19 – Improving organisational structures, page 138, a matrix structure supports a project team approach, which can operate very successfully in small businesses. However, there are other examples which fit into a hierarchical structure: organisation by product or by customer for example. There are also opportunities for team working within firms, based around company-wide concerns such as health and safety or the introduction of new technology. Short-term issues such as relocation to a new site, the Christmas party, fire damage or a security threat, also lend themselves to team working.

What are the benefits and drawbacks of team working?

Team working is designed to unite employees towards a common organisational goal.

Advantages include:

- A feeling of personal responsibility to one's team mates, encouraging the least effective employees to meet team and company standards.
- Higher levels of satisfaction about completing a job.
- Productivity is usually higher.
- Employees are able to learn different skills from others.
- Problem solving is easier in teams.
- Theory suggest that all these factors improve motivation and ensure that each employee is not only efficient, but an effective member of the workforce, because everyone is directly involved in the decision-making process. As a result the quantity and quality of work should increase.

However, there are disadvantages as well as benefits to this approach, which need to be considered when looking at organisational design and motivation.

Disadvantages include:

- Productivity may fall to the level of the weakest worker.
- Too many meetings and discussions on what action to take may waste time and slow down the decision-making process.
- Individual self-worth is diminished.
- Individual team contribution may be hidden, and those with real potential overlooked.
- It may cause difficulties when developing performance measures which are fair.
- Organisational flexibility may be undermined. Cohesive and high-performance teams may be unwilling to change: the success of the team becomes more important than the success of the business.

Business in action

Business Link and True North

Business Link Berkshire and Wiltshire provide advice and support to start-ups and established businesses in the Berkshire and Wiltshire area. Business Link Wiltshire and Swindon had recently acquired Business Link Berkshire and the two businesses needed to integrate efficiently. The aims were:

- to develop a more coordinated operations team
- to raise the profile and the perception of the value of the operations team within the company
- to develop the project management capabilities of the team to be better able to provide skills and resource for projects companywide.

True North, a learning and development consultancy, designed a programme of workshops to develop a better understanding of preferred working styles, team dynamics, team performance and project management techniques. This programme was implemented over multiple sessions, allowing time for the application of new ideas, the review of that application at each subsequent session and gaining commitment to specific changes by individual team members and the team as a whole.

As a result, the team has become more efficient in the way it operates and has been able to support the growth of the company without increasing head count. Morale in the team is now buoyant, with members challenging each other in a positive and constructive manner.

www.truenorthgb.com

Study tip

You will not be asked direct questions about specific motivation theories by examiners, but it is useful that you appreciate how they have been used by businesses to motivate their employees.

Theories of motivation

Motivation has been studied for many years, and there are a number of popular theorists whose work forms the basis of practical motivational techniques.

Frederick Taylor

Taylor was one of the first to look at employee motivation in a mass production setting. His theory was based on an assumption that the only motivator was money. He discovered, through observation, the most efficient way to carry out a task. Taylor believed that any pay scheme should reward those who produced the most, that is, piece rate. He also advocated the close supervision of workers.

Elton Mayo

Mayo looked at how changing physical factors such a light and heat, improved worker's performance. He found out that it wasn't the physical conditions being changed that made people work harder but instead performance increased because social interaction was important, and people worked well if they felt valued. Mayo's work led to the Human Relations School of Motivation, and is the basis for much of the motivational theory that followed.

Abraham Maslow

Maslow's 'hierarchy of needs' is probably the most famous motivation theory. He suggested that within each person there is a hierarchy of needs and the individual must satisfy each level before they move onto the next. There are five hierarchical levels. These are:

Physiological needs, Safety needs, Social needs, Esteem needs and Self actualisation (fulfilment).

Maslow suggested that to motivate an individual an employer needed to know where they believe they were within the hierarchy. Figure 22.7 shows how an organisation might use Maslow's theory.

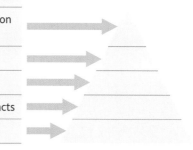

Maslow's level	What the organisation could do
Self actualisation	Allocation of more challenging and stimulating work, delegation of responsibility, training, opportunities for promotion
Esteem	Feedback via appraisal, praise, recognition of success
Social	Work social events, team working
Safety	Safe working conditions, induction training, permanent contracts
Physiological	Competitive salary

Fig. 22.7 *Application of Maslow's hierarchy of human needs*

Frederick Herzberg

Herzberg explored the question 'What do people want from their jobs?'. He found evidence to suggest that there were two types of factor affecting how people felt about work. The first type could lead to job dissatisfaction, for example, how the business was run, too much supervision, working conditions and pay: these he called **hygiene factors**. A second set of factors lead to motivation and these included a sense of achievement, recognition for work well done, the nature of the job role, and the level of responsibility: Herzberg called these **motivators**. There was some cross-over between the two sets of factors: pay, for instance, could cause dissatisfaction if it was believed to be too low, and motivation, if it increased significantly. However, Herzberg believed that the factors which motivate people are not the opposite of those which cause dissatisfaction.

 Key terms

Hygiene factors: according to Herzberg, these are factors such as pay levels and conditions of work which can lead to worker dissatisfaction, but which, even if they are adequate, will not lead to motivation.

Motivators: according to Herzberg, these are factors that can lead to motivation of workers, and include recognition, achievement and responsibility.

 Case study

Foster Yeoman and True North

Foster Yeoman, a family-owned quarrying business with over 700 employees, produces 10 million tonnes of dry-stone aggregate per year. When the company went through a period of significant change it found that several areas of the organisation needed to be improved:

Activity

Look back at the financial and non-financial methods of motivation discussed earlier in this chapter. See if you can link the theories outlined above with the practical techniques used by businesses.

■ The management team needed to be able to undertake and cope with change and use their influence to ensure that new skills were filtered through the organisation.

■ Management skills needed to be developed at lower levels of the hierarchy so that internal promotion into management roles became more realistic and the company could be confident of retaining the experience of its many long serving employees.

■ A reduction in the cost of staff turnover was needed, particularly in the first two years of employment.

The company brought in True North management consultants who analysed the needs of the company and designed and created two distinct programmes for management development:

■ A programme of empowerment for quarry managers designed to build confidence in core management skills such as delegation, time management, planning, communication, performance management, decision making and motivation.

■ A programme for senior managers and directors, which was focused on self-confidence, self-awareness, relationship-building and communication.

The results are that Foster Yeoman has significantly improved internal promotion opportunities and staff are able to deal with and promote change in the organisation. Quarry managers are confident to delegate to others who relish taking on more responsibility. They are working more effectively as a team and as team leaders. The company is more confident of retaining the existing experience, knowledge and family culture which is core to its future success. Many managers and directors have changed their attitude towards personal development and are now actively promoting its value.

www.truenorthgb.com

Show the skills

You will be expected to make some reference to motivational theories in your analysis of answers to questions such as 3 and 4 opposite. However, there will be no direct questions on the motivational theorists.

Questions

1 Explain the term empowerment, using Foster Yeoman as an illustration. (6 marks)

2 Explain why the development of managerial skills at lower levels of the organisational hierarchy might help to reduce staff turnover. (6 marks)

3 Analyse the benefits and drawbacks to Foster Yeoman of using financial methods to motivate their employees. (10 marks)

4 To what extent will changes to the attitudes and training of managers and directors at Foster Yeoman lead to improved motivation of all employees? (14 marks)

5 Research task: http://www.johnlewispartnership.co.uk/work/pay-and-benefits.html

Use this link to read about the pay and benefits offered by John Lewis to its 'partners' – the term the business uses for its employees.

☑ *In this chapter you will have learned to:*

■ discuss financial and non-financial methods of motivating employees

■ examine the links between the structure/design of the organisation and the motivational techniques used by businesses

■ evaluate the extent to which empowering employees can benefit a business

■ analyse the benefits and drawbacks of working in teams to improve the effectiveness of a workforce

■ explain the importance of motivation and motivational theories

For answers to activities and case study questions see **kerboodle**

Practice questions

Chapters 19–22

1   What do you understand by the term 'organisational structure'?   *(3 marks)*

2   List THREE features of a tall organisational structure.   *(3 marks)*

3   Explain briefly TWO benefits to a business of a flat organisational structure.   *(3 marks)*

4   Explain why a growing business might benefit from the delegation of tactical decision making.   *(4 marks)*

5   Describe the main features of the following job roles:
     a)   Supervisor
     b)   Team-leader
     c)   Manager
     d)   Director
     (8 marks)

6   Explain THREE factors that have an influence on effective organisational design.   *(6 marks)*

7   Organic Lunches was set up by two friends in Cardiff who wanted to provide good food to workers on a large industrial estate on the edge of the city. The business was very successful and a retail outlet was opened in the city centre to meet rising demand from office workers for healthier lunches.
     a)   Describe and explain an effective organisational structure for this business.   *(4 marks)*
     b)   Analyse which job roles may be key to the success of Organic Lunches.   *(8 marks)*
     c)   Evaluate the importance of good internal communications to Organic Lunches.   *(11 marks)*

8   Indicate whether each of the following statements are TRUE or FALSE. Briefly explain your decision.
     a)   Voluntary labour turnover is normally lower than involuntary labour turnover.
     b)   The Government prefers to measure UK productivity rather than output per employee.
     c)   If output per employee is falling then efficiency is increasing.
     d)   The CBI believes that high absenteeism is the reason why productivity in the UK is lower than in the USA.
     (3 marks each)

9   Explain why calculating workforce performance is important to businesses.   *(3 marks)*

10   Describe the stages in the recruitment process.   *(6 marks)*

11 Is external recruitment always necessary? Explain your answer. *(3 marks)*

12 What do you understand by the term 'assessment centre'? *(2 marks)*

13 Explain THREE factors that might affect a restaurant's method of selection. *(6 marks)*

14 To what extent can recruitment and selection improve the workforce of a soft toy manufacturing firm where labour turnover is rising and product quality is falling. *(12 marks)*

15 Briefly explain THREE financial methods of employee motivation. *(6 marks)*

16 Why might directors of a construction firm be against the introduction of non-financial methods of motivating their construction workers such as job enrichment and job enlargement. *(8 marks)*

17 To what extent does organisational design help to motivate employees? *(10 marks)*

18 Shipley Sheds design and build wooden constructions for gardens, ranging from tool sheds to summer houses. The directors have decided to introduce team working in an attempt to stop their trained carpenters leaving to work for rival business The World of Wood. They are optimistic that empowering their employees will increase motivation and have organised appropriate off-the-job training at a local college so that all members of staff will feel confident to be involved in decision making.

    a) Explain the difference between 'on-the-job' and 'off-the-job' training. *(4 marks)*

    b) Analyse the possible drawbacks of introducing team working to the business. *(8 marks)*

    c) Evaluate the extent to which empowering employees will benefit Shipley Sheds. *(10 marks)*

Introduction

Toyota is one of the world's largest and most successful car manufacturers – the effectiveness of its operational management has been a major reason for its success.

Think about what you had for breakfast this morning. Unless you live on a farm and you produced the ingredients yourself, the eggs, cereals, bread, milk and jam you may have consumed all passed through a number of different processing stages between the farmer and your table. These processing steps were probably handled by a number of different organisations. The study of operations management looks at how the goods and services that we buy and consume are produced and delivered to us as efficiently as possible using key resources of land, labour and machines.

One definition of Operations Management is 'managing the activities needed to create and deliver an organisation's goods and services'. Some people argue that this definition is too broad and they prefer this alternative:

'Operations management is about producing the right amount of a good or service, at the right time, of the right quality and at the right cost to meet customer expectations.'

Operations managers, then, are responsible for managing activities that are essential for the production of goods and services. These managers will be responsible for a wide variety of different decisions. These are some of the most important areas of an operations manager's decision-making responsibilities:

■ Which production methods to use?
■ Which new products should be developed and designed – linking closely with the marketing department?

■ Which quality standards are necessary to meet customer expectations?

■ What production capacity is needed by the business – and how best to increase it if necessary?

■ What stock levels of materials are needed to produce goods and services?

In order to take these important decisions Operations Managers will need to control and oversee:

■ Important business assets such as buildings, equipment and stock.

■ Cost levels to ensure that production is carried out efficiently whilst maintaining acceptable quality levels.

■ Human resource effectiveness to achieve productivity and quality of acceptable levels – linking closely with the Human Resources department.

This brief introduction emphasises both the importance of and the wide ranging nature of an Operations Manager's responsibilities. If one term sums up these tasks it is 'productive efficiency'. Transforming resources into quality goods and services more efficiently than rival firms is a major competitive advantage. Most industries are now dominated by the most efficient businesses in their fields. This means that they have high 'productive efficiency'. In simple terms this means reducing the cost per unit, in terms of the resources used to produce it, to the lowest possible level. Failure to match the production effectiveness of major competitors is, in most cases, likely to lead to eventual business failure.

The range of activities that make up the responsibilities of operations managers are reflected in the chapter headings for this section:

Chapter 23: Making operational decisions This chapter studies the importance of setting operational targets. Also, making sure that the business has the capacity to meet expected demand requires important operations decisions to be made. This should mean that the Operations Manager is able to match output to demand.

Chapter 24: Developing effective operations: quality This chapter sets out to define quality – and it does not always mean 'the best possible'. The importance of quality control and quality assurance is examined and the benefits of meeting quality standards are assessed.

Chapter 25: Developing effective operations: customer service This chapter explains that Operations Management is not just about the product or service being offered – it includes the way in which customers are treated at all stages of the 'buying experience'. Customer service is becoming increasingly important in competitive markets where products are often of similar design and quality levels. Making customers feel special can deliver a real 'USP'.

Chapter 26: Working with suppliers Effective operations cannot take place without reliable suppliers delivering goods and services at the right time and at the right price. This chapter examines the importance of close coordination with suppliers. This can help a business become more flexible to customer demand and more efficient in delivering quality products 'right first time'.

Chapter 27: Using technology in operations IT has had a huge impact on every aspect of business activity. This is certainly true in the area of Operations Management. This chapter examines the advances in automation, computer aided design programs, stock control programs and retail management IT applications and the effect they are having of improving flexibility and efficiency of operations – but at a cost.

Making operational decisions

Setting the scene

How could we increase efficiency?

Plasma Designs Ltd (PDL) is a relatively small manufacturer of very large plasma TV screens for executive offices and trade shows. It has a good reputation in this specialist field, but like much of UK manufacturing, is now experiencing great competition from imports. This is forcing the business to find new ways of increasing competitiveness. It has a target of introducing at least three new models each year and this helps to maintain customer interest. In fact, demand for the latest models has exceeded expectations and the company's target of meeting all orders within three months is not being met.

There are disagreements amongst the directors as to how this shortage of production capacity should be handled. One wants to see a new workshop built on a larger site which would permanently increase the number of units that could be made. Another option supported by other directors is to ask other local electronic companies to produce goods under PDL's name. Finally, the Human Resources Director prefers the option of hiring part-time staff to work an evening shift in the existing workshop.

Discussion points

1 Why is the company unable to meet its delivery target?

2 How useful is it for a business to have targets for delivery dates, quality levels and new product launches?

3 Which of the three options for expanding output do you think the company should go ahead with? You should also consider the other information that you would find useful in making your decision.

Operational targets – what are they?

Fig. 23.1 indicates the range of different activities involved in a typical operations management department:

These operational activities are interlinked. For example: a) The quality of a product should be related to its reliability. b) The design of a product will influence the cost of making it. Each of these activities will have **operational targets** set for them – and these targets need to be interlinked too.

In the case of a breakfast cereal manufacturer, some of these targets might be:

- Cost – to reduce variable costs of production by 5% annually for the next three years.

- New products – to develop and launch one new breakfast cereal range each year.

- Quality – to keep wastage caused by faulty batches of cereals to below 3% of output.

Key terms

Operational targets: these are specific and usually measurable objectives set for each operations activity of a business.

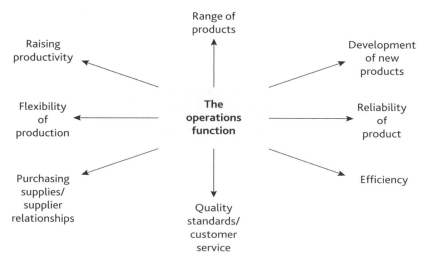

Fig. 23.1 *The operations function*

- Delivery times – to meet supermarket orders within two days of receiving the order.
- Productivity – to increase output per worker by 5% each year.
- Capacity utilisation – to maintain a high level of output compared to total capacity.

These examples of operational targets are taken from the secondary sector. However, all organisations – private sector or public sector, primary or tertiary sector – need to set operational targets that, taken together, should improve productive efficiency. Here are some examples from the primary sector:

- Dairy farm – milk yield per cow
- Forest managed for timber – number of replacement trees planted per month.

For the tertiary sector, operational targets could include:

- Insurance company – number of insurance renewals from existing customers achieved
- Credit card provider – percentage of 'cold telephone calls' converted into eventual new customers
- Hospital – number of patients on waiting lists; number of operations per week.

Why set these operational targets?

The purpose of these targets is to improve operational efficiency. The aim may be to achieve efficiency equal to the best in the industry. Unless targets are set and agreed with operations staff there is likely to be no improvement from one year to the next in the ability of the organisation to convert resources into output efficiently.

■ Capacity utilisation

All firms have a maximum **capacity** output.

Sandwich bars, hospitals, car factories – they all have a maximum number of units of output or customers they can serve in a certain period of time. Most businesses do not work at full capacity all the time. There are often real disadvantages to doing this. For example, there will be no time for repair and maintenance of equipment and the staff will have little time to discuss problems or new ideas for production improvements.

It is useful to measure the proportion of maximum capacity that is being achieved. This is called the rate of **capacity utilisation**.

For example, if a factory produced 300 units last year yet it had the capacity to produce 500, it operated at 60% of capacity.

300/500 × 100 = 60%

Apart from the limitations of always operating at 100 per cent of capacity referred to above, why would it be an advantage to a business to operate at, say, 90 per cent of capacity rather than 50 per cent of capacity? The main benefit is the greater use it makes of the company's fixed assets. This means that the fixed costs are 'spread out' over a higher level of output. It helps to reduce **unit costs** (or average costs).

Example

If total costs of production are £12,000 and output is 5,000 then unit cost is £2.40.

 Key terms

Capacity utilisation: this is the proportion that current output is of full capacity output. It is calculated by the formula:

$$\frac{\text{Current output}}{\text{Maximum output}} \times 100$$

Unit cost: is average cost per unit of output. It is calculated by the formula:

$$\text{Unit cost} = \frac{\text{Total costs}}{\text{Output}}$$

■ **Activity**

Calculate the rate of capacity utilisation in all of the following cases:

Table 23.1

Business	Current output	Maximum annual output	Capacity utilisation %
A	3,500	7,000	
B	26,000	48,000	
C	36	42	
D	550,000	600,000	

Unit cost is of great significance to the competitiveness of any business. If operations managers can reduce this cost to levels equal to or below that of the firm's main rivals and maintain an appropriate level of quality then the profitability of the business will be much higher and its future should be secure. This fact just reinforces the great importance of operational issues and operations managers to the long-term success of any organisation.

 Activity

Copy out this table. Calculate the unit cost at different levels of output:

Table 23.2

Output	Total costs (£)	Unit cost (£)
100	12,000	
200	20,000	
300	26,000	
400	30,000	
500	33,000	
600	35,000	

Other operational issues

Non-standard orders

These are orders for products that the business does not normally produce. Here are some examples:

- Morgan Cars – special colour scheme for a customer's car
- An envelope company – supply a million non-standard sized envelopes
- An insurance company – insure a new design of space satellite
- A restaurant – prepare a complex, special menu for a large group.

Management have to take two important decisions:

Do we accept the order?

This will depend on:

- Revenue gained from the order compared to the cost of producing the non-standard order
- Whether further orders are likely to be received
- The importance of the customer to the supplier
- Whether other potential customers exist for this product.

If so, how do we cope with the operational problems involved?

- Sub-contracting or outsourcing – see Table 23.3. The restaurant in the case above could outsource some parts of the menu to another catering firm
- Hire machines and temporarily employ specialists to operate them
- Job production – meeting special customer demands by producing each product as a separate item. Morgan Cars would find this easier than Ford.

Matching production to consumer demand

This is one of the biggest problems that Operations Managers have to solve. If customer demand is constant or easy to predict accurately then this problem is much reduced. For many businesses though, periods of slack demand and **excess capacity**, followed by high demand and full capacity working create special operational difficulties. Causes of demand fluctuations include seasonal demand patterns and economic factors such as growth or recession in the economy.

The production capacity of the business can be revised, over time, to match demand. In practice, the methods used to match output and demand can have limitations for the business.

Uncertainty does not just exist with customer demand. Machine breakdowns, staff absences and factory fires could all reduce a firm's production capacity to such an extent that it cannot match output to demand.

Ways of matching production with demand

These are the main methods that an organisation could use to try to ensure that output meets demand and customers are not left waiting – or assets are not left lying idle if there is excess capacity.

Activity

Explain why demand is likely to vary frequently, and sometimes unpredictably, for the following goods or services:

- Hospital accident and emergency services
- Barbecue charcoal
- Textbooks
- Luxury cars
- Restaurant meals

Key terms

Excess capacity: when a business has greater production capacity than is likely to be used in the foreseeable future.

Overtime: staff working beyond their contracted hours in exchange for a higher hourly wage.

Temporary staff: workers employed for a fixed period of time after which the employment contract may not be renewed.

Table 23.3 *Methods and their limitations of matching production with demand*

Method – and how it operates	Main limitations
Overtime: This will increase output as staff are available for more hours, using the existing resources of the business.	Staff will be paid a higher hourly wage rate and this will increase unit costs. Workers may 'slow down' production to ensure that overtime is worked.
Temporary staff: They will be employed to cope with higher demand but released when demand falls back.	Temporary staff will still need to be recruited and trained and this may be expensive. These workers may lack the loyalty and commitment of permanent staff
Part-time staff: They will be called in to work at peak periods and will not be needed – or paid – at other times. These may be permanent or temporary contracts.	If these workers have other jobs too, they may not have the loyalty or commitment of full time staff.
Sub-contracting: A supplier will provide all or some of the goods or service that the contracting business produces. This may be for a temporary period only. If the business is a specialist it may provide permanent services that the contracting firm cannot provide itself. Also known as out-sourcing.	This may be more expensive than producing the goods or services 'in-house' as the sub-contractor will add on a profit margin to the cost of the work. Quality assurance becomes more difficult as the sub-contractor will have to agree to meet the same quality standards as the contracting business.
Managing stocks efficiently: Stocks can act as a 'buffer' between production and customer demand. Stocks of both materials and finished goods may be held.	Stock holding is expensive and carries an opportunity cost. Goods can become out of date or may be perishable. Services cannot be stored – they must be produced when the customer is present. Waiting lists and customer queues are a form of 'buffer' for providing services.
Rationalisation: All of the other methods assume that demand exceeds production – rationalisation is often concerned with cutting back on production capacity to match lower demand levels. This is likely to reduce both fixed and variable production costs.	If staff are made redundant then this may reduce job security and motivation of staff remaining. If capacity is cut permanently then if demand increases in the future, capacity shortages will again occur. Cutting costs may mean redesigning peoples' jobs and this can cause uncertainty amongst the staff.

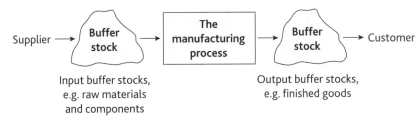

Supplier → **Buffer stock** → **The manufacturing process** → **Buffer stock** → Customer

Input buffer stocks, e.g. raw materials and components

Output buffer stocks, e.g. finished goods

Fig. 23.2 *Holding stocks helps to match output to production*

 Case study

Can we match Swatch?

The last UK based manufacturer of watches, Trutime, was heading towards closure. All of the other UK watchmakers of any size have already been swamped by cheap but often high quality products from Far Eastern makers. But Trutime's Chief Executive, Amir Khan, was determined to have one last go at matching the productive efficiency of the best in the industry.

 Key terms

Part-time staff: workers employed on a less than full weekly hours contract, e.g. 15 hours per week.

Sub-contracting: using a supplier to manufacture part or all of a firm's product or service.

Stocks: materials or finished goods held by a firm as needed to supply customers demand.

Rationalisation: reorganising resources to cut costs – often leading to a cut back in capacity.

Fig. 23.3 *Holding stocks of unsold cars is an expensive way of trying to match supply with changing customer demand.*

Link

If the mismatch of production and customer demand remains a problem in the long term then the business will need to think carefully about its scale of production. For more information, see *AQA Business Studies for A2*.

Show the skills

Be prepared to evaluate 'full capacity working'. It seems to be of great benefit to a business if it is operating at full capacity – it suggests, for example, that demand for its product is high. However, some customers may not be prepared to wait for delivery, workers might have an increased workload, and there is no 'margin for error or breakdown' with machinery. Matching output to demand in an efficient way is one of the great operations management challenges.

'If we use Swatch as an example, we might be able to rescue our business,' he told a recent Board meeting. 'Since the 1980s this company has been able to double the market share of Swiss watches by taking fantastic operational decisions.'

He then listed some of these:

- Plastic cased watch with hundreds of different designs
- Quartz mechanism built directly into the watch using half the components of other watches
- Fully automated manufacture – unit costs are competitive with Asian watches even though Swiss wages are up to 50 times greater
- Variable labour cost has been kept below Swatch's target of 7% of total unit production cost.

'I estimate the unit cost of a typical Swatch to be £5. In contrast, last year we produced 350,000 watches at a total cost of £2.8million at a capacity utilisation of 55 per cent. Low cost, high quality in terms of reliability and time keeping and constantly changing fashionable designs – that must be the way forward for us,' he concluded.

As if to confirm Amir's views, the business news that day carried a story that the demand for Swiss watches exceeded production. Swatch is considering plans to avoid this mismatch between production and customer demand. Should they sub-contract to Asian manufacturers with spare capacity or employ temporary staff to increase production?

Questions

1. Explain what is meant by the term 'productive efficiency'. (3 marks)
2. Calculate Trutime's unit cost of production last year. (3 marks)
3. Explain ONE benefit to the business, with a simple numerical example, of operating at a higher rate of capacity utilisation. (4 marks)
4. Outline TWO operational targets that Trutime might set if it started production of a watch to compete with Swatch. (8 marks)
5. Evaluate TWO of the ways in which a watch manufacturer such as Swatch might deal with a period of demand exceeding production capacity. (14 marks)
6. Research task: Find out how BMW is coping with the high demand for the MINI and its variants.

In this chapter you will have learned to:

- appreciate the huge scope of operational issues
- understand what operational targets are and why they are set
- calculate capacity utilisation and unit costs
- evaluate different ways a business might be able to match production to demand.

For answers to activities and case study questions see **kerboodle**

24 Developing effective operations: quality

In this chapter you will learn to:

- explain the concept of quality
- understand the difference between quality control and quality assurance
- explain the importance of businesses establishing quality assurance systems
- assess the costs and benefits of managing quality
- explain how managing quality effectively can improve the competitiveness of businesses.

Key terms

Quality product: a product or service that meets customers' expectations and is therefore 'fit for purpose'.

Quality standards: the expectations of customers expressed in terms of the minimum acceptable production or service standards.

Fig. 24.1 *Rolls Royce aircraft engine. Customer expectations of quality lead to these being constructed to the highest possible standards*

Setting the scene

Swift Shoes

The Operations Manager at Swift Shoes was proud of the quality standards his business achieved. 'Our sports shoes sell for a retail price of £25 so they are not the best or most stylish on the market. However, only four customers returned shoes because of serious problems over the last year when we sold 50,000 pairs. We always inspect a sample of finished shoes before they are despatched to shops. Of course there are better shoes available, but our customers know what they are getting.'

The Customer Service manager at Exclusive Footwear was about to return a pair of 'hand made leather fashion shoes' to Ital Fashion Shoe producers. 'We retail these for £400 a pair and customers paying such high prices expect, reasonably in my view, a near perfect product. Even the smallest scratch or imperfection means the customers reject them. Even though Ital check every shoe made at each stage of production a few very minor blemishes are sometimes missed.'

Discussion points

1. The consumers of these different types of shoes seem to have different requirements. Why is this the case, do you think?

2. Using just this case study, how would you attempt to explain what 'quality' means?

3. Briefly explain how the two different methods used for achieving quality seem to operate.

What is meant by 'quality'?

A **quality product** does not necessarily have to be the 'best possible'.

As the case study above showed, these consumer expectations will be very different for goods and services sold at different prices. So, we have to make clear from the outset that a quality product does not have to be made with the highest quality materials to the most exacting standards – but it must meet consumer requirements for it.

In certain cases, a product must meet the highest **quality standards** and the high cost of it becomes almost insignificant. Internal parts for a jet engine used on a passenger plane will be expected to have a failure rate of less than 1 in 1 million. However, if fashion clothing was made to the same exacting standards with regards to stitching, buttons, zips and so on – how much would a pair of jeans cost then?! Designing too much quality into a product that consumers do not expect to last for many years can make the product very expensive and uncompetitive.

A quality product does not have to be expensive. If low cost light bulbs and clothes pegs last for several years in normal use then they have still met consumer expectations and have been of the required quality.

■ Activity

Why might a restaurant that buys in the best food ingredients still fail to meet its customers' expectations of quality?

Study tip

Quality is often viewed by students as an absolute concept and not a relative one. Quality must be explained in reference to the expectations of the target market consumers. The level of quality selected by any business must be based on the resources available to it, the needs of the target market and the quality standards of competitors.

■ Key terms

Quality control: this is based on inspection of the product or a sample of products.

Quality assurance: this is a system of agreeing and meeting quality standards at each stage of production to ensure consumer satisfaction.

■ **Business in action**

Achieving quality

Pre-determined quality standards are set and checked on at each stage of the assembly of Nissan cars at the company's Sunderland factory.

First Direct operates its telephone banking system by setting limits on waiting times for calls to be answered, average time taken to fulfil every customer request and assurance standards to monitor that customer requests have been acted on correctly.

So a highly price good may still be of low quality if it fails to come up to consumer requirements. A cheap product can be considered of good quality if it performs as expected. It should now be clear that quality is a relative concept and not an absolute one – it depends on the product's price and the expectations of consumers.

How can consumer 'expectations' or 'requirements' be established by a business? The most common methods would be using market research and by analysing results of consumer feedback data. This research can establish the quality standards that customers expect.

It is easy to think of quality standards in terms of manufactured goods – the reliability of cars or the wear rate of clothes, for example. However, quality is a crucial issue for *service providers* too. For example, the quality of service offered by UK banks is claimed to be inferior to those in other countries in terms of:

- Speed taken to answer the telephone.
- No indication of waiting time on the telephone.
- Queuing time in branches.
- Contact with the same person on each occasion.
- Number of accounts errors made.
- Quality of financial advice given.

■ What are the differences between quality control and quality assurance?

These two terms are used to classify two very different approaches to managing and achieving quality in any business.

Quality control is based on inspection or checking, usually of the completed product or of the service as it is being provided to a consumer.

For example:

An iPod player being tested at the end of the production line for battery charging capability.

A telephone banking adviser having a call to a customer listened to and recorded.

Quality assurance is based on setting agreed quality standards at ALL stages in the production of a product or service in order to ensure that customers' satisfaction is achieved. It does not just focus on the finished product. This approach often involves self-checking by workers of their own output against these agreed quality standards. The key differences between the two methods are that quality assurance:

- Puts much more emphasis on prevention of poor quality rather than inspecting for poor quality products – 'getting it right first time'.
- Stresses the need for workers to get it right first time and reduces the chances of faulty products occurring or expensive reworking of faulty goods.
- Establishes quality standards and targets for each stage of the production process – for both goods and services.
- Ensures components, materials and services bought into the business are checked at the point of arrival or delivery – not at the end of the production process by which stage much time and many resources may have been wasted.

Quality assurance has the following claimed advantages over quality control systems based on final inspection:

- It makes everyone responsible for quality. This can be a form of job enrichment.
- Self-checking and making efforts to improve quality increases motivation.
- The system can be used to 'trace back' quality problems to the stage of the production process where a problem might have been occurring.
- It reduces the need for expensive final inspection and correction or reworking of faulty products.

Why is it important for businesses to establish quality assurance systems?

There are several reasons for this:

- To involve all staff and this can promote teamwork and a sense of belonging which aids motivation.
- To set quality standards for all stages of production so that all materials and all production phases are checked before it is 'too late' and the whole product has been completed.
- To reduce costs of final inspection as this should become less necessary as all stages and sub-sections of the process have been judged against quality standards.
- To reduce total quality costs. By instilling in the whole organisation a culture of quality, it is possible for quality assurance to lead to reduced costs of wastage and faulty products.
- To gain accreditation for quality awards. These can give a business real status or kudos. The most widely recognised quality award within the European Union is **ISO 9000**.

ISO 9000

This award is given to firms that can demonstrate that they have a quality assurance system in place which allows for quality to be regularly measured and for corrective action to be taken if quality falls below these levels. This award does not prove that every product produced or service provided by the business is of good quality. It is an indication that a business has a system of quality in place that has relevant targets set and activities ready to deal with a quality problem.

To achieve ISO 9000 a business must have:

- clear and appropriate quality targets
- a system in place to assure that targets are being met
- a measuring system to record actual results and resources available to correct the problem should one arise.

Total Quality Management

This approach to quality requires the involvement of all employees in an organisation. It is based on the principle that **everyone** within a business has a contribution to make to the overall quality of the finished product or service.

Total Quality Management (TQM) often involves a significant change in the culture of an organisation. Employees can no longer think that quality is someone else's responsibility – instead, the search for quality

Fig. 24.2 *Quality is important in service industries too – failure to meet customer expectations for speed of phone answering and clarity of information given will reduce a firm's competitiveness*

Link

For more information on job enrichment and human resources, see Chapter 22 – Developing and retaining an effective workforce: motivating employees, page 160.

Study tip

Quality is not just an issue for large businesses. Small and medium-sized firms also need to give consideration to this vital operations management area. They must ensure that the quality level selected and the quality assurance methods used are within their resources. In fact, by using quality assurance with the emphasis on reducing wasted faulty products and on staff self-checking quality levels, these businesses can save money in the long term.

Key terms

ISO 9000: an internationally recognised certificate that acknowledges the existence of a quality procedure that meets certain conditions.

Total Quality Management (TQM): an approach to quality that aims to involve all employees in the quality improvement process.

■ **Key terms**

Internal customers: people within the organisation who depend upon the quality of work being done by others.

must affect the attitudes and actions of every employee. When adopting this concept, every worker should think about the quality of the work they are performing because another employee is, in effect, their **internal customer**. Consider these examples:

■ A truck driver who drops off supplies to retailers is the internal customer of the team loading the vehicle – goods must be handled carefully and loaded in the right order. The truck driver has to face the retailer if goods are damaged or the wrong ones delivered.

■ A computer assembly team is the internal customer of the teams producing the individual components – a fault with any of these means the assembled computer will not meet quality standards.

The TQM concept has revolutionised the way all workers are asked to consider quality. To be effective the concept must be fully explained and training given to all staff in its scope and the techniques used to put it into effect.

Study tip

ISO 9000 is not a guarantee of good quality.

Fig. 24.3 *Jaguar use quality assurance systems and they now have one of the highest USA customer satisfaction ratings of any car maker*

■ What are the costs and benefits of introducing and managing quality systems?

All quality checks and quality assurance systems involve incurring costs. In a business that is effectively managed these costs will be covered by the expected revenue gains from producing products of the expected quality. In addition, other costs may be reduced, such as wastage costs and promotion costs to overcome a poor quality image.

■ How can the competitiveness of a business be improved by managing quality effectively?

1 Most markets are now more open to competition than ever before. Globalisation has increased this trend and so has consumer access to the internet. Lowering prices is not the only method of increasing competitiveness and, indeed, it may not be the wisest way, if a

Table 24.1 *The costs and benefits of quality systems*

The potential costs of quality systems	The potential benefits of quality systems
Market research to establish expected customer requirements.	Consumer satisfaction and repeat custom as there is nothing like a good experience with the quality of a product to encourage consumers to buy more – and to tell their friends about it!
Staff training costs to ensure that standards are understood and the operations needed to check them can be undertaken. This will be especially important with TQM.	Good publicity, e.g. from consumer pressure groups and consumer oriented articles in the media.
Material costs – rejecting below standard materials and components before they are used in the production process. This will almost certainly lead to higher expectations from suppliers.	Reputation for quality encourages retailers to stock the firm's products so this will increase the distribution outlets for a product.
Equipment costs for checking standards at each stage, e.g. laser measuring machines for accuracy of panel fit on a vehicle.	Easier to establish new products in the market as consumers will associate the business's good reputation with the new product.
Inspection and checking costs.	Allows the brand to be built around a quality image and branding is an important form of non-price differentiation for businesses.
Reworking of faulty products or rejection wastage costs – the aim of quality assurance is to reduce these to an absolute minimum – 'right first time'.	It may allow a price premium to be charged over other similar products in that market segment. Quality can be used as a 'USP' or unique selling point. This would be a clear demonstration that 'quality pays' as the extra revenue gained should cover the quality costs explained above.
Stopping production to trace and correct quality problems will disrupt output.	

business is unable to reduce its costs at the same rate. Achieving consistent quality is often a more effective method of competing in both domestic and international markets.

2 Consistent high quality can lead to such a well known brand image that higher prices can be justified for this USP.

3 As consumer incomes rise with world economic growth the average consumer buying decision will become more influenced by quality and fitness for purpose. Excess capacity exists in most of the world's manufacturing industries. It is increasingly vital for businesses to differentiate themselves with a quality brand image and, remember, this does not mean 'quality at any price' but regularly and consistently meeting consumers (rising) expectations. Cost factors involved in improving quality must always be weighed up against the expected gains in competitiveness.

Study tip

The costs of quality are often obvious yet the benefits can be long-term and difficult to measure or quantify. This does not mean that they do not exist – in fact long-term survival in competitive markets can be based upon a good quality image.

■ Case study

Quality assurance in practice

The Croydon branch of FatBoyTrims had come bottom of all of the company's branches for customer satisfaction. The number of complaints received at Head Office about this branch and the quality of its haircutting and styling services had been much greater than for any other location. Revenue had fallen in recent months and the number of repeat customers had fallen to 15 per cent of total custom. A competing business nearby, that charged at least 30 per cent more, was always full. As a consequence, this FatBoyTrims branch had spent more on advertising for new business than any other. The revenue per customer was also low as high value services – such as colouring and tinting – were avoided by customers. A new manager had just been appointed to the branch and she immediately set about establishing quality targets for each stage of the 'customer experience'. These included:

maximum time for phone to ring

maximum waiting time for appointment time

maximum times between hairwash and cutting begins

all customers to be offered refreshments

minimum time spent by stylists with each customer

feedback forms to be filled in by 20% of clients and stylists responsible for each client to discuss answers with client.

Each member of staff was given responsibility for at least one of these targets. A record had to be kept of the branch's success at meeting these targets. At first, branch costs increased as an additional staff member had to be recruited to help meet the quality standards. After two months, the number of repeat clients had reached 36 per cent and the branch reduced its advertising expenditure. After four months, revenue had climbed by 38 per cent and the branch had reached third place in the company league table for customer satisfaction. The competing business had reduced many of its prices by 15 per cent.

Show the skills

It is important to be able to evaluate the issue of quality. A 'quality product or service' does not guarantee a successful business if the cost of producing the product is greater than the price customers are willing to pay. The standards of quality set by a business must be in keeping with the expectations of customers.

Questions

1. What do you understand by the terms:

   a quality

   b quality assurance?   (4 marks)

2. Outline TWO drawbacks to this business of not meeting customer expectations.   (4 marks)

3. Analyse the benefits to this service business of improving quality. (6 marks)

4. Do you think the manager was right to introduce the changes she did? Assess the costs and benefits of introducing and managing a quality system in your answer.   (14 marks)

5. Research task: Access the web pages of any TWO UK supermarkets. Discover as much as you can about the approaches to quality of these two businesses. Write a brief report explaining why quality is so important in this industry and how firms try to achieve it.

☑ *In this chapter you will have learned to:*

- explain what quality means and the significance of establishing what customer expectations are

- differentiate between quality control and quality assurance

- analyse the importance of quality to successful businesses

- evaluate the costs of quality control and assurance systems against the benefits to be gained from high quality.

For answers to activities and case study questions see

Developing effective operations: customer service

Fig. 25.1 *Demand for glass conservatories and house extensions has increased significantly in recent years*

Setting the scene

Customer complaints at BriteGlass

BriteGlass was set up in Reigate seven years ago. The business designs and builds glass conservatories and house extensions. Customer demand has increased significantly in recent years. This is due to increasing incomes and rising house prices. People can afford to spend more on their houses and can justify the cost of extensions with a higher selling price.

The business has struggled to cope in recent months. The owner, Bill Smart, has given big incentives to sales staff to get more orders and he has kept prices very competitive. However, the capacity of the firm to meet orders has not increased sufficiently and more errors in design and construction are being reported. One letter of complaint is typical: 'Not only did your workmen not turn up when promised, when they did finally arrive most of the glass sections were the wrong size. Now it is completed, the roof leaks and the tiles on the floor are cracked. I have tried to contact you on the telephone and through your website but have received no reply. I will not pay the final payment unless these errors are rectified'.

Bill took some time to reply as he was busy signing up new customer orders. He offered a 20% price reduction to the customer who complained. He was taken aback when they refused his offer saying 'I am prepared to pay a reasonable price for a good job – you need to do a good job first. You have failed to deliver on all of your so-called quality standards'.

Discussion points

1. List as many examples as you can of what you consider to be poor customer service in this case.

2. Should Bill have been surprised that the customer refused the offer of a discount and demanded the job be completed to a high standard instead?

3. What quality standards of customer service do you think Bill might have originally promised?

4. What do you think will be the future problems for BriteGlass if it does not improve its customer service?

Key terms

Customer service: the provision of service to customers before, during and after purchase to the standard that meets customer expectations.

Customer service – what does it mean?

In a world of competitive markets the idea of offering customers services that meet – and possibly exceed their expectations – is becoming increasingly important. The significance of **customer service** and the levels of it expected by customers will vary by product, industry and customer. For example, an expert customer of IT equipment may need less pre-sales advice than a 'novice'. In the case of a customer purchasing a computer for the first time in a specialist IT retailer, these are the likely expectations of the level of service needed:

- ■ Pre-sales service: Advice on the range of options available, the advantages and disadvantages of different models and brands, explanation of key terms.
- ■ Service at time of purchase: Final assessment that product meets customers expectations, explanation of different purchasing methods, ensuring customer is aware of operation of computer and how to set it up.
- ■ After-sales service: Help line or web service to answer important queries about set up or operation; advice on future upgrades, repair and maintenance.

Offering good customer service is an essential part of the modern concept of 'customer relationship marketing' (CRM) which focuses attention on the importance and profit gains to be made from **keeping** existing customers rather than spending money on attracting **new** customers.

■ Methods of meeting customer expectations

Market research

The most important first step in meeting customer expectations is to find out what customers expect! Unless a business understands customer needs and expectations then it can never hope to fulfil them. This means communication with customers or potential customers and analysis of results to questions such as: 'How quickly do you expect to be served?' and 'What would make you most want to buy from our business again?'

Put customer service as number one priority

Another starting point for achieving good customer service is making it a major business priority. The following research findings make an interesting comparison between the replies from hundreds of management questionnaires in the UK and France:

Table 25.1 *Which of the following is the most important to your company?*

	UK	France
Customer service	46%	22%
Profit	12%	16%
Social responsibility	9%	13%
Environment	10%	7%
Market share	4%	8%
Reputation	12%	20%
Shareholders	3%	5%
Other	4%	9%

Training

This is crucial because no matter how good the market research and no matter how effective quality assurance is, unless staff know what is expected of them, one day they will let the business down with poor customer service. Staff need to know what good customer service means in their industry and what the firm's customer service standards are.

Study tip

Do not confuse 'customer service' with low discounted prices. Many firms that offer rock bottom prices can only do so by offering poor service.

Activity

Think about the levels of customer service expected by customers in the following situations:

1. Buying a holiday
   a from a travel agent, and
   b over the internet.
2. Buying a few groceries at a discount supermarket.
3. A disabled person wanting to deposit money into a bank.
4. A qualified IT engineer purchasing a new mobile phone.

Every member of staff who comes into contact with customers needs enough information and delegated power to make small, customer pleasing decisions without always having to say 'I am not sure so I will have to check with . . .'

Use of quality assurance and quality control

The distinction between these concepts has already been covered in Chapter 24. The maintenance of quality standards throughout the production process (for both goods and services) is an important feature of achieving satisfied customers. The key purpose of quality assurance – 'getting it right first time with zero defects' – should be reflected in the quality standards that a business sets for customer service.

Quality standards

Customers need to know what to expect from the organisation they are purchasing a product from. This allows them to:

- make comparisons between quality standards of competing businesses
- make complaints when the publicised quality standards have not been met.

The quality standards set by Fine Games are typical. The consumer knows what to expect and can compare this service level with that offered by rival businesses. You could walk into most high street stores and either see similar 'promises of quality' or ask to see the shop's customer charter. Another key benefit from clearly stating these quality standards is that staff know precisely what is expected of them and what failings will make customers complain.

🗁 Monitoring and improving customer service

Monitoring customer service

These are some of the most used methods of communicating with customers to monitor customer service:

Satisfaction level surveys

These provide detailed feedback which can be stored on a database and analysed for a number of uses. For example, First Choice holidays gather data from as many returning holiday makers as possible. These results are quickly analysed and results sent back to hotel owners and tour representatives so that feedback may be acted on.

CUSTOMER SATISFACTION SURVEY

The ACME Department Store Group is committed to customer satisfaction and would like to know how well we're doing. Your answers will help us to identify areas needing improvement. If you have questions about this survey, please contact Jayne Wyman (038562189). Thank you for your time and comments.

Which store did you visit?

	Strongly agree	Agree	Neutral	Disagree	Strongly disagree
	O	O	O	O	O
Store hours are convenient for my shopping needs	O	O	O	O	O
Store atmosphere and decor are appealing	O	O	O	O	O
A good selection of products was present	O	O	O	O	O
Store has the most knowledgeable staff in the area	O	O	O	O	O
Merchandise sold is of the highest quality	O	O	O	O	O
The merchandise sold is good value for the money	O	O	O	O	O
Staff are friendly and helpful	O	O	O	O	O
Any complaints I had were dealt with efficiently	O	O	O	O	O

Please indicate your level of agreement or disagreement with each of these statements regarding the store you visited

Overall, how satisfied or dissatisfied are you with the level of customer service you received today?

O Very satisfied
O Satisfied
O Neither satisfied nor dissatisfied
O Dissatisfied
O Very dissatisfied

How satisfied or dissatisfied are you with the *quality* of the merchandise?

O Very satisfied
O Satisfied
O Neither satisfied nor dissatisfied
O Dissatisfied
O Very dissatisfied

Please tell use something we could do to improve our customer service

....

....

Thank you for completing this survey!

Fig. 25.2 *A typical customer satisfaction survey form used by a chain of department stores*

Focus groups

These provide useful insights into customers' views and experiences. Each member of the group hears the reactions of the rest of the group and this can lead to more detailed research findings than a simple survey. The web can now be used to host focus groups where customers join an open forum to discuss views. First Direct bank has extended this concept. They sent out 30,000 emails, received over 1,000 replies and subsequently interviewed and filmed 14 respondents. These customer comments then formed part of the bank's advertisements.

Tracking surveys

These are customer satisfaction surveys that are carried out over time with the same customers/groups of customers to see how the company's performance is changing. Tracking surveys can also be undertaken with different groups of customers, for example, in different regions of the country, to see if they experience different levels of customer service – and why.

Encouraging instant feedback, e.g. by the use of IT

As well as making available a wide range of customer service tools, such as support websites, technology has also created new communication channels to allow customer feedback.

Business in action

Blogging customer feedback

Ewan MacLeod was angry. He had been charged for sending an email from a mobile phone via a package that claimed to offer free, unlimited data usage. He wrote about his experiences on his blog. He was surprised to receive a call from the mobile phone company, 3, inviting him to meet chief finance officer, Frank Sixt. Apparently, someone had posted his comments on the company's blog, set to promote the free service!

'Any big business is a faceless wonder, but a blog gives you the power to let the company and others know how you feel,' said Mr MacLeod. 'I had a call saying Frank would like to meet me. I was proved correct and was refunded. I was entirely satisfied with the result.' The company then invited Mr MacLeod to post another blog, a positive one this time, on the company's website.

The 'Business in Action' above highlights both the tremendous power of IT in providing companies with feedback and also the problems firms have in monitoring the huge amount of feedback being published about them. Blogs, forums, wikis, and even homemade TV clips posted on websites such as YouTube have given everyone the power to publish reports of bad – or good – customer service. National Express, the UK coach company, invites passengers to send text messages of their feedback while riding on the bus! Firms need to respond rapidly and positively to what is being said about them.

Improving customer service

What can any business do – large or small – to improve its levels of customer service? The UK-based Institute of Customer Service (ICS) undertakes regular surveys of large representative samples of UK adult consumers. ICS research found that the top 10 priorities for customer service are:

1 Overall quality of the product or service
2 Being treated as a valued customer
3 Speed of service
4 Friendliness of staff
5 Efficient handling of complaints

Activities

1 Dell, the computer manufacturer, was criticised when it was accused of closing its customer support forums in an attempt to silence negative feedback. How would you advise a business to use new technologies to its advantage when attempting to improve customer service?

2 Some expensive restaurants can charge £50 for a three course meal. The actual food ingredients might only cost £5. Discuss the significance of the priorities indentified by the ICS for such a restaurant. How might the restaurant owner try to make sure that these customer expectations are met?

Activity

Using the list of priorities from the ICS to help you, discuss how the level of customer service in a large department store could be improved.

6 Accurate information provided in response to enquiries

7 Competence of staff

8 Ease of doing business

9 Being kept informed

10 Helpfulness of staff.

Some business consultants believe that there is a basic set of rules for improving customer service:

1 Answer the telephone quickly – going through a series of recorded keypad instructions loses customers.

2 Don't make promises that are unlikely to be kept – not delivering goods when customers have arranged to stay at home is guaranteed to cause offence.

3 Listen to customers – feedback can always be used to improve services for others.

4 Deal with complaints efficiently – perhaps these should be handled by more senior staff.

5 Be helpful even if there is no immediate profit to be made – should a regular customer be charged for a five minute adjustment job on a car's wiper blades?

6 Recruit staff with the right attitude and train staff in customer service.

7 Go the 'extra mile' – if a customer cannot find an item in a large store do not direct them to the correct aisle but take them there and see if he/she has any further requests.

8 Add in something extra – perhaps an expensive dress could be lengthened, if required, free of charge?

The benefits of high levels of customer service

- Better customer service than competitors can give a competitive advantage and lead to higher profits.

- Good customer service may help to clearly differentiate the business from the other firms in the market.

- Slashed prices and special promotions may bring in NEW customers once but unless some of these customers return because of the service they were offered, then the business is unlikely to be profitable for long.

- Good customer service is all about sending customers away happy – as this will bring them back. Happy customers will pass on positive feedback about the business to others who may then try the product for themselves.

- A good customer service reputation can become a unique selling proposition which might allow the business to successfully justify higher than average prices.

Business in action

Pan Book Shop

This is one of the few remaining independent book shops. The market has become increasingly dominated by price discounting internet stores, large book shop chains such as Waterstones and even supermarkets such as Tesco. Even though books are sold for their full cover price, Pan Books survives and thrives because of the personal service it offers. The owner, Robert Topping puts this down to four main factors:

- Wide range of books

- Getting in new titles quickly in response to customer feedback

- Knowledgeable staff with an enthusiasm for books

- Customer friendly ambience and long opening hours to suit them

- Regular special author signings and other events.

www.thepanbookshop.blogspot.com

Business in action

Ritz Carlton Hotels

This international chain of hotels consistently scores one of the industry's highest guest satisfaction ratings – 92 per cent compared to an industry average of 75 per cent. The benefits are obvious. The chain also enjoys one of the highest levels of room occupancy and profitability in the industry.

Customer service and profits are linked. How can this level of customer service be consistently achieved across 50 international hotels with 19,000 employees? The Director of Training has four simple answers:

1 Recruit the right people. The interview process includes a couple of existing employees so they can judge if the new applicant will be a good team member.

2 Each staff member carries a card with 20 rules of customer service and the mantra 'we are ladies and gentlemen serving ladies and gentlemen'.

3 300 hours of structured formal training for new recruits.

4 Daily team briefings to discuss issues of improving customer service.

Case study

Pret a Manger – a cut above the rest?

Companies do not give good customer service, people do. If this view is actually true then Pret a Manger, the sandwich and coffee store, do their best to put it into practice. One shop manager, Anson Read summed up his approach: 'At the end of the day all we do is sell sandwiches. What really matters is the service. People can see through promotional hype – they judge us by what we do.' The firm operates a 'mystery shopper' scheme. An anonymous and impartial third party shopper descends on a shop to test customer service. They check to see if the customer charter is actually carried out in practice:

■ Are customers greeted in a friendly way?

■ Is there a good range of sandwiches available and are they all 'picture perfect'?

■ Is coffee served of the correct strength and volume?

■ Is each customer served within 60 seconds of giving their order?

If the shop scores well in a mystery shopper report then all the staff receive a £30 bonus. The culture of frequent and objective feedback is very strong. Customers are encouraged to fill in report cards and shops are regularly audited for health and safety, food hygiene and food quality. Some customers report that they become so well known to staff members that coffees are made for them as they arrive without asking and first names are used. Staff work as a close knit team. Staff turnover in this industry averages an astonishing 270% per year but at Pret a Manger it is one third of that. People want to work for a business that receives good customer feedback. Ewan Stickley, the Head of Training, recalls that the best thing he heard a customer say was 'I like coming to Pret because I get served by human beings.'

Compare that with your local fast-food joint!

Fig. 25.3 *Pret a Manger: effective staff selection, training and clear customer service standards have contributed to the success of this business*

www.pret.com

Questions

1 What do you understand by the term 'customer service'?   (4 marks)

2 Outline FOUR service expectations that a typical customer at Pret a Manger would have.   (8 marks)

3 Analyse TWO of the long-term benefits to Pret a Manger of developing a good reputation for customer service.   (10 marks)

4 To what extent do you agree with the statement that 'companies do not give good customer service, people do'?   (14 marks)

5 Research task: Look up the Institute of Customer Service website (www.ukcsi.com) and find out how they gather information for companies on levels of customer service.

Show the skills

Some businesses devote many resources to attempting to improve customer service. Setting standards of service, training and retraining employees, providing opportunities for customer feedback – all of these take time and money. These efforts can be evaluated in terms of customer loyalty. If customer loyalty improves because of good customer service, this will save the business money in *the long term*. It is always cheaper to retain existing customers than to attract new ones.

In this chapter you will have learned to:

- understand the concept of customer service – meeting customers' expectations

- analyse the different methods of meeting customer expectations in different business situations

- explain how customer service can be monitored and improved

- evaluate the benefits of high levels of customer service in a range of different industry settings

For answers to activities and case study questions see **kerboodle**

Practice questions

Chapters 23–25

1 What do you understand by the term 'Operations management'? *(3 marks)*

2 List THREE operational targets that a business manufacturing personal computers might establish. *(3 marks)*

3 Explain briefly the benefits to a business of setting operational targets. *(3 marks)*

4 Explain why a bank branch with four cashiers might not plan to operate its service at full capacity all day and every day. *(4 marks)*

5 Explain how unit costs are calculated. *(2 marks)*

6 Write out this table and fill in the missing data: *(3 marks)*

	Current output	Maximum capacity	Rate of capacity utilisation	Total costs at current output (£)	Unit cost at current output	Total costs at maximum capacity	Unit cost at maximum capacity
Firm A	100	200		1,000		1,500	
Firm B	5,000	6,000		150,000		160,000	
Firm C	880	980		4,400		4,704	

7 'Food Direct' specialise in packaging and supplying food hampers containing expensive foods and wines. The demand is very seasonal. Many retailers order these in the summer as consumers buy them as ready made picnics. October to December is also very busy due to the demand for Christmas hampers.

    a) Explain TWO operations problems this seasonal demand pattern causes for Food Direct. *(4 marks)*

    b) Explain why it is important to this business to attempt to match output to order levels. *(6 marks)*

    c) Evaluate TWO ways in which Food Direct could try to match output to seasonal demand patterns. *(8 marks)*

8 Indicate each statement as TRUE or FALSE. Briefly explain your decision. *(3 marks each)*

    a) An expensive product is always of higher quality than a cheaper one.

    b) Insisting on higher quality standards always costs a business more.

    c) ISO 9000 ensures products are of a high quality.

    d) Quality assurance systems can result in lower total costs for a business.

9 Explain why improving quality is important in an increasingly competitive market. *(3 marks)*

10 Differentiate clearly between quality control and quality assurance. Use the example of a small manufacturer of fashion clothing to illustrate your answer. *(6 marks)*

11 Is 'quality' a relative or an absolute concept? Explain your answer. *(3 marks)*

12 What do you understand by the term 'customer service'? *(2 marks)*

13 Explain THREE ways in which a small car repair garage could monitor its customer service. *(6 marks)*

14 Explain why it might be cheaper for a restaurant business to increase its loyalty levels amongst existing customers than to attempt to gain new customers. *(4 marks)*

15 Analyse TWO ways in which a hairdressing salon could try to improve the levels of customer service it offers. *(4 marks)*

16 Why is market research important before establishing the customer service levels for a new fast food take-away café? *(4 marks)*

17 Analyse TWO long term advantages to the café in Q16 of establishing and maintaining very high levels of customer service. *(6 marks)*

18 Bill Ahmed has just bought out a small regional car hire business called 'Kool Kars'. He did not realise until he started talking to customers that the reputation of the business was so poor. Even though car hire charges were the lowest in the area, only 20 per cent of customers returned to hire cars for a second or further occasion. This compares to big national firms who claim 85 per cent customer loyalty. Bill found out that staff had received no training in dealing with customers politely and over 35 per cent of car hire bills were inaccurate too. Kool Kars vehicles had an average age of two years – 18 months older than bigger firms.

    a) Explain TWO ways in which Bill could monitor customer service in future. *(4 marks)*

    b) Analyse TWO ways in which he could try to improve customer service. *(6 marks)*

    c) Evaluate the importance of improving customer service compared to keeping low prices for this car hire business. *(10 marks)*

26 Working with suppliers

Setting the scene

Cheapest not best for Design Light Co.

'I used Yellow Pages to ring around all of the local firms who supply electrical components and they were the cheapest by far.' Clare, the purchasing manager, was explaining to the company Managing Director how SparksBitz had been chosen as the main supplier to the business of the electrical components. The Design Light Co. needed a wide range of parts to assemble the lighting and heating units it produced. The company's products were designed to meet customers' special 'one-off' requirements. SparksBitz had, it is true, kept its prices very low but it had also failed to deliver key components on several occasions. There were also two legal cases the customers had started against the Design Light Co. for supplying dangerous lights that had exploded after just a few hours' use. A faulty part had been traced back to SparksBitz who had obtained them from an unnamed East Asian supplier who had now gone out of business. Replacements could not now be obtained. SparksBitz was now also demanding cash on delivery of any future small orders – its last communication with Design Light Co. had stated that 'we prefer to deal with customers who order large quantities of standard items. Your company's orders are for a few special items that we often have trouble getting hold of.'

Discussion points

1. Was price the key factor in choosing a supplier for Design Light Co.?
2. What factors would you look for in a good supplier if you were purchasing manager of Design Light Co.?
3. What competitive advantages would having good suppliers offer to Design Light Co.?

Why are suppliers important?

Customers provide sales that generate cash and profit so customer relationships are vital for long-term success. Surely business managers should devote all available time and energy into establishing effective links with customers and building their loyalty? This is too simple a view of business activity. To meet customers' expectations consistently it is essential to have reliable suppliers of materials, components and business services. A pizza delivery business might pride itself on a rapid response to all telephoned orders – yet if it fails to meet its promises to customers because it has not received a delivery of important ingredients it will face several problems:

- High labour costs as idle staff wait for ingredients
- Limited choice of products when customers ring up
- Disappointed customers who are left waiting for pizzas.

Supplier relationships: these are links with the companies that supply a business with goods and services.

It pays any business to invest time in choosing the right suppliers and then building good long-term **supplier relationships** with them. The main operational benefits are explained in more detail at the end of this chapter.

💡 Choosing effective suppliers

The most important factors

A lot of companies, especially newly formed ones, focus on just one factor when choosing suppliers – price. Just like the Design Light Co., above. Obviously prices of goods and services are important when operating in a very competitive and cost conscious market – but is it always the most important factor?

Good suppliers should have these qualities:

- Quality of product as this will increase the chances of the final product being of high quality.
- Flexibility to meet special requirements will be important for providers of one-off or unusual goods and services.
- Reliability of delivery – and this may be linked to location. Offering customers 'next day delivery' will be very risky if the suppliers cannot be relied upon. Sometimes, the biggest suppliers can be the most reliable as they have the resources to devote to good transport links and back-up systems. They may lack flexibility when dealing with smaller, specialist business customers, however.
- Value for money – this does not necessarily mean the cheapest. Insisting on the cheapest supplier may lead to poor quality service and goods of dubious quality.
- Good communication links so that frequent contact can be made.
- Operate the same computer software as the purchasing firm to allow immediate orders and requests to be processed.
- Be financially secure – going into liquidation will mean another supplier has to be found quickly.

Although all of these qualities are important, the first step in choosing a supplier is for a business to identify the two most important factors in their particular situation.

1. The most significant strategic goods or services. These can then be differentiated from commodities they also need. Strategic goods are crucial to the success of a business. Commodities are of less importance and can be obtained from many suppliers of equal quality.

Example 1

A business manufacturing quality furniture will have strategic suppliers of wood and leather. The commodities it needs will include nails and screws and stationery for the administration department.

Example 2

A car hire company taking bookings exclusively over the internet will have strategic suppliers of both vehicles and IT software. Commodity needs will include petrol and oil for the cars.

Clearly, businesses will devote more time and effort to developing close relationships with suppliers of strategic goods and services than commodities.

2. The most important factor in choosing a supplier. This could be reliability, quality, value for money or speed. The crucial factor will depend greatly on the nature of the business.

Example 1

Medical product manufacturer – will need high quality suppliers with the highest standards of cleanliness.

Example 2

Insurance company – will require suppliers of legal services with an excellent record of accurate advice.

Example 3

'Value for a £' retailer – empty shelves occasionally will be much less important than low, low prices from suppliers.

How to choose: the supplier selection process

These are the major steps that should be taken in choosing a firm's main suppliers:

1   Make a list of potential suppliers. Details of potential suppliers can be obtained from trade shows, business directories and the internet.

2   Meet them and see how they operate. This may not be possible if they are thousands of miles away. For some businesses it is vital, however. Purchasing managers from Marks and Spencer visit their food suppliers several times a year to check on standards.

3   Discuss reliability and flexibility. These criteria may need to be built into the **service level agreement** – see point 9 below.

4   Payment terms. For small business customers, these may be strictly cash on delivery or one month credit at most. The more flexible the payment terms offered by suppliers the greater the benefit to the purchasing firm's cash flow position.

5   Prices – value for money has already been referred to. As well as 'list prices' from suppliers, additional costs such as delivery and insurance during transit may need to be added. Comparisons between suppliers need to be on a 'like for like' basis. Reducing costs of obtaining important supplies can increase a firm's profitability.

6   Capacity. This is the ability of the supplier to meet increased orders in the future. It may be disruptive to a rapidly expanding business to have to find a new strategic supplier because the original one does not have the capacity to meet increasingly large orders.

7   Quality. This is increasingly important in a world of greater competitiveness and one in which final consumers have higher and higher expectations. Does the supplier have a verified quality assurance system? Can the supplier meet the quality standards expected? Are they so reliable that there will be no further need for quality control checks once supplies arrive at the customer businesses location? This would help to save time and costs.

8   Reliability of deliveries. When a vendor's deliveries start arriving consistently late, incomplete, damaged or otherwise incorrect, it's time to choose another one. On the other hand all firms can have occasional problems and the cause of any one delivery failure may need to be investigated. The need for speedy and utterly reliable deliveries has increased with the trend towards lean production.

Activity

Discuss what you think will be the most important factors to be considered when choosing suppliers by these firms:

- Pizza take-away
- School book shop
- Specialist car manufacturer
- Fashion clothing store.

Key terms

Service level agreement: agreements or contracts with suppliers that clearly lay down the service that they must provide.

Business in action

Internet Service Providers (ISPs) provide the following information in their service level agreement to customers:

- description of the service provided
- commitment to reliability
- responsiveness to problems
- procedure for reporting problems
- consequences of not meeting service obligations
- escape clauses.

Abel and Cole

Abel and Cole operates an organic food box delivery service. It insists that all suppliers are registered with the Soil Association as being organic providers of food. Suppliers must use the absolute minimum of packaging, which must all be recyclable or biodegradable, and must be as local as possible to reduce transport carbon emissions. A food retailing consultant remarked that 'Any bad publicity about any of its suppliers and the methods they use to grow food would be very serious for ethical retailers such as Abel and Cole. Supplier service agreements must be water tight and strictly monitored'.

9 Establish a service level agreement. These contracts will indicate to the supplier:
- The standards of service to be provided
- The delivery timetable
- Payment terms
- Quality levels
- Sources of supplies, e.g. ethically sourced coffee or sustainable supplies of timber
- IT systems to be used to achieve compatibility with the IT system of the purchasing company
- Termination of contract details
- How disputes are to be settled.

These service level agreements are becoming increasingly important in cementing the long-term relationships between a business and its major suppliers. They offer the supplier some confidence that the orders will keep on flowing IF they meet all of the conditions that the agreements contain.

📁💡 Operational benefits of good suppliers

These benefits should already have started to become clear. These are the most significant ones:

1 **Better customer service**. Choosing suppliers who can deliver on time allows promises to be made to customers with an excellent chance of being able to keep them.

2 **Fewer production delays**. Rapid, reliable supplies of parts and components will allow for continuous production and prevent resources lying idle. This is particularly important if a business operates 'lean production' and 'just in time' stock control methods.

3 **Lower costs**. Yes, cost is an important factor – even if it is not always the most important one. Lower supplier costs will allow a business to gain competitive advantage over rivals.

4 **More consistent quality**. Suppliers who can reach and maintain the quality level being aimed at by the purchasing business will mean that there will be far fewer disappointed final consumers of the product or service.

5 **More flexibility to cope with unusual customer requirements**. This will mean that the purchasing business can offer a wider range of products to the final customer.

6 **Improved communications as a result of similar IT systems**. Collaborative software will mean that 'supplier relationship management' (SRM) can be undertaken speedily and accurately. This will allow for automated ordering processes as the computer system at the purchasing firm alerts the suppliers IT system that new supplies are needed.

Study tip

If a question refers to 'operational benefits' don't forget that there could be many of these, not just lower costs of production.

■ Case study

Treat your suppliers like kings

When Mark Balla, Managing Director of MultipliCD Duplication Services, recently organised a dinner for his staff he invited a few of his best suppliers along. 'It seemed like a natural thing to do, they are part of the team and the staff know them well,' Mark says. The company's suppliers have helped his business develop in many ways. One Taiwanese supplier offered £25,000 of credit which allowed Mark to spend more on advertising which helped increase sales. Another supplier fulfilled an order for disks in 14 hours when it would normally take 4–5 days – because one of Mark's own customers was pushing for immediate delivery. Meeting his suppliers face-to-face has also led to Mark being offered low prices that would usually only be offered to much larger businesses.

Carl Robie, Vice President, Strategic Sourcing & Brand Licensing at TGI Fridays, emphasises the importance of innovative products and good communication as being the key advantages of long-term supplier relationships. 'When we recently added shareable starters to our menus our suppliers came up with really good suggestions. They helped us develop this new product. Also, we are constantly kept informed of price changes in food products and suppliers will come up with new ingredients that help to maintain food flavour but at lower cost'.

Fig. 26.1 *TGI Fridays depends on reliable suppliers for quality food and menu suggestions*

Questions

1. What do you understand by the term 'a good supplier relationship'? (4 marks)

2. Outline TWO benefits to MultipliCD of good supplier relationships. (6 marks)

3. Analyse the most important factors that a business such as T.G.I. Friday's would consider in selecting its suppliers. (8 marks)

4. Evaluate the importance of good long-term supplier relationships to the success either of a car manufacturer or a food retailing business. (14 marks)

5. Research task: Use the www.businesslink.gov.uk website to find out more about:
   a Service level agreements, and
   b Supplier relationship management.

Show the skills

Answering a question about 'choosing the best supplier' should give you an opportunity to demonstrate that you understand that the best supplier is very often NOT the one who offers the lowest prices.

In this chapter you will have learned to:

- understand the importance of working with suppliers
- analyse the most important factors that determine which suppliers a business will choose
- evaluate the impact on effective operations of working closely with suppliers.

For answers to activities and case study questions see

27 Using technology in operations

Setting the scene

Using IT helped us improve customer service

The Hi-Technology Group, based in the south east of England, uses IT in many aspects of its business. It offers a total design and specialist manufacturing service. It recently introduced a computerised system to keep in closer contact with both suppliers and customers. This is called supply chain management. 'It allows us to monitor and integrate each customer quote for new contracts, the orders that come in, the purchase of raw materials, scheduling of jobs in our workshop through to transport of the finished goods and sending the bill to the customer. We can keep a check on the progress of everything by using our computers', explained Project Manager Chris Moore.

Hi-Technology Group believes that this use of IT has speeded up customer service and reduced wasted time and resources. Introducing this new IT was not a quick process, however. 'We needed to gain support across the whole business first, from the boardroom to the shop floor', said Chris.

'We set up a project team and involved department heads by asking what they would like to see the new IT software achieve. The installation and testing took several months. Part of the plan included extensive staff training and demonstrations. Everyone knew what to expect when the system was introduced. It was worth taking the time to get it right.'

Discussion points

1. What benefits does the Hi-Technology Group seem to gain from the use of IT?

2. Using supermarkets as an example of a service sector industry, what IT applications do you think these businesses use?

3. Why do you think it was important to Chris and his project team to plan the introduction of the new IT carefully?

Technology – what does it mean?

In its simplest form, technology means the use of tools, machines and science in an industrial context. This chapter is not concerned with the business use of 'low technology' tools and machines such as drills and lathes. Many of these have been in use for hundreds of years. Instead this chapter will analyse the impact on businesses of the introduction of high technology machines and processes that are based on **information technology**. This is a much more recent development.

Key terms

Information technology: the use of electronic technology to gather, store, process and communicate information.

💡 Types of technology in operations management

Robots

Once the preserve of science fiction films, **robots** are now widely used in nearly all manufacturing industries. Using robots for this purpose is called computer-aided manufacturing (CAM).

Manufacturing robots are known for their speed, accuracy and efficiency. When correctly programmed, they increase product quality compared to manual production methods. They are more exact and thorough and they do not take breaks! They are most frequently used for repetitive, hazardous and boring tasks such as spot welding, metal cutting and shaping and circuit board assembly. They free workers to take up more rewarding and challenging work. As they are more accurate than workers, they reduce waste and reject rates – and this has a benefit for the firm's environmental record.

■ **Key terms**

Robot: a computer controlled machine able to perform a physical task.

Fig. 27.1 *Robots increase productivity by performing repetitive tasks quickly and accurately*

Business in action

Land Rover

Land Rover uses advanced robots that can be rapidly adapted to make more than one model on each production line and also allows different features and extras to be added. This allows replacement of the typical 'standardised' product usually associated with production lines with a 'customised' product that meets individual customer's preferences.

A washing machine manufacturer reported a 25 per cent rise in output with no increase in staffing when robots were first used on the production line. Defective products fell from 3 per cent to 0.5 per cent of output. Outline three long-term benefits to the business of these improvements.

Automated stock control programs

Computerised stock control systems run on the same principles as manual ones but they are more flexible and information is easier to retrieve. These are very widely used in service and manufacturing businesses. These IT programs can be used to answer these common key questions:

■ How much is there in stock?

■ What is the current value of stock held?

■ How old is this stock?

■ Which are the fastest moving items of stock and which are the slowest?

Not only will computerised systems allow quick answers to these questions, they will give the following benefits:

■ Automatic stock monitoring, triggering orders when the re-order stock level is reached;

■ Identifying the cheapest and fastest suppliers;

■ Bar coding systems which speed up processing, recording of stock and customer check-outs;

■ Radio Frequency Identification (RFID) can now be used which enables individual products or components to be tracked throughout the supply chain.

Supply chain management programmes

Supply chain management (SCM) is becoming an increasingly significant application of IT. Operations Managers can use SCM programs to improve customer service and gain competitive advantage.

The five main stages of SCM for one customer's large order can all be made more effective by using IT software known as Enterprise Resource Planning (ERP):

■ Plan: Deciding which resources are needed for this order and how many.

■ Suppliers: Choosing the best and most cost effective suppliers of the components needed and ordering them to arrive just in time.

■ Manufacture: Checking the quality and monitoring the rate of progress of the customer's order.

■ Deliver: Picking transport systems that can deliver goods on time, safely and cost effectively.

■ Returns: If there is a problem with the product it will have to be taken back from customers and other items made or the cost reimbursed.

ERP software will monitor all of these stages AND by using the internet, allows the supply chain of a business to be linked into the supply chains of customers and suppliers in a single overall network. This is often referred to as B2B – business to business communication. The following benefits can be gained from ERP software:

■ Supply only according to demand – lean production which avoids waste and helps move the business towards achieving **sustainability** in its operations.

■ Just in time ordering of stocks.

■ Reduces costs at all stages of the supply chain – materials and products are electronically tracked at all stages.

■ Improved delivery times and better customer service.

Key terms

Supply chain: All of the stages in the production process from obtaining raw materials to selling to the consumer – from point of origin to point of consumption.

Study tip

Application is a very important skill to demonstrate when discussing uses of IT. Different types of businesses will find some software applications much more useful than others.

Key terms

Sustainability: production systems that prevent waste by using the minimum of non-renewable resources so that levels of production can be sustained in the future.

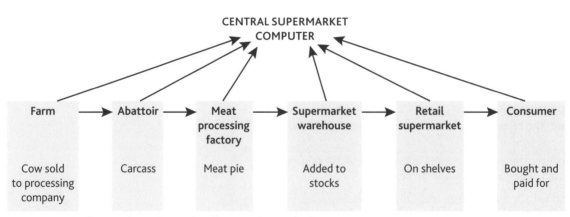

Fig. 27.2 *Technology can be used to track and monitor the supply chain*

Communications technology

Virtually every business will have access to the internet and email. These can be used for external communication with suppliers and customers. An intranet system will allow rapid, cheap and frequent internal communication within the organisation. This can be used to improve the accuracy and speed of passing information between the Operations Management department and other departments of the business. Inter-departmental communication is essential to ensure integrated and consistent policies are adopted and strategies followed. However, too much dependence on IT for communication can have problems too.

Design technology

Computer-aided design (CAD) is the use of a wide range of computer-based tools that assist engineers, architects and other design professionals in their design work. CAD enables designers to lay out and develop their work on screen, print it out in 2-D or 3-D images and save it for future editing. This saves a great deal of time. Due to this greater speed, it takes much less time to develop new products than it used to when designers used manual drawings. This could give a business a real competitive advantage over businesses that do not apply CAD to the same extent. By reducing the product design cycle, updated, revised or completely new products can be launched before those of competitors.

Other benefits of modern CAD systems include:

■ Simulation of designs without building a physical prototype – reducing the use of scarce resources

■ Passing design data directly to computer controlled machines for production – reducing the risk of errors and wastage, and improving the business's environmental image

■ Ability to design a large number of different versions of a standard product – improving the business's ability to focus on different target markets.

■ Activity

Think of three ways in which the efficient operation of your school or college is assisted by communication technology.

Fig. 27.3 *CAD allows quick changes to designs to be made and different variations of the same basic design to be developed*

Overall benefits of using new technology

These can now be summed up as being:

- Lower unit costs of production as technology replaces labour intensive methods increases labour productivity
- Better communications and management information systems
- Quicker and more flexible operations
- Better customer service, for example through internet purchasing
- Improvement in quality and reduction in wastage.

■ Business in action

The modern car manufacturing line is significantly more flexible than in the past, turning out a convertible one minute and an estate car the next. This leads to complex logistics issues, as supplies of doors, wheels and other components have to be ready to be fitted to the correct vehicle.

Barcoded adhesive labels are currently used to identify components and match these to the bar codes on each vehicle passing down the line. These labels can become dirty or scratched. Instead, Powerlase, a UK company, uses solid state lasers to engrave barcodes directly on to aluminium, galvanised steel and stainless steel. Samir Ellwi of Powerlase says, 'The barcodes are indelible and far more robust than adhesive counterparts. Engraved barcodes can be read by scanners even if scratched or painted over.'

🗀 Introducing and updating technology

IT is a part of almost all businesses' everyday life. The software applications above illustrate how businesses can work more effectively and take advantage of new opportunities. However, it is almost too easy for businesses, including start-ups, to spend capital on IT 'solutions' without giving sufficient thought to what the problem is that needs solving. Just purchasing IT applications is not enough – it is very important that the application used is a cost effective solution to a clearly defined business problem. Apart from cost these are other potential problems from introducing and using technology:

- *Staff resistance to change*

  Some workers may be fearful of rapid technological change. Will they be able to cope with the new techniques they will have to learn? Will their jobs be put at risk?

- *Training costs*

  New technology often replaces relatively low skilled jobs – but the programming and maintenance of the software and hardware will require considerable investments in training.

- *Maintenance and updating costs*

  Purchasing or leasing new technology is not the end of capital expenditure – the increasing pace of obsolescence will lead to frequent updating and replacement costs.

- *Breakdown costs and disruption caused by systems not working*

  Dependence on technology has its drawbacks too and customer service can be put at risk by, for example, unreliable computer systems.

■ *IT-based communication systems can create information overload*

Emailing has generated an explosion of messages and these can prevent key information being lost in the sheer volume of communications. Much staff time is spent in sending and reading emails.

To minimise these costs and potential limitations, these are the important stages a business should go through when introducing or updating technology:

■ *Analyse* the potential use of IT and the ways in which it can make the business more effective.

■ *Involve* managers and other staff in assessing the potential benefits and pitfalls of introducing it – better ideas often come from those who will use the system than those responsible for purchasing it.

■ *Evaluate* the different systems and programs available – compare the cost and the expected efficiency and productivity gains. Consider the budget available for this system.

■ *Plan* for the introduction of the new system including extensive training for staff and demonstrations to all users.

■ *Monitor* the introduction and effectiveness of the system – is it giving the expected benefits and if not, what can be done to improve performance?

 Case study

More chips at the supermarket?

The major UK supermarkets have been putting Information Technology at the forefront of their drive for lower costs, improved customer service and more information about their customers. Bar codes, check out scanners, automatic product re-ordering systems, automated stock control programs, robot controlled transport systems in warehouses, chip and pin machines for payment, loyalty cards that record each individual shopper's purchases and internet shopping for customers – the list of IT applications employed by the large supermarkets is almost endless.

Some of these systems have been controversial. For example, centralised ordering and delivery of products reduced the independence and control of individual store managers. The rapid growth of internet shopping left some companies with a shortage of stock and delivery vehicles which led to poor service. Some smaller suppliers who have been unable to cope with the cost of introducing compatible IT systems to take orders from the huge retailers have been dropped.

And now the latest development is causing further controversy. Radio Frequency ID tagging (RFID) involves putting a small chip and coiled antenna, at the initial point of production, into EVERY item sold through the supermarkets. Unlike bar codes that have to be manually scanned, the RFID simply broadcasts its presence and data, such as sell by date, to electronic receivers or readers.

German supermarket chain Metro already use RFID and claims that food can be easily traced back to the farm where it is produced, queues at tills no longer exist as customer's bills are calculated instantly as they pass by a receiver and all products are tracked at each stage of the supply chain – 'we know where everything is!'

There are some concerns, however. Consumer groups suggest that shoppers will be tracked and traceable too – not just the goods they have bought. Isn't this an invasion of privacy? Unions are opposed to it as it could lead to many redundancies due to its non-manual operation. Some supermarket managers fear yet another IT initiative that will mean even more central control over them and they fear breakdowns in the system and lack of training in dealing with problems.

Show the skills

Questions about technology demand answers that are clearly applied to the business in the case study. Many candidates write about `robot technology' even when the case study business is a service provider such as a hotel or restaurant. Try to link different types of technological change relevant to the type of business referred to in the question.

Questions

1 What do you understand by the term 'Information Technology'? (3 marks)

2 Outline how any TWO of the IT systems mentioned in the passage are likely to benefit customers. (6 marks)

3 Analyse the likely benefits of supermarkets using RFID to trace and collect data from every product they sell. (10 marks)

4 Discuss how a supermarket business should effectively introduce the new RFID technology. (14 marks)

5 Research task: Use the internet to research one of the following and write a brief report explaining the potential benefits to any one well known business: CAD; CAM; RFID.

In this chapter you will have learned to:

- explain what information technology means
- analyse the different business applications of technology
- assess the problems of introducing and updating IT applications – and how these might be overcome.

For answers to activities and case study questions see kerboodle

Practice questions

Chapters 26 & 27

1 List THREE of the suppliers that an internet café will need to deal with. *(3 marks)*

2 Explain THREE factors that the manager of the internet café should consider when selecting any ONE of the suppliers you listed in Q1. *(6 marks)*

3 List TWO ways in which the manager of the internet café could discover a list of suitable suppliers for any one product or service required by the café. *(2 marks)*

4 Using a business example, analyse the importance of price and payment terms offered by suppliers to this business. *(6 marks)*

5 Why is the supplier's production capacity a factor to be considered when selecting a supplier for a fast expanding manufacturer of central heating boilers? *(4 marks)*

6 A medium-sized supermarket chain that has most of its branches in the north-east is planning to expand operations to the south-east. This will involve a possible 30 per cent increase in sales over three years. It will stretch the cash flow of the business to the limit. It has a good reputation for good customer service and never running out of stock of major items. The Operations Manager is keen to establish supplier relationships with food and drink manufacturers in the south east. She realises that the choice of suppliers will have an important impact on the success of these new stores.

    a) Define what is meant by 'supplier relationship'. *(2 marks)*

    b) Explain TWO benefits to this business of establishing good links with suppliers. *(6 marks)*

    c) Analyse TWO factors that the Operations Manager should consider when selecting new suppliers for the shops in the south-east. *(8 marks)*

    d) Evaluate the role that its relationship with suppliers will have on the success of this expansion plan. *(10 marks)*

7 What do you understand by the term 'Information technology'? *(2 marks)*

8 List FOUR possible uses of modern technology that a food retailing business might use. *(4 marks)*

9 Differentiate between 'CAD' and 'CAM' technologies. *(3 marks)*

10 Explain what type of business might find CAD useful and why. *(4 marks)*

11 Explain the benefits of using CAM to a motor manufacturer. *(6 marks)*

12 Analyse the possible reasons why a manufacturer of specialist chocolates might keep uses of technology to a minimum. *(6 marks)*

13   'By using the latest computer controlled machinery we were able to increase
productivity,' said the manager of a large dry cleaning business. Explain what
she meant by this.   *(4 marks)*

14   Sarah Cahill owns a business that designs and makes fabrics for curtains
and upholstery. The market is very 'design conscious'. Low prices are less
important than original design and responding quickly to customers
requests for new materials. The business employs 35 specialist designers,
weavers and dyers. The processes used are very labour intensive. Total
sales and market share are falling significantly due to foreign competition
that can respond very rapidly with new fabrics to the latest changes in
colour and design trends. Sarah's business has quite limited finances but
she has asked a business consultant to advise her. He suggested a complete
change of design and manufacturing systems that used technology in place
of most of the skilled employees currently working for the business.

a)   Define the term 'Information Technology'.   *(2 marks)*

b)   Outline TWO possible IT applications that Sarah could employ
within her business.   *(6 marks)*

c)   Analyse the problems that Sarah might experience when
introducing new technology into her business.   *(8 marks)*

d)   To what extent might further application of technology reverse
the fortunes of this business?   *(10 marks)*

Marketing and the competitive environment

Introduction

The next seven chapters build on ideas developed in the first section 'Starting a Business'. In particular, Chapter 5 – Conducting start-up market research, Chapter 6 – Understanding markets and Chapter 25 – Developing effective operations: customer service would be worth re-reading before going any further. Reference to other parts of this book are made throughout this section, which should help you to see how all the elements of a business should be integrated and not seen as distinct from each other. All functional areas rely on each other in a successful business and work together to achieve the goals of the organisation, no matter what its size.

The major issue discussed throughout this section is the competitiveness of a business and the need for any firm to be aware of who their rivals are and what they are doing. This should enable the business to create a competitive advantage through its chosen marketing mix. There are lots of examples of success in highly competitive markets, but it is worth bearing in mind that there are a lot more failures. The aim is to use the marketing mix to ensure success for any size of business.

In this section of the book you should gain an understanding of the importance of marketing to businesses and the huge variety of options available to firms when developing their marketing mix. The results of market research, both primary and secondary, form the basis of developing an appropriate and integrated marketing mix covering the four basic elements of product, price, place and promotion. Firms need to have a very clear understanding of the need of their customers, because mistakes can be very expensive.

Another theme running through this section is the impact of technology on marketing. Developments such as e-commerce are considered in terms of how this has revolutionised the way final consumers and businesses as consumers purchase goods and services to meet their needs.

Chapter 28: Effective marketing This chapter looks at the purpose of marketing and how it can be most effective. What are the benefits and drawbacks of niche and mass marketing? Is there a difference between the *business to business* and *business to consumer* markets?

Chapter 29: Designing an effective marketing mix Here we investigate the influences on the marketing mix which include finance, technology and market research. How important is an integrated marketing mix to the success of a business?

Chapter 30: Using the marketing mix: product This chapter looks in detail at the product element of the marketing mix. What are the influences on the development of new goods and services? The possibilities include technology, competitors' actions and the entrepreneurial skills of managers and owners. What are the advantages to a business of creating a unique selling point, and are there any other ways to differentiate one product from another? In answering these questions you will be introduced to product portfolio analysis and will learn how to use the Boston Matrix and interpret the Product Life Cycle diagram.

Chapter 31: Using the marketing mix: promotion This covers the second element of the marketing mix: promotion. What are the elements of the promotional mix? How important are factors such as branding, merchandising, sales promotions, direct selling and advertising? Why do businesses get involved in public relations? What are the influences on the promotional mix chosen by a firm, apart from the finances available?

Chapter 32: Using the marketing mix: pricing Pricing strategies are discussed in this chapter. What is the difference between price skimming and penetration pricing? Is a strategy the same as a tactic? What is psychological pricing? How does a firm decide on the price to charge for its goods and services? The concept of elasticity of demand is introduced. Why does a change in price benefit some firms/products and not others?

Chapter 33: Using the marketing mix: place This chapter covers the fourth main element of the marketing mix: place. The impact of technology is particularly evident here because the internet has changed the balance of distribution for many smaller businesses, away from traditional routes. What types of distribution channels are available to businesses? Which are the most appropriate outlets or distributors for a firm?

Chapter 34: Marketing and competitiveness This section is brought to a close by considering the relationship between marketing and competitiveness. You will look at the range of market conditions facing firms from those where a small number of businesses dominate to others where there are lots of similar, small firms. How do market conditions influence the design of the marketing mix? What is competitiveness and how can it be improved?

Key terms

Marketing: identifying and meeting customer needs.

Niche marketing: focusing marketing on selling differentiated products to a small, specific part of a larger market.

Market: the group of customers who are interested in buying a product with the ability to purchase it.

Setting the scene

Rapha

Selling cycling shirts, capes and jackets for up to £140 each requires effective marketing. Rapha is a specialised retailer of top quality cycling wear and its success is due largely to trying not to compete with 'household name' sportswear businesses. Rapha is aimed squarely at the most committed of cycling niches. Very keen amateur riders, competing at the top level but without professional support, are prepared to pay top prices for the highest quality cycling clothing. Rapha knows its market well and communicates with customers constantly through Twitter, Facebook and blogs. Marketing expenditure is around 20% of sales, but this is not directed towards conventional advertising. Effective marketing is done through participation at cycling events and electronic marketing, as Rapha is largely an online retailer.

Discussion points

1 Why is niche marketing key to Rapha's success?

2 How can marketing be made more effective by constant communication with customers?

The purpose of marketing

Many new businesses do not succeed because they have not clearly identified their customers. This starts with good market research, (Chapter 5 – Conducting start-up market research) which must then be translated into an effective **marketing** mix. Many new firms also underestimate the competition they will face when they enter the market. To be successful, any new business must quickly establish a competitive advantage which will persuade potential customers to choose them rather than their existing supplier, or the nearest rival offering a similar product or service. Customers will always have at least one choice: to buy or not to buy. The purpose of marketing is to ensure that the customer picks the first option rather than the second.

There are two main strands to successful marketing:

- Identifying customer needs: in other words finding out what the customers want that is not already being provided to a sufficiently high standard (Chapter 5)

- Meeting customer needs: making sure that your product or service is exactly what customers are looking for (Chapters 29–34).

Niche marketing and mass marketing

Niche marketing

This involves meeting the needs of a small **market**, or a small section of a large market. Small firms often use this approach because they can concentrate on establishing a strong position in the market. Niche markets are usually too small to attract the interest of larger businesses. Delicious

Alchemy (see the Business in Action case study below) is a good example of such a business because it is aimed at people who suffer from food allergies.

Advantages of niche marketing:

- The ability to focus specific products on the needs of individual customers and respond quickly to changes in these needs.
- The return on marketing expenditure is often high because it can be so well targeted.
- There is little competition which makes it easy to gain market share.
- It may be possible to charge premium prices because of the lack of direct competition. This will lead to increased profitability.
- In a new niche market, it may be possible to achieve first mover advantage. For a completely new product, where the potential market is unknown or very difficult to estimate, it may be possible for a small business to gain a significant market share and a strong brand image before larger firms get involved. This is even more likely if the innovation is protected by a patent.

Disadvantages of niche marketing:

- The degree of specialisation makes niche markets vulnerable to changes in market conditions.
- It can be costly to use research to identify market niches and develop products to satisfy customers within them.
- A successful niche may attract the interest of large, multi-national companies. Once such organisations enter the market, small firms will find it difficult to compete.
- Sales levels may be relatively low which could cause problems if costs rise unexpectedly, and profit margins are squeezed. This is one of the reasons why many businesses operating in niche markets have found greater success through the internet and e-commerce: operating costs are much lower, therefore giving higher profit margins.

Activity

Can you identify the needs being met by the three businesses described in the *Customer needs* Business in Action?

Business in action

Customer needs

facebook.com, the social networking website was started in 2004 as a small project for Harvard students in the US. It has now grown into a world-wide phenomenon. It is the fact that you can control who sees your profile that currently gives Facebook the edge over its rivals.

Celebrity Castoffs is an internet auction site where celebrities donate their high-profile clothes, which are so unique that they cannot be worn more than once. The additional incentive of donating 70% of the proceeds to charity made the proposition even more attractive. It is the brainchild of Hayley Smith, who came up with the idea whilst reading a celebrity magazine. Her first move was to register the domain name, and she didn't launch the business until she had researched the idea thoroughly.

Delicious Alchemy is a business selling wheat-, gluten- and lactose-free foods. It was founded by Emma Killilea after she was diagnosed with having severe wheat intolerance. She decided to specialise in baking allergen-free food for hotels and restaurants, and started by exhibiting some of her range at a food show in Yorkshire. Emma sub-contracts work to a baker who produces food such as mocha-syrup sponges and ginger mini-loaves on a commercial scale.

Mass marketing

Many businesses start life with niche market products, but as they grow their goal becomes the mass market. The Body Shop was started by Anita Roddick as a firm which targeted a small group of consumers for whom ethical trading was important. However, the perceptions of the general public changed, in no small part due to the efforts of the Body Shop's founder: the values she championed, for example ingredients not tested on animals, were what most consumers came to expect when buying cosmetics and toiletries.

Other firms have always aimed at the mass market, although they may have begun by concentrating on a particular geographical area. Wilkinson's started with one hardware store in Leicester in 1930, and now has 285 shops nationwide.

Advantages of mass marketing:

▪ High sales, at low prices, mean that costs are spread over a greater number of units. This may mean, for example, that a firm in the mass market can afford expensive advertising. Profit margins may be low, but actual profits can still be very high due to the high volume sold.

▪ As products are aimed at a large range of potential customers, it is likely that revenue will be regular, and cash flow problems are less likely.

Disadvantages of mass marketing:

▪ High profits will attract a lot of competitors into the market which can drive down prices and reduce profit margins.

▪ It may be very difficult to spot changes in consumer needs because the market is so large, which could lead to a loss of market share.

▪ It is very difficult for small or medium-sized businesses to compete with the small number of very large organisations operating in many mass markets.

Which is best – niche or mass?

As you probably realise, there is no right or wrong answer to this question. The decision will depend on the individual business context. However, there is a growing body of evidence to suggest that due to the growth of e-commerce, it is now possible for niche businesses to operate in the global market. Therefore, there might not be the same need to enter the mass market in order to grow. You will also have noticed that many of the advantages of the niche market are disadvantages of the mass market and vice versa. The question you will need to ask is whether the potential for growth in the market is really limited, and what the aspirations of the directors of the firm really are.

Consumer marketing and business to business marketing

We are all consumers and it is easy to forget that many firms do not do business with the public, but meet the needs of other organisations. Do they still need to do marketing? Yes of course they do. The environment in which most firms operate is still competitive.

Consumer marketing is aimed at the general public who are the final users of the product. In other words, the product is not being bought to be resold, but to meet the personal needs of the buyer. Consumer markets typically have a large number of potential buyers and purchasing alternatives. Consumer markets may contain millions of individual consumers. It is very difficult to predict or forecast changes in consumer

Key terms

Mass marketing: selling undifferentiated products to the whole market – no attempt made to identify specific niche sections of the market.

Business in action

Torchshop

Torchshop sells only Mag-lite flashlights and accessories, via its website, and offers a very high level of customer service to the people who are interested in their products. Another example from the US is Buymybrokenipod, which offers consumers a very simple way to sell their broken or unused iPods, again via the internet.

Link

For more information on revenue and cash flow, see Chapter 17 – Improving cash flow, page 119.

Activity

Prepare a marketing proposal for a niche product or service aimed at the 16–25 year olds market in your area. Try to give your product some element that differentiates it from the competition it may face.

Key terms

Consumer marketing: creating and delivering products to meet consumers' needs.

tastes or consumer behaviour. Consumer marketing must rely on the statistics gained from a larger population to predict this behaviour.

Business marketing is concerned with one company identifying the needs of a potential customer who is buying the product as part of their own business process. Business to business markets (B2B) typically contain significantly fewer possible purchasing alternatives than consumer markets. It may be possible to identify all possible buying organisations in a particular niche business market, gather information about each of them and approach them individually.

Is marketing important?

It does not matter whether a business is small or growing, in the consumer or the business market, effective marketing is always important. Any business must ensure that potential consumers are aware of the goods and/or services on offer, or they will not survive. Marketing is effective if it achieves the goal of increasing customer awareness to the extent that they choose to become a customer of your business.

Case study

Jack's of London has been developed by Sue Whitehead who ran a successful unisex hairdressing salon in Wimbledon. She noticed that she didn't have many male clients and conducted a lot of market research to discover that men really wanted:

- their hair cut in a male environment
- to be able to walk in and get a haircut
- their hair cut before or after work.

Sue created a business with a different feel to a regular barbers shop: there are plasma screens, internet access, free beer and the right magazines. There is a webcam so customers can see if there is a queue, and the salon opens for 12 hours a day, 7 days a week.

This is a niche market with a lot of potential for growth by franchising the business concept. Prices are mid-range and the business exploits the huge growth in the men's grooming market. The marketing mix is built around a strong brand image. The internet, the innovative queue webcam system, on-line style guide and product sales, and an in-house magazine 'Evolve' featuring competitions, gadgets, latest style collections and grooming tips all support the brand and increase awareness. Most recently, Jack's of London has been nominated for the finals of the annual British Hairdressing Awards.

Questions

1. Use the case study to explain the term 'niche market'. (4 marks)
2. Explain the advantages to Jack's of London of niche marketing. (8 marks)
3. To what extent has the effective marketing of Jack's of London been the cause of the firm's success? (14 marks)
4. Research task: Use this link to discover more about B2B marketing and the support available for businesses that market products to other businesses. http://www.b2bmarketing.net/

Key terms

Business marketing: serving the needs of a business or businesses within one or more industries.

Study tip

Don't assume that all businesses want to grow into multinational corporations. Many entrepreneurs are only interested in a niche market existence, and can achieve high profits by operating efficiently in their chosen specialist area.

Business in action

Lapel Men's Hire

Lapel Men's Hire trade through the hire and retail of menswear for special occasions, weddings and black tie events. They market themselves through Yellow Pages, advertising and weddings shows, and most recently via a website.

Business in action

Venom

Venom RIBs (Rigid Inflatable Boats) is a business targeting the professional RIB user: lifeguards and sailing instructors. This means that their marketing needs to be tailored to meet the specific needs of their customers. Their website includes a lot of technical data which is very important to potential business clients.

✔️ *In this chapter you will have learned to:*

- explain the purpose of marketing
- discuss the benefits and drawbacks of niche and mass marketing
- discuss the difference between *business to business* and *business to consumer* marketing
- evaluate the importance of effective marketing for small and medium-sized businesses.

For answers to activities and case study questions see

Show the skills

So many candidates write answers to marketing questions without referring to the case study business. It is very important to identify whether the business is selling to consumers or other businesses – for example, both the promotion methods and the channels used to distribute the products will be different.

Designing an effective marketing mix

Fig. 29.1 *Coco Ribbon is a luxury company*

Key terms

Marketing mix: the integration of product, place, promotion and pricing designed to achieve the marketing objectives of the business.

Setting the scene

Coco Ribbon

Coco Ribbon is the ultimate in luxury – a shop for people with an almost unlimited budget. Sophie and Alison set it up in 2002 and the long list of celebrity customers includes Jamie Oliver, Jennifer Love Hewitt, Elizabeth Jagger and Minnie Driver. It sells a carefully selected range of products from perfume to clothes to homeware which must have the 'wow!' factor. The shop is located in the coolest part of London – Notting Hill – and it has had lots of attention from upmarket magazines. There are hundreds of shops selling perfume, clothes and homeware but Sophie and Alison seem to have found something different – Coco Ribbon has gone for a niche.

Sophie and Alison have to be very careful about what they sell in the shop so customers continue to feel that it is special. They buy 'wide but shallow' – not too much of any one thing because it's better to run out than have stock left over. It makes every item feel even more exclusive. Nothing is cheap at Coco Ribbon but getting the price right can be tricky. Sophie and Alison need to know what customers are prepared to pay before they set the price. This means looking carefully at the competition. If they set the price too low, customers won't buy because they think the product isn't good enough. If it's too high, they won't buy either.

Discussion points

1. Sophie and Alison seem to have done something right. What do you think it is?

2. Why do you think Coco Ribbon has a different pricing strategy from Ikea, Gap or Tesco?

3. Why was Notting Hill a good place for this small business to start?

4. How have Sophie and Alison promoted their shop?

5. Running out of stock annoys Marks & Spencer's customers but has its benefits for Coco Ribbon. Why?

The marketing mix

The **marketing mix** refers to all those elements of marketing which help to meet identified customer needs. These elements are generally referred to as the 4Ps, although there have been additions to this number, for example packaging and people.

1. Product

Product refers to the features and functions of the product or service being offered. If a product has a unique selling point/proposition, it

Fig. 29.2 *Diagram to show the marketing mix available to businesses*

means that one of these features or functions is not available anywhere else. The development of new and existing products should be based on market research which has identified the needs of consumers in the market.

2. Promotion

Promotion concerns communication with the consumers. A new product could meet all the needs of customers, as identified in primary market research (Chapter 5 – Conducting start-up market research, page 27), but unless they are aware of its existence, the product or service will not be bought. Promotion is not just about advertising: it covers all opportunities to inform the market about a firm's products from trade fairs to an item on the local radio.

3. Place

Place is where the purchase can be made by the consumer. Traditionally many products were purchased through retail outlets or catalogues. Today, the growth of e-commerce is such that an increasing amount of purchasing is via the internet. This development applies to both the consumer and business markets (Chapter 28 – Effective marketing, page 211).

4. Price

Price refers to how much the consumer is expected to pay for the product or service. The price should give an indication of the value of the product, and can be altered as demand for the product changes. New, innovative products are usually given a very high price to reflect their unique qualities, whereas new products launched into a very crowded and competitive market such as biscuits or soft drinks could have a low price to attract the attention of consumers.

Business in action
Divine Chocolate

Divine Chocolate, the leading UK fair trade chocolate business, was founded in 1997. In February 2007 the company launched a new US firm in Washington, with a news event and chocolate tasting at the Old Ebbitt Grill, the capital city's oldest restaurant, where Ghanaian-born chef Marion Pitcher created the 'Divine Double chocolate Torte'. The product will be sold in independent retail locations and natural food stores, but the hope is to expand to major supermarket chains later in the year, to gain a share of the $13 billion US chocolate market. The price will be set in line with other high quality chocolate bars.

Study tip

It is more important to be able to apply your knowledge of the marketing mix, than to be able to regurgitate definitions learned by heart.

■ Key terms

Integrated marketing mix: this makes sure that the 4Ps give a consistent and coherent message to customers about the product.

■ Activity

Write a short news item outlining the launch of a new live music venue in your area. You should describe an integrated marketing mix which supports a clear message to the target audience.

Fig. 29.3 *Promotions such as this require financing*

Packaging and people

Packaging and people are often identified as other important elements of any marketing mix because both can play such an important role in the buying decision. Huge amounts of money are spent every year by businesses to ensure that their product looks appealing to consumers. The importance of people in marketing relates to the principles of TQM (Chapter 24 – Developing effective operations: quality, page 179) which suggests that every employee is part of the marketing of a business.

💡🗂 An integrated marketing mix

A detailed analysis of the marketing mix will be considered in Chapters 30–33. However, it is important at this stage to understand that the elements outlined above must be used effectively and coherently, and do not contradict each other. There is no point spending millions of pounds on advertising a product if it is not available to purchase for another six months; the price charged should reflect the quality of the product – nobody would expect to pay £350 for a pair of shoes sold in a supermarket. In the same way, if you buy a watch for £5, you would not expect it to be gift-wrapped, offered with a life-time guarantee and a free pair of diamond studs. Making mistakes with the coordination of the mix can be very costly to businesses both large and small.

Divine Chocolate (page 217) illustrates the importance of an integrated marketing mix. All the elements of the marketing mix work well together to ensure that the message is clear. The product has the fair trade unique selling point and is made using the highest quality cocoa beans, which is reflected in the above average prices that Divine charge. They are targeting people who don't make their decisions based on the price of the chocolate, but on the quality of the product. Products are placed at independent retailers and health food stores where consumers would expect to find Divine Chocolate. Finally, the promotion was very exclusive: the oldest restaurant in the capital city of the USA! Note also that the launch promotion does not include an expensive advertising campaign, but uses free news coverage.

Influences on the marketing mix

There are many factors which could influence the composition of the marketing mix.

Finance

How much money does a firm need to spend on marketing? Multinational organisations such as Unilever, Coca Cola and Colgate, spend billions of pounds on marketing, whereas small businesses may have a marketing budget of £500 per year. This does not mean that small business marketing is not going to be effective – if the elements of the mix are used in an integrated and creative way, the impact on customers can be just as positive.

The needs of the market/market research

The marketing mix should be based on the identified needs of customers which in turn should come from market research (Chapter 5 – Conducting start-up market research, page 27). It is also important for firms to continue carrying out market research as their business grows. The needs of customers change over time and the marketing mix may have to be adapted to take this into account.

Business in action

Marketing on a Shoestring

Marketing on a Shoestring is an agency for small businesses, with limited budgets. One of their clients, Silverwell Dental Surgery, is a successful and busy surgery in the town centre of Bolton. The dental partners wanted to encourage their current patients to think more broadly about their dental health and appearance and also to generate greater levels of referrals for dental implant treatments from other local dentists. Marketing on a Shoestring conducted market research, developed a range of printed items, a direct mail pack and a website to meet the specific needs of the dental surgery. The dental partners were very happy with the results of the new approach to marketing and the increased take-up of the services they offered.

Competitor actions

Any marketing mix should be seen as ever-evolving rather than something fixed and permanent. It can be used as the basis of a response to the actions of competitors in the market. For example, if a major competitor brings out a new product or lowers prices, other firms in the market must react to safeguard their position and retain their market share. This may involve taking similar action such as introducing a rival product, or matching the new prices, but there are other options available to businesses that are prepared to use the whole marketing mix in a creative way.

Technology

There have been big changes in recent years which have affected the marketing mix. The most obvious area is the 'place' where goods are bought and sold, with the internet becoming a major source of business. This has been particularly useful for small businesses as the costs are so low. However, pricing strategies should also reflect technological change, for example charging less for buying and booking online. Marketing by mobile phone has also increased rapidly, with the technology becoming available to almost all consumers.

Business in action

Harry Tuffins

Harry Tuffins is a small chain of six supermarkets. All of the stores are within 25 miles of each other on the Shropshire/Wales border. The store in Ludlow, opened in 2007, competes with a large Tesco store. Tesco had been keeping a watchful eye on the development of the Harry Tuffin's store as it was being built. Before the new store opened, Tesco sent round a mailshot to shoppers within 10 miles of Ludlow offering two money-off vouchers for their local Tesco branch. One voucher offered £10 off a £30 shop in the fortnight before Tuffins opened, and the other offered the same deal, but in the fortnight after Tuffins opened.

Harry Tuffins' managing director claimed that this was an example of predatory pricing. His stores hit back at Tesco by offering 10p off a litre of fuel for all shoppers who spent over £60. The ability of small companies to continue to thrive in the face of competition

Activity

If you were in charge of Harry Tuffins' marketing mix, what would you do in response to the Tesco campaign?

from some of the UK's biggest retailers depends not just on price, but on their range of products, convenience and effective local promotions.

Study tip

A successful marketing mix will reflect the marketing objectives of the business. Make sure you understand what it is that the firm is trying to achieve.

Case study

Alara

Alara is a specialist muesli manufacturer. It has been trading since 1975 and has a history of growth and change. The firm currently has 50 per cent of the organic muesli market and exports 20 per cent of its products. The factory is located in Kings Cross, in the heart of London where the firm plays an active part in a diverse and vibrant local community. Operating from a modern unit, production is done in adherence to British Retail Consortium higher-level quality standards. The product is the centre-piece of the business's marketing mix: they provide very high quality products to meet specific requirements including organic, gluten free, kosher, fair trade and small production runs of customer specified blends using a unique database control solution they have developed. At the moment there are 250 different kinds of muesli for sale online, and a smaller choice is also available through health food shops. Some major supermarket groups stock Alara gluten-free muesli. Prices online range from £1.85 for a 500g box of Organic Rich to £3.85 for 750g of Goji and Yacon. In 2006 Alara won two prestigious awards: the Gold Great Taste Award from the Guild of Fine Food Retailers and the Best Food and Drink Product at the Natural Trade Show in Harrogate. 2007 saw the launch of the firm's first major promotional campaign which included consumer media relations, sampling activities and advertising.

Show the skills

If asked to evaluate the marketing mix of a business, it will be important to assess two points in particular:

a) Is the mix well focused towards the objectives of the business?

b) Is the mix an integrated one – do all parts of the mix give consumers the same message about the product?

Questions

1 Outline the main elements of Alara's marketing mix. (8 marks)

2 How might the actions of a major manufacturer like Nestle affect the components of the marketing mix for Alara? (8 marks)

3 Analyse the advantages and disadvantages to Alara of making the product the centre-piece of its marketing mix. (8 marks)

4 Should Alara aim to increase sales in the major supermarkets in the UK, or continue to expand its overseas business? Justify your answer. (14 marks)

5 Research task: Use Alara's website to undertake more research into the company's marketing mix. Write a brief report on the marketing mix, including your opinion on whether the mix is an 'integrated' one.

☑ *In this chapter you will have learned to:*

- discuss the components of the marketing mix

- analyse the importance of an integrated marketing mix

- discuss the relative importance of the factors influencing the marketing mix.

For answers to activities and case study questions see

30 Using the marketing mix: product

Key terms

Product development: changing aspects of goods and services to meet the changing needs of existing customers or to target a different market.

Product line: a set of related goods or services.

Product mix: the full range of products offered by a business, also known as product portfolio.

Setting the scene

Space-pod – hotdesking!

There are many problems with offices, and all too often workers have to 'hotdesk' (share their desk and computer with colleagues). Space-pod has created a mobile workstation which is a fully integrated, self-contained office space that folds out from a very small unit and is completely mobile. The Macro-pod contains a computer, printer, phone, chair and filing. Pods can be joined together to create a team environment and there is a Macroscreen for team meetings and one-to-one interviews. Customers include media centres, local authorities, banks, airports and hospitals as well as the target market of blue chip corporate giants.

Discussion points

1. Why has the business changed the appearance and function of the office?

2. Why is product possibly the most important element of the marketing mix for the Space-pod?

What does product development mean and why is it so important?

Product development involves looking at the market for a product or service and identifying how customer needs have changed and can be met better. By modifying aspects of a product, by adding to an existing **product line**, or extending the **product mix**, a business can meet a wider range of customer needs and/or aim the product at a different target market. For example, an independent health food store may offer fair trade as well as organic food and drink, essential oils in a larger variety of sizes and a new range of locally produced jewellery. Product development is very important to small and growing businesses because it comes from identifying the needs of customers who should always be the focus of an organisation. Product development is also important because no market stands still forever. Although the rate of change will vary, it would be dangerous for any business to assume that a successful product will be just as popular in a year's time!

The product development process

A product development process is needed in a business of any size, because it helps to control the costs and the time taken to develop a new good or service. Successful firms divide development up into a number of identifiable stages which can be applied to goods and services, to product differentiation, to the extension of an existing product line, and the expansion of an organisation's product mix.

1. Creativity: coming up with new ideas to meet consumer needs.
2. Defining the concept: turning an idea into a real business opportunity.

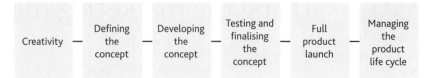

Fig. 30.1 *The product development process*

3 Developing the concept: defining the customer requirements, creating a prototype or pilot service.

4 Testing and finalising the concept: controlled release to test the market.

5 Full product launch: employing all elements of the marketing mix.

6 Managing the product life cycle: monitoring sales and improving features to increase longevity (see page 226).

💡 The unique selling point/proposition

Product development is also important because it can create a **unique selling point (USP)**. If there is something about the design of the product or what it can do which makes it identifiably different to others on the market, the business can use this as the basis for their marketing mix.

■ **Key terms**

Unique selling point (USP): a feature or function of a product that makes it different to any other on the market.

Product differentiation: creating a perceived difference for a product in a competitive market.

Even if it is not possible to create and maintain a USP, businesses will try to achieve **product differentiation** by making their product different in some way from others on the market. This will make it easier to apply the other elements of the marketing mix, because there is something specific to identify the product or service. It could be as simple as saying that a plumbing company has been established for 40 years, or that a shampoo has just won 'Product of the Year', or offering a 24/7 service. However it is achieved, product differentiation is very useful in a competitive market, because it is a way of distinguishing one business from another, and gives customers a reason to select one firm rather than any other. This can lead to benefits such as repeat business and personal recommendation. A successful USP can also make the demand for a product less sensitive to price rises, and it might allow for premium pricing. In other words, the business that achieves product differentiation is more likely to be successful.

■ **Activity**

Does the Space-pod *Macro-pod* have a USP, and if so what is it?

■ What factors influence product development?

The product mix offered by a firm should not stay exactly the same over time. As you have already seen, customer needs will change and businesses must respond positively to retain their share of the market.

However, there are other influences on the market which might appear to pose a threat to a business, but which can also provide opportunities to be exploited by those with a strong entrepreneurial drive.

Advances in technology

Technology has led to significant changes in most areas of business. Technology such as robotics and automated stock control (Chapter 27 – Using technology in operations, page 200) may be beyond the budget of many small businesses, and this could lead to fears that such firms cannot compete against organisations able to achieve lower costs and improved product quality. However, by searching out niche markets, and developing their product lines and product mix, small businesses may still be able to offer clients a product to meet their specific requirements, which larger

organisations aiming at the mass market may not be willing or able to supply. At the same time, advances in communication technology have created opportunities to enter new markets. Small businesses can now trade in the global market place via the internet. However, this in itself can be a threat, as the number of competitors in the market has also increased.

The actions of competitors

Competitors may threaten market share, and lead to the necessity of new product development. A large company, with a reputation for high quality products at low prices, may decide to move into a new market. Existing firms in that market, particularly the smaller ones, may not be able to compete on price, so what should they do? One solution may be to extend their product mix to meet the needs of a wider range of consumers, or develop their existing product lines to provide a greater range of options. A more high risk option may be to develop completely new products.

The entrepreneurial skills of managers and owners

Managers and owners, through their creative thinking and risk-taking, move products/brands in new directions. Examples include Richard Branson and his use of the Virgin brand and Stelios and the growth of Stelio's Easy.com to incorporate 15 diverse product ranges from easyJet to easyPizza! It also includes hairdressers such as Trevor Sorbie who have taken their talent from the salon onto the high street. It is the ability to see an opportunity and develop the product to exploit it that can make the difference between a successful small business, that survives in a competitive market and increases its share of the market, and a firm that joins the large percentage of new businesses that fail within the first three years.

■ Business in action

Hair today

The hairdressing salon, Hair Today, discovered that a new salon, part of a national chain which also offered self-tanning facilities, was opening close by. Many regular customers made it clear that they would be trying out the new alternative as soon as it opened. In response, the owner of Hair Today, Stacey Smith commissioned some primary market research in the area and discovered that 40 per cent of customers would prefer the additional of a nail care service: gel nail enhancements, natural nail overlays, French manicure, and a range of nail art. Stacey recruited a nail technician and reorganised the salon to cater for this extra service. As a result, she gained new customers as well as keeping most of her existing clients and increased her share of the market.

■ Product portfolio analysis

All businesses, no matter how small, should regularly assess their marketing performance: how well each of the products in its product portfolio is doing. This process should ensure that the money allocated to the marketing budget is used effectively. **Product portfolio analysis** is a technique used to identify the position of every product in a firm's portfolio within its market.

■ Business in action
Today is boring

The development of digital television and downloading films online has seen the decline of the local video shop. However one business which has developed this generic product in its own way is Today is Boring, a video shop with a difference in Shoreditch, London. The selection of 2,500 titles comes from the interests and preferences of the local residents and community. Special offers include money off pizza from the local food shop 'The Grocery' when you hire a film.

■ Activity

Returning to the initial case study on page 221, which factors influenced the development of the Space-pod *Macro-pod*?

■ Link

For more information on entrepreneurs, see Chapters 1 and 2.

■ Key terms

Product portfolio analysis: analysing the existing product mix to help develop a balanced range of goods and services.

Boston Matrix: a method of analysing the products in a firm's portfolio based on relative market share and market growth.

The Boston Matrix

The **Boston Matrix** is a model which analyses the goods or services offered by a business in terms of their share of the market, and whether the market itself is growing. Using this method, a firm can quickly assess the position of all their products in their relative markets. From this assessment, decisions can be made about how each product should be treated in the future. The descriptions of each quadrant are deliberately humorous: to help you remember them!

The Question Mark/Problem Child

A new product with a small share of a growing market; high maintenance: needing relatively high levels of investment to become well established in the market; high failure rate but potential for future success.

The Rising Star

High share of a growing market; high maintenance: marketing resources and effort should be concentrated on this type of product so that market share is maintained; fierce competition is likely.

The Cash Cow

High share in a low growth market; any increase in sales will be at the expense of a competitor; low maintenance; little marketing expenditure needed; relatively high profits.

The Dog

Low share of a declining market; may be kept going because they complete a product line; can possibly be revived, but likely to be withdrawn.

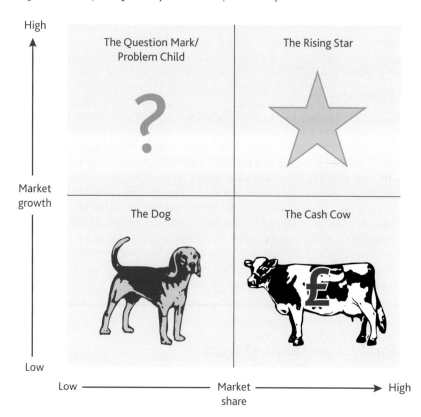

Fig. 30.3 *The Boston Matrix*

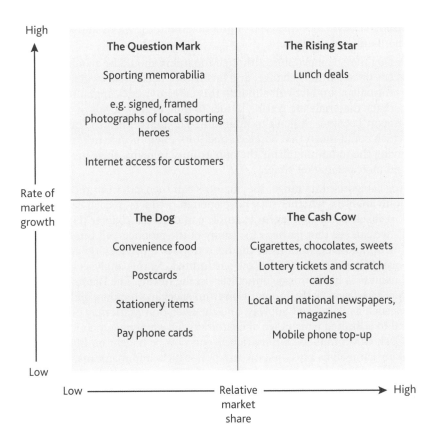

High

The Question Mark

Sporting memorabilia

e.g. signed, framed photographs of local sporting heroes

Internet access for customers

The Rising Star

Lunch deals

Rate of market growth

The Dog

Convenience food

Postcards

Stationery items

Pay phone cards

The Cash Cow

Cigarettes, chocolates, sweets

Lottery tickets and scratch cards

Local and national newspapers, magazines

Mobile phone top-up

Low

Low ——————————— Relative ——————————→ High
market
share

Fig. 30.4 The Boston Matrix for an independent newsagent

Figure 30.4 shows an example of how the Boston Matrix can be used to classify the range of products offered by an independent newsagent. The business sells the following items: national and local newspapers, sweets and chocolate snacks, lunch deals comprising a sandwich, drink and snack; convenience food such as bread and milk; postcards of local views; stationary items such as envelopes; pay phone cards; cigarettes, National Lottery tickets and scratch cards, specialist magazines and mobile phone top ups.

How can a business use the Boston Matrix to analyse the suitability of their product portfolio?

Any business, no matter how big or small, should ideally have a balance between the four types of products shown in the Boston Matrix. The profits from Cash Cows can be used to help finance the Rising Stars and any investment in the Question Marks. Having decided which categories the product portfolio falls into the following analysis is useful:

1 A **Question Mark/Problem Child** helps to ensure that the business is meeting the needs of customers in the market; it is a Star of the future. Without new product development the firm could miss opportunities and lose market share.

2 A **Rising Star** is potentially the real revenue-earner. It brings new customers to the business, who may well become loyal to the brand and buy other products within the portfolio, including Question Marks and Cash Cows. However, it may still need a great deal of cash investment to remain competitive in the face of fierce competition.

3 A **Cash Cow** can be 'milked' to provide the finance needed to pay for the marketing of Question Marks and Rising Stars. Most businesses

will have several of this type of product, often the goods and services that launched the firm.

4 A **Dog** may be inevitable, although too many should be avoided. The needs of consumers change, and businesses need to be aware that eventually a product will slip into this category: sales are falling, perhaps materials are getting harder to find, or high levels of customer support becomes difficult to maintain. The market is also stagnant which could mean that some competitors might decide to leave, giving the remaining firms the opportunity to revive their products and increase market share.

Having categorised its range, the business can then carry out product portfolio analysis; whether they have enough products in each category. Looking back at the newsagent example earlier in the chapter (Figure 30.4), we can see that perhaps too many of the products fall into the Cash Cow and Dog sections of the Boston Matrix, particularly as the life-span of some of the Cash Cow's is limited. As this analysis shows, the business is likely to face difficulties in the future. The Rising Star product faces very fierce competition from specialist retailers and large stores such as Boots and Subway, and the Question Mark may only appeal to a limited percentage of customers. Of even greater concern are the Cash Cow products: lottery tickets can now be bought on line, anti-smoking campaigns are constant and newspapers and magazines can all be purchased in supermarkets or delivered. The owners of this business need to consider very carefully how to attract more customers and what products they should supply to their market.

Are there any drawbacks to using the Boston Matrix?

As an aid to decision making, when deciding on product development, the Boston Matrix is a quick and easy way to make general decisions. However, it is based on two assumptions which are flawed:

1 Market share is the best way to measure the success of a product: a great deal will depend on the type of market and the overall market size. If a firm is trading in a very competitive market, with many other businesses, then a relatively small market share is perfectly acceptable. If the product is competing in a very large, global market, however, a small market share could be a seen as successful.

2 A fast growing market is the most important quadrant to be in. This may be true for an entrepreneurial business that thrives on risk-taking and cutting-edge innovation, but there is plenty of scope for success for businesses involved in a slow moving market as well.

As with many business models you will come across, the Boston Matrix should be treated with caution, and certainly not taken too literally. It can be used best as an analysis of the current product portfolio of a business and as the starting point for discussions about future product development and maintaining share of a particular market.

◨ What is the product life cycle?

Figure 30.5 illustrates the path of a product from its development to its disappearance from a business's portfolio (**the product life cycle**). The time scale will vary – some products only last a few months (think World Cup T-shirts) while others seem to go on forever (think chocolate biscuits). During the introduction or launch stage, sales will often grow slowly. This may be followed by a sharp rise in sales as the product

---

Study tip

Products don't go backwards through the Boston Matrix! It follows a logical progression from Question Mark through to Dog. It applies to the products of one business and is not used to make comparisons with products offered by competitors. It is not necessary to draw the matrix or describe the four elements in detail.

■ Key terms

The product life cycle: the sales path of a product from its introduction onto the market, to its eventual disappearance from that market.

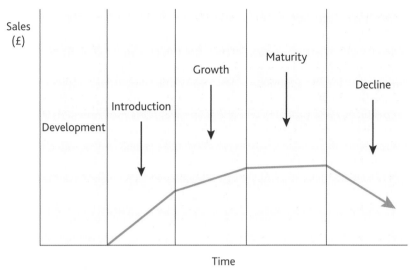

Fig. 30.5 *Product life cycle*

becomes better known. At some point, sales stabilise into the maturity phase, before being overtaken by new product developments or changes in consumer needs, causing a decline in sales.

Why is the product life cycle significant?

■ At the **development stage** the product is being researched and prepared for introduction to the market. No sales are made during this phase.

■ At the **introduction stage** the product is being launched onto the market. There will be a lot of money spent on product development and sales promotion, and because sales are low at this stage, cash inflows are likely to be less than cash outflows. The firm needs to have sufficient finance available to support the new product, and should use techniques such as budgeting and cash flow forecasting to make sure that this stage of the product life cycle does not lead the firm into financial difficulties.

Fig. 30.6 *This product has been in the maturity phase of its life cycle for many years*

■ The **growth stage** should see sales increase significantly, and the product should achieve break-even. The issues at this stage will be about maintaining the expansion of sales and operational decisions will be very important.

■ The **maturity stage** occurs when sales level off and revenue generated by the product stabilises. Customer loyalty has been achieved and less needs to be spent on promotion. Expenditure on the product can be reduced and possibly transferred to others in the introduction and growth stages.

■ **Decline** starts when sales begin to decline, and is perhaps the most difficult stage to spot. Fluctuations in the level of sales can occur for any number of reasons, but is it the start of a long-term decline in the popularity of the product? Businesses can take one of two options at this stage: they can consider extension strategies where modifications are made to the product or service to meet the changing needs of customers (think mobile phones and electronic gaming products); or the product can be allowed to decline with little on-going expenditure by the business (think chocolate bars that you remember from your childhood that no longer exist).

Fig. 30.7 *Slight changes were made to this model in 2013 to extend its life cycle*

Extension strategies

In terms of product development, the maturity stage of the product life cycle is particularly significant. The aim of marketing will be to maintain this level of sales for as long as possible, perhaps even increasing sales through product development. This is when modifications can be introduced to extend the life of the product. Consider mobile phones or electronic gaming products where updated versions are launched on a regular basis. Businesses must prepare for this stage, and make sure that the revised version is ready when needed and (as ever) meets the needs of the customers. It is important to note that any element of the marketing mix can be changed to maintain or increase sales (see Chapters 31–33).

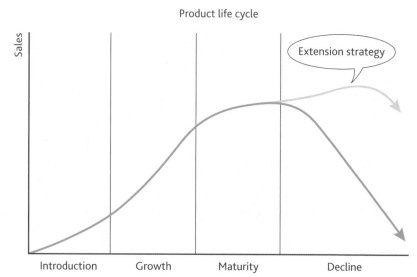

Fig. 30.8 *Diagram to show the effect of an extension strategy on sales*

How useful is the product life cycle?

As with the Boston Matrix, the product life cycle should be treated with caution. It is useful for analysing past sales figures, but it is very difficult to say with any certainty where exactly a product is on the graph at any particular time. There is also a danger that firms may anticipate stages in the product life cycle and react too quickly to variations in sales: reducing marketing activities because they believe that a product has gone into decline, rather than looking for any other explanation for a dip in sales. In fact, there are a range of factors that affect sales, such as the activities of competitors and changes in tastes and fashion, and a product's declining sales may be due to an inappropriate marketing mix rather than any intrinsic problem with the product. There are goods and services that have been on the market for a very long time, such as Monopoly, which prove that with product development, new packaging, new designs and new distribution channels, the maturity stage might never end.

■ **Activity**

How does the product life cycle relate to the Boston Matrix?

■ **Case study**

G.B. Kent & Sons

G.B. Kent & Sons Ltd, manufacturers of brushes since the eighteenth century, is one of the oldest established companies in Great Britain.

Kent Brushes was founded in 1777 by William Kent in the reign of George III. The Kent family continued to run the company for six generations until 1932 when Mr Eric L.H. Cosby, owner of Cosby Brushes Ltd, entered into an association with G.B. Kent & Sons, and since that time the company has been under the creative and dynamic direction of the Cosby family.

The company continues to retain the craftsmanship and unprecedented quality that is Kent's reputation. Even in today's fast moving, mass-produced assembly, Kent are proud to still be manufacturing many of their original brushes by hand, which gives them a product life cycle of at least 230 years!

Nevertheless, Kent Brushes is committed to developing new products and enhancing its existing products. It uses the latest hi-tech manufacturing processes, whilst building on the time-honoured traditional methods to create the world's finest example of each and every brush that leaves their factory.

Kent Brushes currently manufacture an exceptional choice of products, with ranges for hair, body, clothes, make-up, teeth and shaving. Part of Kent Brushes' success with major retailers has been built on their reputation for efficiency and quality. Kent have been supplying stores such as John Lewis, Selfridges, Harrods and Fortnum and Mason along with leading chemists in the UK for over 200 years. They also distribute to over 50 countries worldwide, including USA, Hong Kong, Canada, Australia, Japan, Europe, Scandinavia and the Middle East.

Kent's range is now so vast, that it has a selection of over 250 brushes to choose from. The most comprehensive of these is the hairbrush range, providing brushes for use on any hair type, style and length and for every budget. With a selection of styling brushes, radials, ceramics, vents, ionic, paddle, volumising and pure bristle, Kent are now the perfect choice for salon use and retail.

Questions

1. Use examples from Kent Ltd to explain the meaning of the term 'the product life cycle'   (4 marks)

2. Explain why it is important to a business such as Kent Ltd to develop new products as well as enhance existing ones.   (8 marks)

3. Analyse the benefits to Kent Ltd of attempting to classify its products according to the Boston Matrix model.   (8 marks)

4. To what extent is the future success of Kent Ltd likely to depend upon product portfolio analysis?   (14 marks)

5. Research task: By referring to a car manufacturer or a soft drinks manufacturer, use the product life cycle model to analyse the range of products sold by the business. Explain the decisions that the manufacturer could make with products at different stages of their cycles.

Show the skills

Showing knowledge of both the product life cycle and the Boston Matrix is essential if a question is based on 'product portfolio analysis'. Understanding how to assess a product in terms of its market share, and the growth of the market it is sold in, allows businesses to take appropriate decisions about the future of the product. Your ability to evaluate the usefulness of both forms of portfolio analysis in the context of the case study business may be examined too.

✔ *In this chapter you will have learned to:*

■ explain why the development of goods and services is important

■ explain why a USP and product differentiation are important to a business

■ discuss factors influencing the development of new goods and services

■ explain the meaning of a product portfolio

■ discuss the meaning and significance of the product life cycle

■ evaluate the value of the Boston Matrix and the product life cycle for marketing decision making.

For answers to activities and case study questions see **kerboodle**

Practice questions

Chapters 28–30

1   Explain the purpose of marketing. *(2 marks)*

2   Explain the difference between a niche market and a mass market. *(2 marks)*

3   What is the difference between a consumer market and a business market? *(2 marks)*

4   Ferrets UK is a niche market business which sells everything to do with this increasingly popular pet. The owner Karen Parker operates her business via the internet and has customers from all over the world. Before launching the website and trade-marking the name, Karen conducted a lot of internet market research to ensure that her idea was commercially viable.

    a)   Explain TWO advantages of operating in a niche market. *(4 marks)*

    b)   Karen is hoping to get into the mass market with a series of children's stories called Ferret Tales. Analyse the advantages and drawbacks of this plan. *(8 marks)*

    c)   Evaluate the importance of good market research to the successful marketing of Ferrets UK. *(10 marks)*

5   Identify and explain the main components of the marketing mix. *(6 marks)*

6   Explain the importance of an integrated marketing mix to the success of a business selling to a niche market comprising high income consumers. *(6 marks)*

7   ABC Cabs is a family run taxi business which is facing strong competition from a new business that has just opened in the same town, offering lower fares and quicker response times. Jerry Smith, the marketing director for ABC Cabs has decided to revamp the existing marketing mix in response to this development in the market.

    a)   Identify the four main influences on the marketing mix of a business. *(4 marks)*

    b)   Jerry thought that customers were most interested in clean vehicles and a reliable service. Explain why ABC Cabs needs to keep in touch with the changing needs of consumers. *(4 marks)*

    c)   One of the drivers for ABC Cabs suggested that an online booking service might help to increase market share. To what extent should changes in technology influence the marketing mix for this business? *(10 marks)*

8   What do you understand by the term 'product development'? *(2 marks)*

9   Explain the stages in the process of product development. *(4 marks)*

10 Explain the difference between product differentiation and a unique selling point. *(4 marks)*

11 Explain how developments in technology can effect product development. *(3 marks)*

12   Explain the term 'product portfolio analysis'.   *(2 marks)*

13   The owners of Johnson's, an independent grocery and flower shop, used the Boston Matrix to analyse its product range: potted plants, cut flowers, dried flowers, imitation flowers, traditional fruit and vegetables, organic, locally grown fruit and vegetables.

    a)   What is the Boston Matrix?   *(2 marks)*

    b)   Analyse the benefits to Johnson's of using the Boston Matrix to assess the suitability of their product portfolio.   *(8 marks)*

14   What is the product life cycle?   *(2 marks)*

15   Should Johnson's use the product life cycle, as well as the Boston Matrix to analyse their product portfolio?   *(10 marks)*

16   Evaluate the importance of product portfolio analysis to the marketing mix decisions of a food manufacturing business.   *(14 marks)*

In this chapter you will learn to:

- explain the aims of promotion

- discuss the range of promotional activities available to a business

- explain the meaning of a promotional mix

- discuss factors that might be considered when choosing the promotional mix

- evaluate the final choice of the activities included within a promotional mix.

Key terms

Promotion: bringing a product or range of products to the attention of existing and potential customers.

Sales promotion: offers designed to increase sales.

Promotional activities: the ways in which a business can communicate with its potential and existing customers with the aim of increasing sales.

Setting the scene

Burberry boosts digital promotions

For the first time, the famous fashion brand is to allow customers to purchase clothes through a campaign gallery and short film on Burberry.com. The campaign will run across all of the digital platforms that Burberry currently uses to communicate with its customers including Facebook, Twitter, Google+, Instagram and Pinterest.

The campaign is supported by adverts which focus on Burberry's British heritage. Chris Bailey, the chief creative officer at the company, said that the promotion campaign is 'celebrating our brand … through imagery, film, music and our iconic outerwear in a very British way'.

Discussion points

1. Why is it important for a business to 'communicate with its customers'?

2. What factors might influence the choice of promotional activities and media used by a business?

The aims of promotion

Promotion is the element of the marketing mix concerned with ensuring that customers and potential customers are aware of current and new products in a firm's range. As a result of this awareness, the business hopes to increase sales to existing and new customers.

There are also a number of secondary purposes of promotion which may apply to a particular business:

- To persuade customers that one product is better than others on the market, thereby encouraging people to change their buying habits

- To increase awareness among a greater number of potential customers, for example those spread over a large geographical area

- To remind consumers about a product, for example during the maturity stage in the product life cycle when marketing expenditure may be reduced (Chapter 30). This can encourage repeat purchasing and may attract new customers

- To establish an identity for a business rather than a specific product.

The range of promotional activities available to a business

Sales promotions

These are offers designed to increase short-term sales by giving consumers incentives to purchase one product or service rather than another. **Sales promotions** and **promotional activities** will hopefully lead to longer-term loyalty.

Fig. 31.1 *The range of promotional activities available to businesses*

Business in action

Nando's

Nando's Chicken Restaurant in Manchester wanted to:

- increase sales in its Manchester branch by 10% on the average weekly sales (calculated over the four weeks before the campaign)
- increase sales over the lunch period by £1,000 per week
- Introduce new customers to the store.

The sales promotion chosen was to send a lunch box with a typical sandwich pack and free lunch vouchers worth £4 to offices in the local area. The vouchers were redeemable between 12 noon and 3pm Monday to Friday and customers were invited to telephone their final orders in advance. On redemption of the vouchers they received a 'bounce back' offer for a return visit (buy one get one free). As a result weekly sales increased by 19 per cent, total vouchers redeemed was 17 per cent and sales per week over the lunch period increased by over £1,500. The tick box on the voucher revealed that the sales promotion had attracted over 40 per cent new customers.

Options available to businesses include:

- Money-off vouchers; discounts; loyalty cards; buy-one-get-one-free. These techniques are commonly used by large high street retailers, but smaller firms can also use them just as successfully.
- Competitions with prizes to encourage people to make a purchase.
- Endorsements from respected personalities. Again, although major brand endorsements are very familiar, small, local firms can also use this technique quite successfully.

■ Free gifts offers when a purchase is made.

■ There are other options such as credit terms and product placement, which may be possible for growing businesses, but could prove to be too costly or risky for smaller firms.

Direct selling

Direct selling can be split into two parts:

Personal selling

This accounts for total sales of more than £2 billion per year in the UK. It is usually made face-to-face, either where a product is demonstrated in the home or a catalogue is left with the customer. In the business to business market, firms will employ sales representatives who make direct personal contact with potential clients.

There are several **advantages** of this method of promotion:

■ The features and functions of the product or service can be fully explained and questions answered.

■ Orders can be collected and delivered.

■ Feedback can be gathered directly from customers.

However, there are also **disadvantages** with this option:

■ It can be expensive to maintain a sales team.

■ Some customers dislike 'cold callers'.

■ There are legal issues to protect consumers from being intimidated by forceful sales people, which may be difficult to monitor, and may require expensive induction training.

Direct mailing

Direct mailing involves sending information about a product to potential customers through the post. This may be seen as 'junk mail' by some consumers, but this form of promotion can be very successful, particularly for small and new businesses who want to get a foothold in a market.

> ### Key terms
>
> **Direct selling**: a way of selling directly to the final consumer without another intermediary.

Fig. 31.2 *Merchandising helps to support the Twinings brand*

Business in action

Twinings

Twinings speciality teas provide merchandising support for their products including cards and signs, display stands and boxes, guides and leaflets. The company believes that their merchandising projects a quality image which is the basis for all their marketing. Because their products are sold in such a wide range of outlets, supplying the merchandising material helps Twinings to control its brand image.

Merchandising

Merchandising is about the visual presentation of a product to the consumer at the point of sale. Merchandising attracts the customers to buy a particular product in a shop, and is often targeted at impulse buyers, and takes advantage of pester power – children trying to persuade parents to buy them a gift. The features of good merchandising include high quality display material, full shelves and the layout of products

> ### Key terms
>
> **Merchandising**: the visual presentation of a product to the consumer at the point of sale.

within a store being well planned: putting very popular items at the back of the store so shoppers have to pass all the other items first for example. Appealing to people's senses is also a successful technique: clever lighting and enticing aromas can attract people into a store.

Advertising

This is probably the most familiar method of promotion and involves the use of media such as billboards, newspapers, trade and technical press, TV, radio, directories, internet and cinema, to communicate with consumers. It can be local or national, relatively cheap or incredibly expensive! **Advertising** is known as 'above the line' promotion, whereas all other types of promotion are called 'below the line'. It is generally a longer-term option compared to some of the other promotional techniques, and advertising is categorised into two main types, each with a different objective:

- **Persuasive**: trying to convince consumers to buy a product. This can be the most controversial type of advertising and has lead to controls being placed on advertisers, for example the Trades Descriptions Act 1968 and the Advertising Standards Authority which regulates the content of advertisements, sales promotions and direct marketing in the UK has outlawed Pester Power. Advertisements should not actively encourage children to make a nuisance of themselves to parents or others.

- **Informative**: increasing consumer awareness of a product, by providing details of its features. This sort of advertising is less controversial and, it is argued, enables the consumer to make a rational choice about which product or service to buy.

There are advantages and disadvantages to every type of advertising, and not all of them are appropriate for smaller businesses. In general terms, firms need to consider the following factors when deciding between advertising media:

- Cost – most small organisations will have to think about which media they can afford to use.
- The audience reached by the media – it is better to concentrate on the target audience only, for example through specialist magazines to maximise impact.
- Competitors' advertising, if successful, will indicate the best media for a business to use.
- The law may have an impact on how and where a firm can advertise.

Public relations

The aim is to increase sales by enhancing the reputation of the business. **Public relations** is a planned and sustained effort to make sure that customers have a good opinion of the organisation. Options include press releases, launch parties, editorial features, media events, charity support, sponsorship and competitions.

Branding

Branding is a means of identification for consumers of a business or one or more of its products. Successful **branding** promotes the strengths, and increasingly, the values of the business. Although the concept of branding is most familiar with household names such as Coca-Cola and Pepsi, where millions of customers are loyal to one brand and will not buy another, smaller firms can create brand loyalty. This could be a family-run business that gains such a good reputation for excellent quality and

Key terms

Advertising: the use of media to communicate with consumers.

Activity

Go to Burberry.com and comment on the advantages and disadvantages of the ways used by this company to advertise and promote the brand and its products.

Key terms

Public relations: communicating with the media and other interested parties to enhance the image of the business and its products, and thereby increase sales.

Branding: creating an identity for a business and its products to differentiate it from rivals in the market.

customer service, that when a new range of products is launched, the loyalty of previous customers to the brand ensures a steady stream of business. For many firms, the aim of branding is to become the brand leader in their particular market. The most successful branding occurs where the generic name for the product is replaced by the name of the brand – when you talk about a MacDonald's rather than a burger for instance. Obviously, if a small business is competing in the mass market it will be very difficult to have the most well known brand, but for firms operating in niche markets the opportunity to develop the leading brand is always a possibility.

Business in action

Attenborough Saffron and Blue Dragon

Attenborough Saffron is a Public Relations company with a wide range of clients including Blue Dragon, importers and manufacturers of oriental speciality food. To reinforce and support Blue Dragon's authentic marketing, Attenborough Saffron organised sponsorship of the Chinese State Circus tour to the UK, negotiated extensive on-site product placement, for example in the programme and banners in the 'big-top', set up regional press competitions to win tickets to local performances and offered tickets to VIPs within the trade media and for sales force use.

Business in action

Apple

Apple is a particularly interesting case study. Saved from bankruptcy in the 1990s, it has transformed its product range and brand image to become one of the most widely recognised and respected names in global business. The Apple brand is successful for a number of reasons. Many Apple users say it is because of the way its phones and other equipment operate. Some psychologists suggest that it is because of the social relationship built up between the company and its consumers. Other people still believe its success is down to one man, the late Steve Jobs, and his flair for creativity and funky, quirky designs.

Fig. 31.3 *The iPhone supports Apple's image-conscious brand*

Key terms

Promotional mix: the combination of promotional activities which make up a campaign to communicate with a target market.

💡 The promotional mix

All businesses will use a combination of these methods to make up the promotional element of the marketing mix. This is called the **promotional mix** and the combination chosen will depend on a number of factors, which could include the following.

Costs

For many small and growing businesses, the marketing budget is not likely to be very large, and so the choice of promotional mix may not include high cost options such as television advertising, high-profile endorsements and expensive competition prizes.

Competitors

The promotional mix of rival companies can have an impact on activities selected by a business: do you match their sales promotions for instance, or offer something better? What is important is that an organisation is aware of what competitors are doing in terms of promotion, so that they are not caught out and lose valuable customers.

Target market

Any business should have a clear idea about which consumer group they are aiming a particular promotional campaign at. If the target market for a new magazine is children, the publishers will use a different promotional mix to that of a new magazine aimed at retired people.

The product

If it is a new product or service, being launched onto the market, the emphasis will be on product awareness, and the promotional mix should reflect this, with more emphasis on advertising and sales promotion. Later, when the product has become established in the market, the focus could change to developing brand loyalty and a comprehensive merchandising package.

The market

If the business is operating in the consumer market, the target for advertising and branding will be the end consumer. In the business to business market, personal selling may be much more important than any other elements of the promotional mix.

The other elements of the marketing mix

In any decision about which mix of promotional activities to select, the point of reference should be full integration with the other elements of the marketing mix, which in itself comes from an understanding of what the business is trying to achieve. Only if there is full integration between all parts of the marketing mix will sales success be maximised.

Case study

Tourism Ireland

Tourism Ireland is responsible for marketing the island of Ireland to over 20 markets across the world. It has an annual promotional budget of over £50 million. It aimed, in 2012, to increase tourist numbers by 7%. Before developing new promotional mix activities for each market, it analysed the types of tourists who visit Ireland from each market. For example, in 2012, it attracted over 850,000 visitors from the USA. This is the second largest number from any one country after the UK. A higher proportion of US tourists hire a car during their holiday than tourists from any other country. 81% of the US tourists travelled to Ireland for sightseeing and culture holidays in 2012, and 71% visited for the first time.

The Gathering 2013 was Ireland's biggest ever tourism initiative. This year-long series of fairs, festivals and cultural events is designed to attract the 70 million people around the globe who claim ancestral links to Ireland. *The Gathering* was promoted with a mix of TV adverts under the banner of 'Jump into Ireland', promotional fairs including 'Ireland Days' in certain foreign cities, and press and radio advertising. A developing theme with Tourism Ireland's promotion is the increasing importance of e-Marketing. Over 25% of the total budget is now allocated to online promotions, and these include 41 websites in 19 different languages.

Activity

Promotion is communication, so it is very important to understand the behaviour of the target market. Avon failed to anticipate the size of the response to a campaign offering a free Orange mobile phone to customers who spent £15 or more on skincare products. Many customers were disappointed and this caused negative publicity for the business.

How can firms avoid this type of mistake?

Business in action

Media Communications

Media Communications have Chartered Institute of Marketing qualified staff and therefore are able to fully understand the client's needs before producing design work. They ask questions, sometimes difficult ones, so they can understand the purpose of a firm's marketing literature and therefore ensure it is targeted correctly at the clients. 'With advertising, the approach should always be targeted, never random.'

Study tip

Promotion is more than advertising and the budget available will affect promotion possibilities.

■ Show the skills

Keep up to date with the latest developments in promotion via social media and other forms of digital communication. You might have an opportunity to evaluate whether such methods are suitable for all businesses or not.

Questions

1 What do you understand by the term 'promotional mix'? (4 marks)

2 Explain why it is important, using evidence from the case study, to conduct market research in target markets before deciding on the promotional mix to be used. (8 marks)

3 Analyse the likely reasons why e-Marketing methods are becoming more important to Tourism Ireland. (10 marks)

4 Evaluate appropriate ways in which Tourism Ireland could promote holidays in Ireland to tourists from a country such as China that currently sends few visitors to Ireland. (14 marks)

5 Research task: Find out the most popular tourist destination in your region. Examine the ways in which this destination promotes itself to potential visitors.

☑ *In this chapter you will have learned to:*

- explain the aims of promotion
- describe the range of promotional activities available to a business
- discuss the creation of a promotional mix
- analyse factors that might be considered when choosing the promotional mix
- discuss the final choice of the activities included within a promotional mix.

For answers to activities and case study questions see **kerboodle**

Using the marketing mix: pricing

Key terms

Pricing strategies: long-term pricing plans which take into account the objectives of the business and the value associated with the product.

Price skimming: entering a market with a high price to attract early adopters and recoup high development costs.

Penetration pricing: below market pricing to gain a foothold in an established and competitive market.

Setting the scene

Kate Moss @ Topshop

When Topshop launched the Kate Moss range of clothing in its 225 UK stores, customers were only allowed to buy five items per person to prevent the clothes being re-sold on eBay. The clothes were competitively priced and sold out in record time. The target market of young, fashion conscious female shoppers wanted to buy into the Kate Moss look. The most popular item was a £45 floral print dress. When the range was launched in the Barneys store in New York it sold out within one hour. One New York fashion critic commented that the studded real leather clutch bag selling for US$125 was indistinguishable from a designer bag that would sell for US$400 elsewhere.

Discussion points

1. Why is price important to customers?

2. What factors might have influenced the pricing decisions taken by Topshop when launching the Kate Moss collection?

Pricing strategies

When a new product is launched onto the market, the firm must decide how much to charge. If the price is too high or too low for the market, it can at best limit the growth of the business and at worst cause sales and cash flow problems. At a basic level, a firm needs to know approximately how much it costs to provide a product or service, and then make sure that the price charged is above that figure. The **pricing strategy** should reflect the perceived value of the benefits a product provides for customers, always bearing in mind what competitors are charging of course!

Pricing strategies for new products

Price skimming

Price skimming is used for the launch of a new product which faces little initial direct competition, for example the product has a unique selling point/proposition. The launch price is high so the product is bought by a small number of consumers, known as 'early adopters', who are not very concerned about the price. The profit margin is high, but this is often necessary to recover very large research and development costs. At some point the price is lowered. This is either because competitors have launched a rival product or because the objective of the business is now to sell the product in large numbers.

Penetration pricing

Penetration pricing is the opposite approach to skimming, although it is also used for the launch of a new product. The aim is not to sell to an exclusive segment of the market, but to capture a large share of the market as quickly as possible. It is a strategy used mostly in a very competitive market where there is little real product differentiation. The pricing policy will be supported by other elements of the marketing mix such as promotion to try and establish brand loyalty. If this can be achieved, then the price can be gradually increased. The legend 'introductory offer' suggests penetration pricing.

Link

For more information on pricing and costs, see Chapter 11 – Calculating costs, revenues and profits, page 75.

Business in action

Skimming in action

The Apple iPad Mini, Playstations 1–3, Panasonic plasma screen TVs and Sky Sports have all been launched using this strategy.

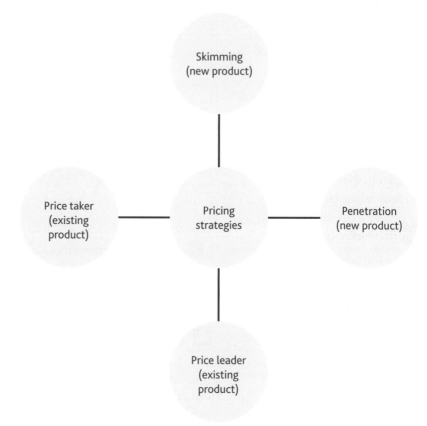

Fig. 32.1 *The main pricing strategies available to businesses*

Pricing strategies for existing products

Price leaders

These are businesses that dominate a market and can set the price for certain products. Every other business in the market has to follow their lead. This **price leader** strategy can be used when one business has a very strong brand image, and the product differentiation is minimal.

For smaller businesses it may be possible to dominate a local market with a very strong brand, for example a taxi service, and operate as a price leader.

Price takers

These are firms that have no option but to charge the market price for their products. This applies when there are many small businesses, with very little difference, as far as consumers are concerned, between one product on the market and another, or where one or a few companies dominate a market which also has many small firms. Businesses that are **price takers** will use other elements of the marketing mix to try and establish product differentiation, which may give them more freedom when it comes to price setting.

Key terms

Price leader: a product that has significant market share and can influence the market price.

Price taker: a firm which sets its prices at the same or similar level to those of the dominant firm in the industry.

Pricing tactics

Pricing tactics are short-term pricing plans designed to achieve a particular business objective such as increasing market share or to increase the sales of a product range.

Loss leaders

Loss leaders are products sold for less than it costs to make or buy from the manufacturer/wholesaler. The aim is to create interest and encourage customers to visit the shop, website, or catalogue. Once the consumer is 'captured' they are likely to buy other products in the firm's range, therefore increasing the total value of sales.

Psychological pricing

This is the use of prices that seem to be significantly lower than other very similar prices and so appear to the consumer to offer better value for money, for example £5.99 rather than £6.00. **Psychological pricing** is also known as odd value pricing and only really works if price is an essential part of the consumer's buying decision, that is when there are lots of very similar products at around the same price.

Business in action

Harry Potter

The final Harry Potter book *Harry Potter and the Deathly Hallows* was distributed wholesale for £10.74, and had a Recommended Retail Price of £17.99. However, Waterstones, WH Smith and Amazon priced it at just £8.99 and Asda and Tesco sold it for even less. When questioned about this tactic, Waterstones, for example, were confident that once the Potter fans were in the store they would buy other titles, thereby increasing total sales.

Activity

Amazon may offer a DVD for £10.98, Play.com for £9.99.

1. Which DVD supplier would you choose?
2. Would your decision change if you knew that Amazon would deliver the product to you in two days, whilst Play.com would take one week?
3. Is there any length of delivery time at which your purchasing decision would change?

Influences on pricing decisions

When a company decides on its pricing structure, there are several factors that must be taken into consideration.

Costs

Even if a business elects to use a loss leader pricing tactic, this can only operate in the short term, unless there are other products to cover the losses made (see Cash Cow, Chapter 30). One of the main reasons for new business failure is poor planning, and this includes understanding costs, profit and margins. If the price charged is wrong and costs are not

Key terms

Pricing tactics: the manipulation of price to achieve a specific short-term objective.

Loss leaders: products sold at less than cost to attract customers to a product range.

Psychological pricing: the use of odd number pricing to increase the value-for-money appeal of a product.

Activity

Why was the final Harry Potter book sold as a loss leader by the supermarket chains Asda and Tesco?

Link

For more information on the using marketing mix, see Chapter 30 – Using the marketing mix: product, page 221.

Business in action

Boots as price takers

Independent chemists and even large businesses like Boots are price takers in a market now dominated by the large supermarkets. They emphasise high quality customer service and promotional techniques to attract consumers instead. Other examples will include independent garages offering vehicle repair and maintenance and sandwich shops.

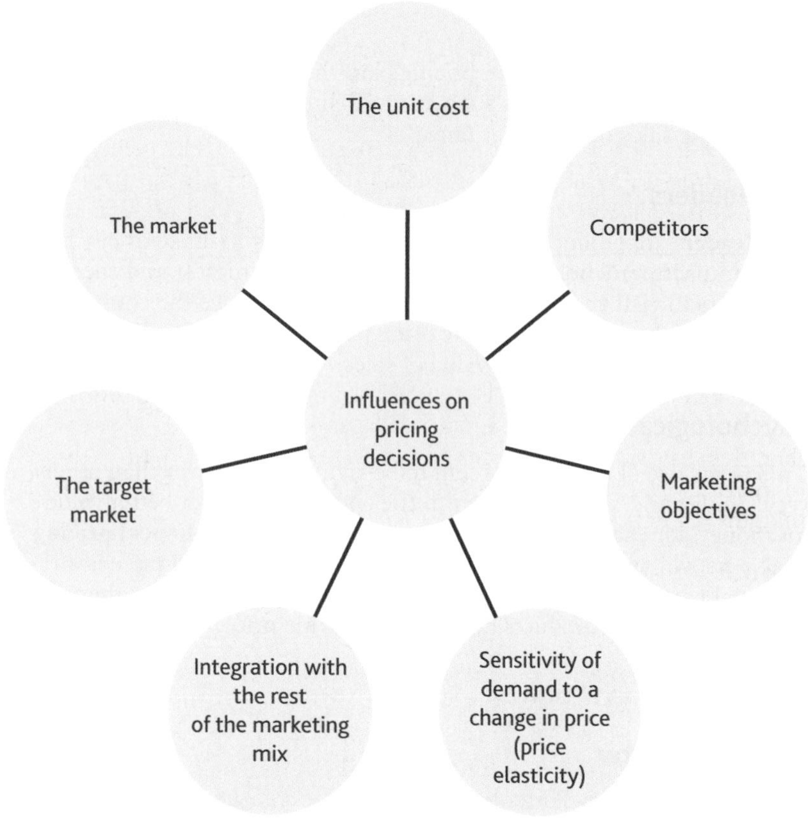

Fig. 32.2 *Influences on pricing decisions*

Study tip

Cost is not the same as price. Make sure that you always use the terms correctly, otherwise your answer may appear confused. The cost of a product is what a business *incurs* when it pays its suppliers; the price is what the business *charges* its customers.

covered, the business will have cash flow problems and is unlikely to survive (see Chapter 17 – Improving cash flow, page 119).

Competitors

Competitors will have a big impact on pricing decisions. The price that rivals in a market charge will be very important if the product being sold is perceived as very similar by consumers. If one business in the market decides to drop its price in an attempt to increase market share, others will have to decide whether or not to follow suit. If rivals decide to match the lower price, a price war may begin which will reduce the profit margin for all businesses in the market and can lead to shortages and restriction on consumer purchases. The nature of the product is also important, and businesses will use the marketing mix to try and persuade consumers that their product is in some way superior to that of competitors, thereby justifying a higher price.

Activity

Under what market conditions might rival companies enter a price war, and when might competitors not respond by changing price?

The market

The market itself has a significant influence on pricing decisions. The fast rate of change in one market may lead firms to believe that their product has a relatively short life cycle. The decision may be made to try and exploit the 'early adopter' consumers with a price skimming strategy. If the market is not growing very quickly and products have reached the maturity stage of the product life cycle, a change in price may be used as a way of regenerating interest in a product to extend its life.

Business in action

In 2013, Tesco introduced its 'price promise'. Tesco shoppers have their basket of goods checked against prices at Asda, Sainsbury and Morrisons. If comparable goods could have been bought cheaper there, customers are given a voucher for the price difference.

The target market

This will have an impact on the pricing decisions made by a business. There is no point putting a very high price on a product when the target consumer group is low to middle income earners. This has certainly been an issue facing drugs companies producing chronic disease medication such as drugs to treat HIV/AIDS. Should they operate a differentiated pricing structure based on socioeconomic indicators to make them equally affordable to people and countries with different incomes and disease burdens, or skim the market to recover the very high research and development costs?

The objectives of the business

Business objectives will also be important in the decision-making process. If the organisation wants to maximise profits in the short term, then the price should reflect that. On the other hand, if the firm wants to increase its share of the market, then a lower price and reduced profit margins may be more appropriate.

The other elements of the marketing mix

The rest of the marketing mix will influence the price, because the elements must be fully integrated for the mix to be effective. If the product is sold online as well as in retail outlets, there may need to be different prices for each market. In the same way, a product which is differentiated from others on the market may enable the business to charge a higher price. Price must be integrated with the other elements of the marketing mix.

Sensitivity of demand to price changes

The relationship between demand and price is called **price elasticity of demand** and is particularly important for a business considering price changes. For most products it is safe to suggest that if the price increases, demand for the product will fall and vice versa. However, by how much will the demand change? Price elasticity of demand theory attempts to predict the impact a change in price will have on demand and therefore total revenue and profit.

Fig. 32.3 *Prices must be integrated with the rest of the marketing mix*

■ Key terms

Price elasticity of demand: the responsiveness of demand for a product to a change in its price.

■ Link

For more information on price, revenue and demand, see Chapter 11 – Calculating costs, revenues and profits, page 75.

■ Price elasticity of demand (PED)

If Apple cut the price of its iPads by 10% but demand only increased by 5%, would this have been a good decision? It seems that demand is not very responsive to this price cut – so the total sales revenue (i.e. price × quantity) will actually fall.

Our answer to this question: 'Is it a good decision?' would be helped by calculating the price elasticity of demand. The following formula is used:

$$\text{Price elasticity of demand} = \frac{\%\ \text{change in demand}}{\%\ \text{change in price}}$$

Using the iPad data above, the PED will be:

$$\text{PED} = \frac{5\%}{-10\%} = -0.5$$

This result means that, for every 1% change in price, demand only changes by 0.5% but in the opposite direction! So if the price rises, demand falls and vice versa. This is what we would expect. This simple relationship between the price of a product and the demand for it will mean that the

Activity

Prove to yourself (by using the formula above) that if the price of Polo mints increased by 4% but demand for them *fell* by 8%, then the PED result will be –2.

PED results will be *negative*. As nearly all PED results are negative, it is common practice to ignore the minus sign when discussing elasticity.

When the demand for a product is very responsive to a change in price, PED is said to be elastic. The value of PED will be greater than 1 (ignoring the minus sign!). When the demand for a product is very unresponsive to a price change, PED is inelastic. The result will be less than 1 (ignoring the minus sign).

So, the PED calculation results in a number that is either greater or less than 1 (ignoring the minus sign). This PED result indicates to a business whether a change in prices will have a positive or a negative effect on total sales revenue. Marketing managers will want to take price decisions that increase total sales revenue. How can knowing PED help them take the right price decision? By working through the following two examples we will be able to make some simple statements about how the PED result can influence pricing decisions:

Example 1: Car tyres

a A car tyre business sells 500 tyres per week. The average selling price is £50.
Total weekly sales revenue = 500 × £50 = £25,000

b The manager estimates the PED for car tyres sold by his garage is −2 (i.e. demand is elastic).

c One week, he reduces tyre prices by 10% to £45.

d Using the PED coefficient of −2 and the % change in price of 10%, the manager can now calculate the % change in demand:

$$-2 = \frac{\% \text{ change in demand}}{-10\%}$$

Therefore the change in demand is 20%

$$-2 = \frac{20\%}{-10\%}$$

e Demand was 500 and has now increased by 20%

$$500 \times 0.20 = 100$$

Therefore new demand = 500 + 100 = 600 tyres

f Total weekly sales revenue = 600 × £45 = £27,000 (*more* than it was originally)

This shows that total sales revenue will *increase* if prices are reduced when PED is *elastic*.

Activity

Calculate the total weekly sales revenue if the tyre business increased tyre prices by 5% from £50 to £52.50.

Example 2: Florist

a A flower shop sells 300 bunches of flowers each week for an average of £10.
Total weekly sales revenue = 300 × £10 = £3,000

b The manager estimates that PED for flowers sold from her shop is − 0.5 (i.e. demand is inelastic)

c One week, she reduces prices by 10% to £9.

d Using the PED coefficient of −0.5 and the % change in price of 10%, the manager can now calculate the % change in demand:

$$-0.5 = \frac{\% \text{ change in demand}}{-10\%}$$

Therefore the change in demand is 5%

$$-0.5 = \frac{5\%}{-10\%}$$

e Demand was 300 and has now increased by 5%

$$300 \times 0.05 = 15$$

Therefore new demand is 300 + 15 = 315 bunches

f Total weekly sales revenue = 315 × £9 = £2,835 (*less* than it was originally)

This shows that total sales revenue will *fall* if prices are reduced when PED is *inelastic*.

The following table should now help to make clear the impact of elasticity on sales revenue following price changes:

Table 32.1 *Price elasticity of demand and the impact on total revenue*

PED result	Price change	Demand change	Impact on total revenue
Between 0 and 1 (ignore minus sign) e.g. 0.5	Rise	Fall (but by a smaller proportion)	Increase
	Fall	Rise (but by a smaller proportion)	Decrease
Greater than 1 (ignore minus sign) e.g. 2.5	Rise	Fall (but by a greater proportion)	Decrease
	Fall	Rise (but by a greater proportion)	Increase

Case study

PED of Pizza

Jane and Ashif run a pizza takeaway business. Based on their past experience, they estimate that their products have a price elasticity of demand of −0.6. The average price per pizza is £6.50 and they sell 200 per week. Total weekly revenue is 200 × £6.50 = £1,300.

Their landlord has recently increased the rent on the shop. Jane and Ashif have reluctantly decided to increase the prices of their pizzas by 20% to £7.80. They were relieved to find that sales only fell to 176 per week because the PED estimate was correct. Sales fell by 24 pizzas which is 12% of the original 200.

$$PED = \frac{-12\%}{20\%} = -0.6$$

Total weekly sales rose to £1,372.80.

Total weekly sales revenue = 176 × £7.80 = £1,372.80

Three months after the price increase another takeaway business opened up in the same street. This charged lower prices than Jane and Ashif's business. They realised that demand for their pizzas would now be more elastic than before. For one week only, they lowered the prices of the largest pizzas from £10 to £8 (−20%). Sales shot up by 30% from 50 to 65 during this week.

Questions

1 Calculate the total sales revenue from the large pizzas
   a before the price reduction
   b after the price reduction   (4 marks)

2 Do your results mean that the demand for these pizzas was elastic or inelastic?   (4 marks)

3 Explain why new competition has made the demand for pizzas more elastic.   (4 marks)

What determines a product's price elasticity of demand?

The number of similar products available to consumers

If there are lots of competing products PED is likely to be elastic because a rise or fall in price will cause customers to switch from one supplier to another. Don't forget though, that if a business can achieve strong customer loyalty, they can reduce the PED.

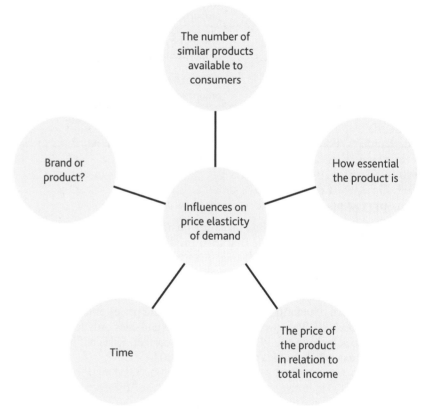

Fig. 32.4 *Influences on price elasticity of demand*

Key terms

Price inelastic demand: the demand for a product changes relatively less than the change in price.

How essential is the product?

This will also affect consumers' reactions to changes in price. If the product is a necessity, or very addictive, customers will continue to buy the same quantity even though the price changes. This suggests that essential and very addictive products are **price inelastic**.

The price of the product in relation to the total income of the consumer

This may also be significant because price becomes a more important consideration. This would suggest that when the product is expensive (a large percentage of disposable income, for example a car, a house, a holiday) the product will be **price elastic**, whereas a cheap product, for example a packet of crisps is likely to be price inelastic. Note that this refers to product groups rather than individual brands or makes.

Time will affect price elasticity

In the short term consumers are often loyal to their chosen brand and won't change their buying habits even if the price changes. This makes products more price inelastic in the short term. In the longer term they may look for alternatives, particularly if satisfaction in the brand decreases, making demand more price elastic.

Brand or product?

The demand for petrol is likely to be price inelastic due to the essential nature of the product. However, the demand for any one *brand* of petrol could be elastic if only one company, Shell for example, increased their prices. Car owners would quickly switch to Esso and other retailers.

In some markets, though, brand loyalty is very strong, helped by promotion and brand image. So if the price of Jimmy Choo shoes increased, for instance, the sales of them might not be much affected, as demand is inelastic.

Are there any problems with measuring price elasticity?

- The main difficulty is getting accurate information about consumer demand at different prices. This requires market research which can be time-consuming and expensive if it is to be reliable.
- Price elasticity does not stay the same at every price and the reaction of consumers to a very small change in price may be different to their buying behaviour if price change is significant in their eyes.
- It is not always possible to attribute changes in demand for a product directly to a change in price. As we have already seen there are other elements of the marketing mix, and external factors such as competitor's actions to consider.

Key terms

Price elastic demand: the demand for a product changes relatively more than the change in price.

Case study

Levi's sustainable denim

Levi's recently launched what it claimed to be the first fully sustainable denims from a major brand. The jeans, made with completely organic material went on sale at 20 Levi's stores in the UK. A spokesperson for the company said that market research showed customers were becoming interested in clothes made using sustainable production methods, but still wanted style and quality. Levi's produced 30,000 pairs of jeans for the launch across Europe and initially stocked them in just 2 per cent of stores. This was partly due to the limited availability of organic cotton. The price tag was £80 which suggested that demand is price inelastic: a small number of consumers wanting to buy organic products. Interestingly, the jeans were only available in Europe: Levi's claimed that European consumers were more interested in products that have been made in a sustainable way than customers in the USA and Asia.

■ Show the skills

Use your understanding of the business in the case study to help answer questions on pricing decisions. For example, if the business has a product with a USP, it might successfully be able to charge a high price as PED is likely to be low (inelastic). If it sells a product which is difficult to differentiate from other rival products, then lower, more competitive prices will have to be set.

Questions

1 What is meant by the phrase 'demand is price inelastic'? (4 marks)

2 Calculate the total revenue the company would achieve if it sold all 30,000 pairs of organic jeans. (4 marks)

3 If the price elasticity coefficient for organic Levi jeans was -0.5, what would be the new total revenue if they raised the price of the jeans by 5%? (4 marks)

4 Would you expect the PED for Levi jeans to be elastic or inelastic? Explain your answer. (8 marks)

5 Analyse how Levis could try to ensure that the whole marketing mix for its jeans reflects the premium prices being charged. (10 marks)

6 To what extent is the cost of materials likely to be the most important factor determining the £80 price tag on Levi's 'green jeans'? (14 marks)

7 Research task: Next time you go shopping for clothes, note down the prices of five different brands of jeans. How would you explain the different prices?

💡✅ *In this chapter you will have learned to:*

- describe the pricing strategies used by businesses

- describe the pricing tactics used by businesses

- discuss the importance of price within the marketing mix and how it can be used to deal with competition and meet the needs of the target market

- analyse the factors influencing the price decision

- discuss the significance, determinants and the problems of measurement of price elasticity

- use the price elasticity coefficient to show the effects of price changes on total revenue.

For answers to activities and case study questions see

33   Using the marketing mix: place

Setting the scene

Old Oak Insurance

Old Oak Insurance was established in 1938 by Peter Evans and Hugh Williams, who have invested considerable time and resources growing the company to its current size. They have three different offices in West Wales and service their clients with ten different types of cover including home, marine, farm, travel, taxi, church and pet insurance. Although they can be contacted via email, and have a comprehensive website, they encourage clients to 'talk to us to find out how we can help you with your insurance.'

However, the number of consumers searching for and arranging insurance online is increasing rapidly. Insurance-related searches for insurance were up 18% in January 2011 compared to a year earlier – and car and travel insurance increased by 84%. Confused.com was the first insurance price comparison website in the UK, but it has been followed by many others. These now account for a very high proportion of new insurance business.

The selling and distribution of other products is also changing. 2.6 million children's e-books were sold online in the first six months of 2012 compared to 1 million in 2011.

Discussion points

1. What factors are likely to influence a business's choice of retail outlet or online selling for its products?

2. Does it matter where a business decides to sell its products?

3. How could Old Oak Insurance try to compete with sites such as Confused.com?

What is 'place'?

This element of the marketing mix is concerned with the distribution of the product to the purchaser, whether it is another business or the final consumer. The aim is to ensure that the product gets to the right place at the right time. A fantastic product can be priced correctly and promoted cleverly, but if it is not available to buy, it will not be really successful.

Distribution channels

Companies can be involved in consumer marketing and business to business marketing, which may be significant when considering how customers gain access to a firm's products. There are a wide range of **distribution channels** used by businesses selling to final consumers and other companies, some are the same, but others are more specific to one or other type of market.

Key terms

Distribution channel: method by which a product is sold to the customer.

249

Direct distribution

A **direct sale** is where the product or service is sold by the supplier to the final consumer without the intervention of any **intermediaries**. The development of e-commerce has made the direct sale an increasingly realistic option for many smaller firms because it can keep the price that the final consumer pays to a minimum. Examples include farmers' markets, hand-made furniture makers and chiropodists.

Fig. 33.1 *Direct channel of distribution*

Traditional distribution

For many firms, whose customers are geographically dispersed or who need to reduce the quantity sold into smaller units, intermediaries such as wholesalers, retailers and agents are used. Examples include soft toy manufacturers who use regional wholesalers to distribute their products to local retailers, market gardeners who distribute their produce directly to retailers and educational book publishers who use agents to distribute their products to schools and colleges.

Business to consumer markets

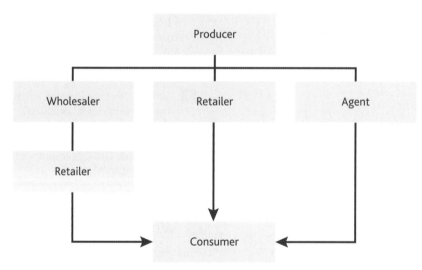

Fig. 33.2 *Traditional channels of distribution*

Retail

This covers everything from a market stall to a hypermarket. There have been trends away from high street retailing over the past 20 years, but there is growing pressure for urban renewal and incentives are available to attract businesses back to town centres. This is an expensive form of distribution because the costs for premises and staff are higher than other alternatives.

Mail order

Catalogues can give access to a greater number of potential customers or can be used to target a particular consumer group. Costs are lower than for retailing.

Direct selling

The producer sells straight to the final consumer of the product or service, without intermediaries such as wholesalers or retailers. It includes door to door selling, telephone sales and product parties. It is particularly successful for high-value and complex products such as building work, double-glazing and life insurance.

Internet/e-commerce

Selling goods and services via a website, using search engines, web links and pop-ups. It has grown to become a very important method of distribution, particularly for small, start-up businesses because of the low initial cost. The development of secure methods of payment has increased the use of this option by consumers.

Multi-channel

Businesses using more than one channel of distribution. The coordination of these different options has been made possible by related developments in technology.

Business to business markets

Wholesaling is used by many small and medium-sized businesses. It provides a link between manufacturers and retailers and allows for goods to be bought in manageable quantities.

Direct sales

Without the use of any intermediaries, direct sales are very important in the **business to business market** because many products or services are high-value and complex. For example, expensive machine tools will be sold directly from the manufacturers to the factory planning to use them.

E-commerce

This is of growing importance in this market, particularly for small businesses wanting to sell goods and services, for example website design services, via the internet. There are a growing number of intermediary sites that facilitate the distribution process on the web. Businesses can display examples of work and include testimonials and case study examples from existing clients.

Mail order/catalogue

This method of selling is used in particular by businesses that have a wide range of product options for clients to choose from. It can be used to display examples of previous work. Many offices still purchase stationery and supplies from mail order catalogues.

Multi-channel distribution

This is also growing in importance in the business to business market.

Intermediaries

In both markets, the role of intermediaries can be very important. These individuals or organisations act on behalf of the business, but are not employed by them. In many case, intermediaries in the chain of distribution will act on behalf of many different businesses such as wholesale businesses.

In the **business to consumer market** many insurance businesses use brokers rather than dealing directly with customers, and holiday

Activity

1. Select a product or service. What are the advantages and disadvantages of each method of distribution for this good or service?

2. Why are an increasing number of businesses using multi-channel distribution?

Key terms

Business to business markets: companies meeting the needs of other businesses in the market place.

Business to consumer markets: companies meeting the needs of final consumers of goods and services.

Multi-channel distribution: the use of a variety of selling/distribution methods to give customers a choice of how to purchase a product.

Fig. 33.3 *Retail stores are just one of the distribution channels used by Next plc*

companies use travel agents, and cosmetics and toiletry manufacturers use high street retailers and supermarkets.

In the business to business market, agents are also commonplace, particularly when a company is new to the market and needs their expertise.

Choosing appropriate outlets or distributors

Businesses will take several factors into consideration when selecting the best outlets or distributors for their products.

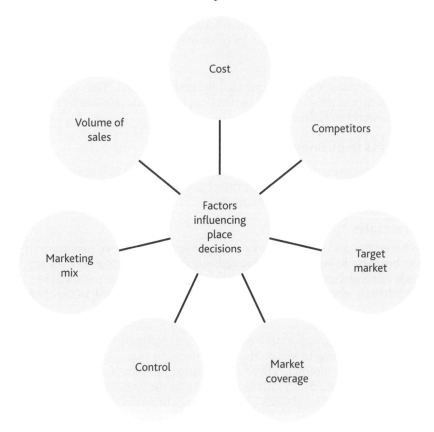

Fig. 33.4 *Factors influencing the choice of outlets/distributors*

Cost

Cost will be important. In both the business to consumer and business to business markets, fixed and variable costs need to be calculated and comparisons made. Many small businesses now distribute their products via the internet because the start-up and running costs are much lower.

Competitors

The competition should also be taken into consideration. If most suppliers of a particular product or service use one channel of distribution, one company might increase market share by using a different one. However, if customers expect to buy through an established route, this strategy could be risky. For example, it took Amazon many years to become profitable when it introduced internet shopping for products normally bought through retail outlets.

The target market

The target market should always be considered when selecting appropriate outlets. For example, locating a fashion clothing store with a target market of teenage girls, at an out-of-town retail park, may not be as successful as a city/town centre location.

Market coverage

Consider the need of suppliers to reach a large number of potential consumers. This may not be possible for the producer without the help of intermediaries who can spread the coverage over a wider geographical area.

Control

Control over the distribution process is also very important, and the more intermediaries a business uses, the less influence the original supplier may have.

Fig. 33.5 *To distribute its crisps to the Chinese market, Tyrrell's linked up with Sinodis, a specialist importing and distributing business*

The marketing mix

The other elements of the marketing mix will also have an impact on the choice of distributor and outlets. As we have seen before, the mix must be integrated, and the place element is no exception.

Volume of sales

Sales volume will be an important consideration. If the business needs high volume to cover costs and achieve profit, there must be an appropriate distribution network in place. If the firm is aiming for exclusivity this should be reflected in the quality and quantity of chosen outlets.

Case study

Exhibitions – a form of direct selling

It is claimed that in the business to business world, the best channel of distribution, offering the highest return on investment, is the exhibition. They offer suppliers the opportunity to demonstrate products, answer questions, overcome objections and build relationships directly with customers. According to the latest research, exhibitions are seen as the best marketing channel for building relationships with customers, above direct selling, PR, advertising and the internet. Visitors are already expressing an interest and are pre-qualified, so there are few time-wasters. Businesses can be sure that those people are worth talking to. It is the best chance to have face-to-face contact, and it is most likely to lead to a fruitful business relationship. The advantage for the smaller business is you are getting the same access to prospects as the larger companies. If you do your pre- and post-marketing, then there is no reason why you can't compete with your larger competitors.

Exhibitions are not only about sales, there are a host of other objectives that can be met successfully at the show, such as educating the market or raising brand awareness.

Exhibitions also make good platforms when you need to re-position the company or launch a new range.

They offer a cost-effective opportunity to encourage trial of your product and give out samples. And that's not all. You can use a show to build a database or to conduct market research or even test the market for a new product. Many companies find exhibitions are also the best place to secure new dealers and distributors as well as being the ideal forum for finding new personnel. Do your preparation, chase the leads and remember you are only as good as your follow-up.

Questions

1 What is direct selling? (2 marks)

2 Analyse the benefits and disadvantages to a wedding dress maker of selling through exhibitions. (10 marks)

3 A wedding dress maker, who already sells directly through wedding fairs, is considering an additional distribution channel. Evaluate which one of these following two methods should be used:

a retail shops

b online selling.

Assess the advantages and disadvantages of each method before making a final recommendation. (14 marks)

4 Research task: Undertake research into the estate agency market in the UK. Do you think that traditional estate agencies will be replaced by online selling over the next 10 years?

Show the skills

An evaluative question on methods of distribution – or 'place' – should not lead to an answer that is just full of knowledge about the alternative methods. Mere description of shops, online selling and so on will gain very little credit. Apply carefully the methods selected to the type of product referred to in the question. Consider both advantages and disadvantages and make a justified final conclusion.

In this chapter you will have learned to:

- explain the various distribution channels used by businesses in the consumer and business to business markets

- analyse the factors influencing the choice of suitable distributors/outlets.

For answers to activities and case study questions see

34 Marketing and competitiveness

Fig. 34.1 *The pricing of the final Harry Potter book was very competitive*

Key terms

Degree of competition: the number and size of businesses operating in a given market, be it local, regional, national or international.

Setting the scene

The World of Harry Potter

In July 2007, Waterstones and WH Smith expected to lose money on the final Harry Potter novel as they tried to match the aggressive pricing of Tesco, Asda and Amazon. They hoped that through publicity stunts and midnight openings the book would act as a loss leader, encouraging other book purchases from customers once inside the store. Independent book retailers didn't even try to compete in the price war.

Market conditions have changed and increasingly a small number of blockbuster titles are sold at a heavy discount through supermarkets and over the net. High street retailers are struggling: Waterstones bought Ottakar's in 2006 which reduced the direct competition. There are fewer independent book shops and competition for the best sellers is now concentrated amongst a small number of very large retailers who buy the top 200 titles in such quantities that they can sell them on at prices which independent book shops and book shop chains cannot match. Retailers have to respond by looking to other elements of the marketing mix: promotional offers, a bright appealing environment and almost instant delivery.

Discussion points

1. How could the market for books be segmented by retailers?

2. Why are book retailers likely to continue to struggle against the supermarket giants and internet businesses?

3. Why might consumers prefer to browse in a bookshop rather than buy books off the internet or with their weekly shop?

■ Market conditions: do all businesses face the same amount of competition?

It is very unusual for a business in the UK to have no competitors. In the past, when there was a public sector (owned by the State), which included gas and electricity supplies, telephone services, postal delivery, and steel and coal production, there was only one supplier. Now all these markets are competitive to a certain extent: even the Royal Mail does not control 100 per cent of letter-post deliveries and faces a high **degree of competition** in the parcel delivery market.

Classification of markets

The number and size of firms operating in a market can be a useful way of describing the conditions facing a firm.

■ A highly competitive market will exist where there are many firms all offering a very similar product or service. Firms will be price takers and to ensure survival, will have to keep costs low by using all their

Study tip

If more businesses enter a market, it does not necessarily mean that the market grows in size. Market size measures the value or volume of sales, not the number of businesses doing the selling. If the number of firms in the market increases, that does mean more competition however.

resources efficiently. Businesses start up and close down/change ownership regularly and it is not difficult to achieve a share of the market. The promotional element of the marketing mix is very important for a firm in this market, because it can be used to attract the attention of potential consumers. Examples include hairdressers, fish and chip shops and car mechanics.

- Some markets are dominated by a few large firms that tend to compete through the non-price elements of the marketing mix: place, promotion and product. The actions and reactions of competitors is a very important consideration when choosing the marketing mix. Firms try not to compete on price for any length of time, because they fear a price war (Chapter 32). Examples of this type of market in the UK include supermarkets, breakfast cereal manufacturers, bus companies and banks.
- In a few cases, there is only one business that operates in the market, or controls a significant share of that market. This tends to be where there are very high barriers to entry (for example start-up costs) or the business has built up their position over many years. Examples include East Midlands Trains and Airbus.

	Great competition ⟵	⟶	Less competition
	Many small firms (e.g. hairdressing)	**A few large firms dominate industry (e.g. supermarkets)**	**One dominant firm-monopoly (e.g. London Underground)**
Key features	Similar product – but try to differentiate	Try to differentiate products or service – may be difficult	Little consumer choice – may lead to inefficiency
	Price takers – may not be able to charge prices different to competitors	Price competition could lead to price wars	Price maker
	Competition will force firms to be cost efficient	High marketing and promotional spending aimed at building customer loyalty	May not have incentive to develop new products or services or become more efficient

Fig. 34.2 *Market classification based on competition*

Key terms

Market conditions: the nature of the product, the needs of consumers, the number of firms and the ease of entry to the market.

How do market conditions impact on the marketing mix?

Markets are not always this simple to categorise in reality, but the features of each example can be a useful reference point when making decisions about how to develop a successful marketing mix. A lot will depend on whether or not the market is local, national or international: does the business want to attract customers from anywhere in the UK to buy their products, or do consumers in a specific area form the target market? Although a small firm may be one of many thousands of providers of a product or service nationally, there is a possibility in a local area for a firm to be in a situation where it dominates the market. It is also important to remember that firms in the business to business market will have a marketing mix in just the same way as a business in the consumer market.

Activity

Select one product from each of the primary (e.g. farming, fishing, forestry, mineral/oil extraction), secondary (e.g. manufacturing, construction, processing, refining) and tertiary (services to business and/or consumers) sectors and write a brief assessment of the market conditions facing one business.

Try to include at least one business to business market.

Table 34.1 *Examples of the impact that market conditions may have on the marketing mix*

Marketing mix	Market conditions: very competitive with many small to medium-sized firms	Market conditions: a few firms dominate	Market conditions: one firm controls the market
Product	All products are very similar and firms must try to develop and differentiate their goods and services to meet the needs of their particular customers, e.g. offering a higher level customer service	New product development, USPs and extension strategies enable firms to compete. Smaller firms may find a niche in the market and offer a narrower range of specialist products	There is no pressure on the business to improve their products or innovate, unless there is another market that acts as competition, e.g. train travel, short haul air travel.
Promotion	Cost is an important factor in the choice of promotional mix. Businesses need to find out the best way to reach their customers and how to attract their attention. Word-of-mouth promotion is particularly cost-effective	Branding is very important, and firms will compete by trying to establish brand loyalty. High cost advertising such as television, is popular	The promotional mix is likely to concentrate information advertising to consumers and Public Relations
Pricing	Firms are price takers, and do not usually use pricing as a way of competing with rivals	Pricing can be very competitive, particularly where the market is not growing very quickly and one firm tries to take market share off its rivals. The largest of the dominant firms may become the price leader. However, there is a reluctance to compete too heavily on price because of the possibility of a price war	Pricing is not competitive although it may be regulated by a government agency
Place	Cost is an important consideration so that efficiency is maximised. Direct selling is becoming an increasingly popular channel of distribution: using the internet rather than traditional channels	Technology will be used to great effect by large businesses with the resources to pay for the latest expertise. All possible channels of distribution will be exploited to gain a competitive advantage	The channels of distribution will depend on the market, but need to be convenient rather than competitive

💡 Competitiveness

Competitiveness will enable a business to survive and grow in a market: consumers will be attracted to buy the product because it meets their needs. The marketing mix, when used successfully, differentiates one firm sufficiently from its rivals and therefore gives that business a **competitive advantage**.

Methods of improving competitiveness

A firm facing any market conditions has the choice of whether to take action to increase its competitiveness, or to react to the actions taken by rivals in the market. In markets dominated by a small number of larger businesses, smaller firms may tend to be reactive rather than proactive. However, that need not be the case, because larger firms may not be as aware of changes in consumer wants and needs. Smaller firms may be able to make short terms gains because they take action to increase their competitiveness.

In more competitive markets, with many small and medium-sized firms, those businesses that take action may be able to gain a long-term competitive advantage over rivals of a similar size.

■ **Key terms**

Competitiveness: characteristics that permit a firm to compete effectively with other businesses.

Competitive advantage: discovering and using methods of competing which are distinct and offer consumers greater perceived value, than those of rivals in the market.

Fig. 34.3 *Why would it be difficult for a small haulage firm to compete in this market?*

Marketing methods to increase competitiveness

As we have seen, marketing can be used to improve the competitiveness of a business in many ways.

Market research

This should be a significant influence on the marketing mix because it will identify the needs of consumers which can be met by the business through an effective integration of the main elements. Markets are not static, and the firm that is aware of the changing needs of consumers and reacts to those changes can gain a competitive advantage over rivals.

Product

Product developments can be made to existing products during the product life cycle, and new products can be launched onto the market, possibly with a USP or at least clear differentiation.

Promotion

By using the full range of options available, a firm can create a promotional mix that will attract the attention of consumers and encourage them to choose one business over others in the market. This does not have to be expensive: word of mouth is one of the most effective ways of increasing market share, and it costs nothing! As with the marketing mix as a whole the promotional mix must be integrated to achieve maximum impact. Small businesses need to be very clear about what they hope to achieve from promotional activities so that the outcomes can be evaluated.

Pricing

Pricing is a difficult element for smaller firms to use, because they are not free to choose the prices they charge. Instead they must select the best tactics to make short-term gains such as loss leaders to increase overall sales. The importance of elasticity of demand should not be underestimated. A very small short-term drop in price can have a positive impact on total revenue, particularly in a competitive market.

'Place'

Place is the area of the marketing mix that has seen most change for smaller businesses, because the internet has opened up a new channel of distribution that potentially has lower costs than other alternatives, particularly in the retailing sector. By keeping up with e-commerce developments, one business can gain a significant cost advantage over rivals. Using the most appropriate outlets and distributors can certainly help to create a competitive advantage.

Non-marketing methods to increase competitiveness

As well as using the marketing mix to increase competitiveness, non-marketing methods can also be effective.

Reducing costs

If labour costs can be reduced, cheaper sources for raw materials found, or indirect costs cut, then a business has the option to reduce price and still maintain its profit margin. This is particularly important in a competitive market and can enable a firm to make use of more elements in the marketing mix.

Quality

Product is one of the elements of the marketing mix, so improvements in quality can be integrated with the promotional mix and help to achieve a competitive advantage. In the same way, we have seen throughout this section that small firms use the quality of service they offer to customers as their method of product differentiation. This highlights the need for an integrated approach, involving all parts of the business to achieve increased competitiveness.

Staff training and improving customer service

There are many examples of small businesses that have found that when employees are better trained, sales increase. It might be that a wider range of services can be offered, or that costs are reduced because labour turnover falls.

Link

Chapter 24 – Developing effective operations: quality, page 179, and Chapter 25 – Developing effective operations: customer service, page 185, look at how the quality of products and customer service can be improved.

Case study

Petrol retailing in the UK

The marketing strategies of the major UK petrol retailers – including supermarkets – are driving small petrol stations out of business. There has been a dramatic decline in the number of filling stations from 18,000 in 1990 to 9,000 at the end of 2011. The growth of the market share of supermarkets in petrol retailing has been very rapid. Although only accounting for 15% of all filling stations in 2012, they controlled 39% of the UK fuel market. Petrol retailing is a high volume, low profit margin business. Increased competition has meant that smaller, independent petrol stations are no longer profitable. The combination of higher consumer expectations of filling station service levels and stricter environmental legislation means that many sites cannot justify the investment needed to keep up with modern standards. However, apart from the power of existing fuel retailers, there are few barriers to entry into the petrol retailing market. Although there are only seven oil refineries in the UK, the Office of Fair Trading has tried to promote local competition and prevent the owner of a refinery developing a dominant local position.

Show the skills

When evaluating 'competitiveness' and 'ways to improve competitiveness' remember to explain that it is not just about 'lowest possible prices'. Low prices might be very important in some markets, but in others, factors such as the product, brand image and levels of customer service are even more important.

Questions

1 Explain the changes in the competitive environment in UK petrol/diesel retailing in recent years. (8 marks)

2 Analyse TWO likely reasons why UK supermarket businesses are keen to increase market share in fuel retailing. (8 marks)

3 Evaluate ways in which an independent petrol/diesel retailer could compete more effectively in this market. (14 marks)

4 Research task: Investigate the competitive environment in ONE other UK market, for example airlines or mobile phone services. Examine how market conditions have changed in recent years.

☑ *In this chapter you will have learned to:*

- describe a range of market conditions facing businesses
- analyse the possible impacts of market conditions on the marketing mix
- explain competitiveness
- evaluate the extent to which businesses can use marketing and non-marketing methods to improve competitiveness.

For answers to activities and case study questions see **kerboodle**

Practice questions

Chapters 31–34

1   What do you understand by the term 'promotion'? *(2 marks)*

2   Explain THREE aims of promotion. *(6 marks)*

3   Describe and briefly explain FOUR types of sales promotion available to businesses. *(8 marks)*

4   Explain the difference between direct selling and direct mailing. *(2 marks)*

5   Merchandising: Eye Level is Buy Level – When you go to a supermarket you can notice that the high profit earning products are always placed on the upper shelves, because retailers know customers don't readily view the lower shelves.

   a)   What is merchandising? *(2 marks)*

   b)   Explain TWO features of successful merchandising. *(4 marks)*

   c)   Analyse the benefits to a producer of getting their products on the eye level shelves in supermarkets. *(6 marks)*

6   Analyse the factors which might affect the choice of promotional mix for a regional supplier of organic fruit and vegetables? *(8 marks)*

7   What is the difference between a pricing strategy and a pricing tactic? *(2 marks)*

8   Explain TWO pricing strategies available for the launch of new products. *(4 marks)*

9   Explain the difference between a price leader and a price taker. *(2 marks)*

10 Many car manufacturers now fit DAB digital radios to their models. It is possible to have these fitted to existing cars that did not have them built-in during manufacture. C and G Electronics offer a supply and fitting service for leading makes of DAB car radios. The owner of the business is considering a change in prices to make the business more competitive.

   a)   If price elasticity of demand for DAB car radios is estimated to be – 1.25, what would be the likely impact on C and G Electronics' total revenue if it reduced prices by 10%? *(4 marks)*

   b)   Explain FOUR other factors, apart from PED, which might influence the pricing decisions of C and G Electronics. *(10 marks)*

   c)   To what extent will pricing decisions be the most important factor influencing C and G Electronics' level of sales? *(12 marks)*

11 Evaluate the advantages and drawbacks of using price elasticity of demand to make pricing decisions. *(10 marks)*

12   What do you understand by the term 'place' in the marketing mix?   *(2 marks)*

13   Explain the difference between direct distribution and traditional distribution.   *(4 marks)*

14   Analyse the factors that might influence the channels of distribution decisions made by a business selling hand-made hats and scarves.   *(8 marks)*

15   Three years ago Wilfred Emmanuel-Jones launched his food brand 'The Black Farmer', daring to take on the big stores and their own labels dominating the market at the time. Based in Devon, his range of sausages, burgers and barbeque products is now stocked in major supermarkets across the UK.

    a)   The Black Farmer is operating in the business to business market. Explain THREE channels of distribution that he could use for his products.   *(6 marks)*

    b)   What type of market is the Black Farmer competing in?   *(4 marks)*

    c)   Analyse the impact that market conditions might have on the Black Farmer's marketing mix.   *(8 marks)*

    d)   To what extent can The Black Farmer use marketing and non-marketing methods to improve his competitiveness?   *(12 marks)*

35   Examination skills

The AQA AS Business Studies Examinations

There are two examination papers that make up the AQA AS Business Studies qualification.

Unit 1 BUSS1 – Planning and Financing a Business

- This is worth 40% of the final AS level grade (20% of the A level grade).
- The examination is 1 hour 15 minutes long.
- The total marks awarded to all questions is 60.
- There are **two** compulsory structured questions both based on a mini business case study.
- Question 1 will contain short answer questions including calculations.
- Question 2 will contain questions requiring longer written answers.

All questions will be based on the Unit 1 section of the specification and this book:

1 Starting a Business – introduction to Business Studies and an overview of activities involved in setting up a small business.

2 Financial Planning – essential financial concepts and the basic relationships between finance and other business functions.

Unit 2 BUSS2 – Managing a Business

- This is worth 60% of the final AS level grade (30% of the A level grade).
- The examination is 1 hour 30 minutes long.
- The total marks awarded to all questions is 80.
- There are two compulsory multi- part data response questions. There will be questions requiring calculations and questions requiring extended written answers.

All questions will be based on the Unit 2 section of the specification and this book:

1 Finance – using budgets, improving cash flow and profits

2 People in Business – organisational design, recruitment, selection, training, motivation.

3 Operations Management – operational decisions, quality, customer service, suppliers, technology.

4 Marketing and the Competitive Environment – designing and using an effective marketing mix, market conditions and competitiveness.

Examination entries

Both Unit 1 and Unit 2 are offered in June each year. Most schools and colleges will enter candidates for both Units at the end of Year 12, after one year of teaching. Candidates will then be entered for Unit 3 and Unit 4 at the end of the second year of teaching, in the June of Year 13.

There is an option to retake Unit 1, Unit 2 or both Units in June of the second year.

In some schools and colleges, candidates might be entered for all four Units at the end of the teaching course (either 1 or 2 years). This would be called a 'linear' mode of entry as there would be no opportunity to study one or two sections or modules of the course, take the Unit examinations and then progress to the rest of the course.

What examiners are looking for – the assessment objectives

'Assessment objectives' is a technical term for 'examination skills'. These are the particular abilities that you will be expected to demonstrate in your examination answers. They are the skills that examiners will be awarding marks for as they assess your exam. paper. So, it is very important that you:

- Understand what these examination skills – or assessment objectives – are.
- Know how you can demonstrate them in your answers.
- Understand how examiners will award marks for them.

There are four assessment objectives. This is what the specification says about them:

Table 35.1 *Assessment objectives*

AO1 – Assessment Objective 1	Knowledge and understanding	Knowledge and understanding can be demonstrated by: ■ accurate definitions of relevant terms ■ identifying a relevant point in answer to a question.
AO2 – Assessment Objective 2	Application	Application of knowledge and understanding to the business context. This is NOT done just by stating the name of the business. Application can be shown by: ■ recognition of a specific aspect of the business relevant to the question ■ referring to the problems or issues faced by the business.
AO3 – Assessment Objective 3	Analysis	Using relevant business theory and information from a range of source to analyse business problems and situations. This can be demonstrated by: ■ building an argument that shows understanding of cause and effect.
AO4 – Assessment Objective 4	Evaluation	Evaluating evidence to reach reasoned judgements. This skill can be demonstrated by: ■ weighing up an argument and coming to a conclusion based on it ■ giving a support recommendation.
Quality of written communication	The quality of written communication is assessed in all assessment units where candidates are required to produce extended written answers. Candidates are assessed according to their ability to: ■ ensure text is legible and that spelling, punctuation and grammar are accurate ■ select and use a form and style of writing appropriate to the subject matter ■ organise information clearly and coherently. The assessment of the quality of written communication is included in AO4.	

Assessment Objective 1 – 'Knowledge'

Table 35.2 *Achieving AO1 (Knowledge)*

What the examiner is looking for	Checklist of how to show the skill
■ Evidence that you have relevant knowledge and understanding of Business Studies terms ■ Evidence that you have responded to the demand in the question for 'Two factors' or 'Two items' by identifying relevant points ■ Evidence that you remember basic formulae or calculation methods, e.g. profit	■ Identify the key Business Studies terms referred to in the question ■ Define terms or 'explain what is meant by it'. ■ Identify what else you are asked to do, e.g. 'List two factors'. ■ Use your knowledge and the case study to help you list the points you have been asked for.

Command words that test only 'Knowledge'

There will be surprisingly few questions that only test knowledge. These will appear in Unit 1 Question 1. **All other** questions will carry knowledge marks – but will also test other skills. We will look at some of the 'command words' that are used in these questions later. For now you just need to know that when the following command words are used only knowledge is being examined:

Table 35.3 *Examples of command words testing only AO1 (Knowledge)*

Command words/terms	Examples
Define . . .	Define 'budget'. Define 'market growth'. Define 'adding value'.
What is meant by . . .?	What is meant by 'entrepreneurs'? What is meant by 'opportunity cost'? What is meant by 'fixed costs'?
List . . .	List two factors that are included in a cash flow forecast. List two types of employees used in small businesses. List two factors that influence the choice of sampling method.
State . . .	State two methods of market research data. State two sources of new business ideas. State two factors influencing start-up locations.

Questions that are expecting *only* knowledge to be shown will usually be worth *just* two marks:

■ 1 mark for 'some understanding of the term', or
■ 2 marks for 'good understanding of the term'.

Examination examples

All of the points that have been made about the examination skill of knowledge can now be illustrated by looking at an example Unit 1 Paper and the THREE 'knowledge only' questions that are based upon it:

Unit 1

Decoplates Ltd

The idea for Decoplates came to Ian after his young son told him about a game played at a party he had been invited to. This was a competition to decorate a plate with paints. These were then sent away to be 'glazed and fired' in a kiln so everyone had a permanent record of the party. This was incredibly messy but great fun! Ian's own career as a designer was in a rut and he was looking for a fresh challenge offering independence. Why not open a studio to allow people of all ages to decorate plates, vases and other pottery pieces? The studio could also offer fully decorated plates as souvenirs of important events such as birthdays, weddings and anniversaries.

He discussed his idea with a neighbour, Kate, who had experience in running a clothing shop. She was enthusiastic but warned Ian that being an entrepreneur offered great independence but involved considerable risks too. She offered to invest £5,000 in the venture if he would match this, which he did. Over the next few weeks they decided to form a private limited company called Decoplate Ltd., and started to draw up a business plan.

Market research proved to be a problem. They had little experience of gathering primary data but the feedback from friends and relatives about the idea was positive. Ian tried to collect secondary data about the market for 'pottery shops' but none was available. He did find that the total market for 'Art and creative products' grew from £4.5m in 2005 to £8m in 2007.

They realised that £10,000 would not be enough to finance the business start-up. A bank loan would be necessary. They were disappointed that the local bank initially rejected their business plan. 'We need to see some figures. The basic ideas are fine and the location you suggest has potential – but financial forecasts are essential before we can agree a loan,' explained the Small Business Adviser of the bank.

The revised Business Plan contained much more financial information including the following cost, price and customer forecasts:

Decoplate Ltd: first year: forecasted cost, price and customer numbers	
Variable cost per customer	£2
Annual fixed costs	£27,500
Average price per customer	£7.50
Annual customers	8,000

A cash flow forecast for the first year's trading was included and this indicated that a loan of £20,000 would be needed. The interest on this would add to the fixed costs of the business. Kate had wondered if another shareholder should be accepted into the business or if venture capitalists should be approached but the couple agreed that they wanted to keep full control.

In the first year of trading, the profits of the business exceeded budget. Interest in the original product being offered had been much greater than expected and customers were spending more, on average, than forecast in the Business Plan. Farah, a parent of one of the younger customers was so taken by the business idea that she proposed to Kate and Ian that she could open a similar shop in a nearby town. She wanted to be allowed to operate the business as a franchise operation, using the name and same suppliers as Decoplate Ltd. She owned a shop in the town which had recently traded as a hairdressing salon but had closed. It seemed to be well located on the High Street. Kate and Ian were keen on the idea but they explained that the market in the local town needed to be researched. They were not sure if the same marketing mix would be successful in this town. In addition, they had been very lucky in employing some part-time staff who were really hard working and enthusiastic. Would Farah be this lucky?

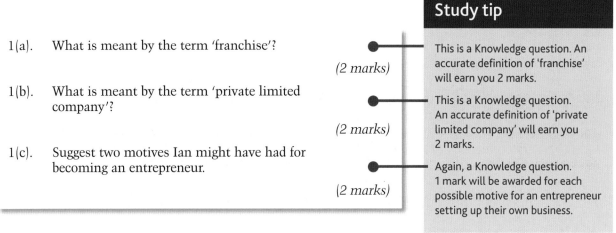

1(a). What is meant by the term 'franchise'?

(2 marks)

Study tip

This is a Knowledge question. An accurate definition of 'franchise' will earn you 2 marks.

1(b). What is meant by the term 'private limited company'?

(2 marks)

This is a Knowledge question. An accurate definition of 'private limited company' will earn you 2 marks.

1(c). Suggest two motives Ian might have had for becoming an entrepreneur.

(2 marks)

Again, a Knowledge question. 1 mark will be awarded for each possible motive for an entrepreneur setting up their own business.

Assessment Objective 2 – 'Application'

Table 35.4 *Achieving AO2 (Application)*

What the examiner is looking for	Checklist of how to show the skill
■ Evidence that you have read and understood the case study and realise how it can be used to support your answers. ■ Evidence that you can use the case study and the issues it covers to illustrate the knowledge point that you are making. ■ Evidence that you can accurately extract relevant figures and complete the calculation asked for. ■ Evidence that you can answer the questions in the context of the business study	■ Read the case study before answering any questions! Never assume that questions can be answered without understanding what the case is about. ■ Identify sections of the case study that are relevant to each question. ■ Use quotes and phrases from the passage in your answer that illustrate or support the point being made. ■ Be careful to use the right figures from the case if a calculation is asked for. ■ Think about how the question affects the business study in order to demonstrate application

Command words that test only 'Knowledge' and 'Application'

It is very important to remember that there will be NO marks given for copying out parts of the case study in an answer if no relevant subject knowledge has been demonstrated. In fact, we can go further than this, without SOME relevant subject content (knowledge and understanding) in all of your answers then they will not gain any marks at all! Demonstrating relevant subject knowledge in each and every answer is essential for any marks to be gained for the other assessment objectives too. So, there is no such thing as 'a well applied or analysed answer with no appropriate subject knowledge'!

Table 35.5 *Examples of command words testing AO2 (Application)*

Command words/terms	Examples
Explain with an example what is meant by . . .	Explain, with a numerical example, what is meant by the phrase 'falling net profit margin'. Explain, with an example from the case, what is meant by 'the legal structure of business'.
Explain why . . .	Explain one reason why the owners might have decided to use primary market research. Explain one factor that might have influenced the owners' decision to locate in the town centre.
Outline . . .	Outline one benefit to this business of using a business consultant. Outline one disadvantage to this business of using niche marketing.
Calculate . . .	Using the information in the table, calculate the net profit margin for this business. Calculate the company's profit variance for May.

Study tip

This question carries 2 knowledge marks. These will both be awarded for an answer that demonstrates a good understanding of what a cash flow is and/or one reason why it is important to include it in a business plan. The question also carries 2 marks for APPLICATION of the answer to the case study.

Examination examples

These questions are based on the Unit 1 paper 'Decoplates Ltd' (see page 266).

(d). Explain ONE reason why the bank insisted on a cash flow forecast in the Business Plan.

(4 marks)

(e). Use the information in the table to calculate:

i) The number of customers required to break-even.

(3 marks)

ii) The total forecasted profit in the first year.

(3 marks)

(f). Calculate the percentage growth in the UK market for 'Art and creative materials' from 2005 to 2007.

(4 marks)

Assessment Objective 3 – 'Analysis'

Table 35.6 *Achieving AO3 (Analysis)*

What the examiner is looking for	Checklist of how to show the skill
■ Evidence that you can explain an answer using logical and reasoned arguments, e.g. X leads to Y which may cause Z! ■ Evidence that you can explain points made with supporting use of Business Studies theory and ideas. ■ Evidence of appropriate use and understanding of numerical and non numerical techniques.	■ Most importantly, you should firstly establish that the question is asking for detailed explanations. If the question uses the command words referred to in Table 35.5 then time will be wasted analysing your answer in detail – time that should be spent on those questions that need this development. ■ Identify the Business Studies techniques and ideas that could be used to support the points made, e.g. price elasticity when analysing the impact of a proposed price change. ■ Build up an argument showing, for example, how a business decision might have either a positive or negative impact on it. ■ **Only** if asked to, build up arguments both for and against the point made in the question.

Command words that test 'Analysis'

There will be three main ways in which examiners will ask for this skill to be shown. Don't forget, though, that your answer must contain appropriate knowledge and this will often be best demonstrated by defining the business term in the question. Questions which demand analysis will always also carry application marks – so your answer should be based on case study evidence too!

You will notice that 'Explain how' is included in this list. To answer this type of question effectively it is necessary to use powers of analysis. Compare this with 'Explain why' in Assessment Objective 2 which only requires an applied use of knowledge – not analysis.

Table 35.7 *Examples of command words testing AO3 (Analysis)*

Command words/terms	Examples
Analyse . . .	Analyse the importance of monitoring quality to . . .
	Analyse TWO advantages to the business of using internal recruitment in this case.
Examine . . .	Examine TWO possible reasons why the net profit margin has fallen.
	Examine TWO ways in which the business might increase sales of this product.
Explain how . . . might . . .	Explain how . . . might develop a more effective workforce.
	Explain how . . . might improve customer service.

Examination examples

These examples are based on the Unit 1 paper 'Decoplates Ltd' (see page 266)

2(a).   Examine the possible reasons for the profit target being exceeded.

(10 marks)

2(b).   Analyse TWO benefits to Kate and Ian of producing the more detailed Business Plan.

(10 marks)

Study tip

Don't forget that although these are 'analyse' questions it is essential that your answers are also 'applied' and show key 'knowledge' too. Without relevant knowledge, NO marks will be awarded. Without any application of the answer to the business a *maximum* of Level 2 and 4 marks will be awarded. To achieve Level 5 and 10 marks, the answer must contain both 'good analysis' AND 'good application'.

Assessment Objective 4 – 'Evaluation'

Table 35.8 *Achieving AO4 (Evaluation)*

What the examiner is looking for	Checklist of how to show the skill
■ Evidence that a judgement has been made in the answer or the conclusion to the answer. ■ Evidence that the arguments used have been weighed up and the most important one(s) identified. ■ Evidence that a recommendation has been given, if asked for, which is supported by the arguments used. ■ Evidence that the case study business and the issues it faces have been built into the judgement and that evaluation is not just made up of pre-learned phrases such as 'on the other hand . . .'	■ Check that the question requires judgement – this depends on the command word. So much time is wasted by students making judgements or coming to conclusions when none was asked for! ■ Decide on what matters most in this case – and support your judgement. ■ Compare and contrast 'arguments for' and 'arguments against' an issue. ■ Conclude the answer with a clear conclusion and/or recommendation which is based on the arguments used.

Study tip

Look at past paper mark schemes to see how examiners award different Levels and Marks to answers.

Table 35.9 *Examples of command words testing AO4 (Evaluation)*

Command words/terms	Examples
Evaluate . . .	Evaluate the actions that CP Crisps might take to improve its profitability.
Discuss . . .	Discuss the case for this business introducing a system of quality assurance.
To what extent . . .	To what extent do you agree with Paul's view that drawing up cash flow forecasts is vital for the company's long run success?
Recommend . . . Justify your answer.	Recommend appropriate financial methods of motivation in this case. Justify your answer.

Study tip

To gain access to high Levels and Marks (see past paper mark schemes) your answers must include a supported judgement. This should balance the arguments for and against the issue in the question. You must give a reasoned conclusion. To reach Level 5, your answer must show 'good application AND good analysis AND contain a judgement with well supported justification'. In addition, do not forget the marks awarded for 'Quality of written communication'.

Examination examples

This example is taken from the Unit 1 paper 'Decoplates Ltd' (see page 266).

3(a). If you had been advising Ian and Kate, would you have recommended raising the extra £20,000 from other shareholders rather than a bank loan? Explain your answer.

15 marks

3(b). To what extent might the new studio's location determine the future success of the franchised outlet?

15 marks

Unit 2

These further examples are taken from this Unit 2 case study question. See if you can now identify which assessment objectives are being examined in each of the questions that follows.

Gardiner Stores plc

Gardiner Stores plc is one of the UK's smaller supermarket chains. The company operates 50 supermarkets mainly in the Midlands and the South East of England. It was founded in Birmingham and still owns undeveloped land in the city. The company sells only groceries and it aims to supply quality products and to provide excellent customer service. Gardiner Stores plc charges premium prices and expects each sale to make a contribution towards overheads.

The company's financial position is improving slowly. It has made small but rising profits over recent years, and its share price on the Stock Exchange has increased. The company gives the managers of each supermarket responsibility for setting and monitoring budgets for their stores. Gardiner Stores plc has pursued a policy of steady expansion, opening two or three stores every two years, and this has led to occasional cash flow problems.

In 2006, Gardiner Stores plc opened a new supermarket in Oxfordshire. The forecast and actual figures for the first two months of trading for this supermarket are shown in Table 10 below:

Table 10 *Actual and budgeted sales, costs and profits for Oxfordshire store*

| | April | | May | |
	Budget £000s	Actual £000s	Budget £000s	Actual £000s
Sales revenue	966	y	957	967
Purchases of stock	606	630	611	615
Wages/salaries	241	250	245	249
Other costs	98	96	97	97
Total costs	x	976	953	961
Profit/(Loss)	21	(79)	4	z

Gardiner Stores plc is planning further expansion. Two new stores are planned in Surrey, a county with many wealthy consumers. The Human Resources director plans to recruit the new store managers and departmental managers internally from within other company stores. The Operations Director is determined to apply the latest I.T. to these new stores. He is planning to trial a Radio Frequency ID tagging system for all groceries. He is convinced that this will be the key factor in the company maintaining its reputation for excellent customer service. He told his staff that 'Buying the latest I.T. equipment is the most important operational issue for Gardiner Stores plc'.

1(a). i) Calculate the value of Gardiner Stores plc's BUDGETED total costs and ACTUAL sales revenue for April 2008.

(2 marks)

ii) Calculate the company's total profit variance for the Oxfordshire store for the two month period, April–May 2008. Show your workings. State whether this variance is adverse or favourable.

(6 marks)

2(b). Analyse TWO advantages to Gardiner Stores plc of using internal recruitment to appoint new store managers.

(8 marks)

Study tip

Examiner's mark scheme: Level 5 and 13 marks for 'good application' and 'good analysis' PLUS judgement with well supported justification. (Do not forget the quality of written communication!)

2(c). To what extent do you agree with Chris that, 'Buying the latest I.T. equipment is the most important operational issue . . .' for this business?

(13 marks)

2(d). Evaluate the actions that Gardiner Stores plc might take to improve its profitability.

(13 marks)

Examination skills – final advice

1 Read the case study carefully.

2 Identify the key command word in each question.

3 Define/explain the key business term in each question no matter what the command word – knowledge marks are awarded for this in all questions.

4 Allocate time carefully between each question – after reading the case study material you will have around '1 minute per mark' to spend on each question.

5 Do not waste time on unnecessary analysis or evaluation if the command words do not require these skills.

6 Write in full sentences.

7 Use separate paragraphs for each separate point being made.

8 Show all numerical working and lay this out as clearly as you can – marks can still be awarded for incorrect results if the working has some logic to it.

Index

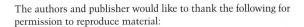

Acknowledgements

The authors and publisher would like to thank the following for permission to reproduce material:

Text permissions

p7, numbers of different sizes in various sectors licensed under the Open Government Licence v1.0.; p7, Case Study: UK business start-ups rise to new highs: information adapted from Global Entrepreneurship Monitor; p11, Case Study: The Pure Package Idea, The Pure Package, www.purepackage.com; p21, Setting the scene: AKC Home Support Services, www.businesslink.gov.uk, licenced under the Open Government Licence v2.0.; p24, Government agencies, www.businesslink.gov.uk, licenced under the Open Government Licence v2.0.; pp30–31, Case Study: Market research at Bladonmore, www.businesslink.gov.uk, licenced under the Open Government Licence v2.0.; p34, Setting the scene: New Horizons Travel, www.statistics.gov.uk, licensed under the Open Government Licence v1.0.; p63, Setting the scene: part-time and temporary employment in the UK, Labour Force Survey and TUC, adapted from data from the Office for National Statistics licensed under the Open Government Licence v.1.0. and Trades Union Congress (TUC), www.tuc.org; p66, Employee jobs: by industry 1978 and 2005, Employee Jobs; p67, Average weekly hours worked in the UK, www.ons.gov.uk, adapted from data from the Office for National Statistics licensed under the Open Government Licence v.1.0.; pp68–69, Case Study: Slivers-of-Time, www.slivers.com, Slivers-of-Time; p89, Business in Action: Cheet: Bags of Style, permission kindly granted by Emily Cheetham, www.cheetlondon.com; p110, Case Study: The difference between success and failure, www.leviroots.com; p134, Setting the scene: Family business, copyright Guardian News & Media Ltd 2006; p141, Case Study: Charlie Bigham's, www.bighams.com, FRANK PR/ Bighams; p152, Using technology to cut recruitment costs, www.personneltoday.com; pp166–168, Business in action: Business Link and True North and Case Study: Foster Yeoman and True North, www.truenorthgb.com, Truth North; p168, John Lewis Partnership weblink; p191, Case Study: Pret a Manger – a cut above the rest?, www.pret.com, LEWIS PR – Global Communications; p204, quote from Samir Ellwi of Powerlase; p211, Setting the scene: Rapha, www.rapha.cc; p232, quote from Chris Bailey of Burberry; p259, Case Study: Petrol retailing in the UK, UK Petroleum Industry Association Ltd.

Images

p1: ROBERT GALBRAITH/Reuters/Corbis; p3: Eddie Mulholland/Rex Features; p4: ZUMA Press, Inc./Alamy; p13: Domino's; p16, top to bottom: Shutterstock, Imagestate Media Partners Limited Impact Photos/Alamy, iStockphoto; p23: Bytestart Ltd; p28: hibu plc; p30: Fotolia; p37: Newscast/Alamy; p48: Stephen Shepherd/Alamy; p50, various images: iStockphoto; p54, logos: The Prince's Trust, The Prince's Initiative for Mature Enterprise, Department for Business Enterprise & Regulatory Reform (BERR) logo licenced under the Open Government Licence v2.0; p61: Regus; p65: Paula Solloway/Alamy; p73: Alex Segre/Alamy; p78: Justin Leighton/Alamy; p89, Catherine Harhalakis Photography; p103: Getty Images; p105: iStockphoto; p110: Nick Randall/Rex Features; p112: PSL Images/Alamy; p129: Chris Howes/Wild Places Photography/Alamy; p134: YogaBugs; p157: Apex Radio Systems Ltd; p161: Kevin Foy/Alamy; p171: vario images GmbH & Co.KG/Alamy; p178: Adrian Sherratt/Alamy; p179: vario images GmbH & Co.KG/Alamy; p181: Stan Gamester/Alamy; p182: Bloomberg/Getty Images; p185: iStockphoto; p191, Pret a Manger logo: LEWIS PR - Global Communications; p199: Peppercomm/TGI Fridays; p201: vario images GmbH & Co.KG/Alamy; p203: Sam Tinson/Rex Features; p216: Getty Images; p218: Marc Serota/AP/Press Association Images; p222: scooterMAN; p227: iStockphoto; p228: Shutterstock; p233: Michael Kemp/Alamy; p234: Shutterstock; p236 and 243: iStockphoto; p251: B2B Index.co.uk logo; p252: Alex Segre/Alamy; p253: studiomode/Alamy; p255: Phil Rees/Rex Features; p258: Justin Kase zsixz/Alamy.

Every effort has been made to trace the copyright holders but if any have been inadvertently overlooked the publisher will be pleased to make the necessary arrangements at the first opportunity.